FABULOUS FOOD
FROM EVERY SMALL GARDEN

This book is dedicated to everyone who ever sank their teeth into a tasteless tomato and knew there had to be a better choice; for anyone who ever felt dismay at rising food prices; for everyone who ever wondered where their food came from and what was in it; and most of all, for the children, yours and mine.

FABULOUS FOOD
FROM EVERY SMALL GARDEN

MARY HORSFALL

CSIRO PUBLISHING GARDENING GUIDES

© Mary Horsfall 2009

All rights reserved. Except under the conditions described in the *Australian Copyright Act* 1968 and subsequent amendments, no part of this publication may be reproduced, stored in a retrieval system or transmitted in any form or by any means, electronic, mechanical, photocopying, recording, duplicating or otherwise, without the prior permission of the copyright owner. Contact **CSIRO** PUBLISHING for all permission requests.

National Library of Australia Cataloguing-in-Publication entry

> Horsfall, Mary, 1949–
> Fabulous food from every small garden/Mary Horsfall.
>
> 9780643095977 (pbk.)
>
> CSIRO Publishing gardening guides.
>
> Includes index.
> Bibliography.
>
> Vegetable gardening – Australia.
> Plants, Edible – Australia.
> Fruit-culture – Australia.
> Small gardens – Australia.
>
> 635

Published by

CSIRO PUBLISHING
150 Oxford Street (PO Box 1139)
Collingwood VIC 3066
Australia

Telephone: +61 3 9662 7666
Local call: 1300 788 000 (Australia only)
Fax: +61 3 9662 7555
Email: publishing.sales@csiro.au
Web site: www.publish.csiro.au

Front cover (clockwise, from top right): Swiss chard; tomatoes (EarthBox Australia); broccoli; native raspberry (Happy Earth).

Back cover (clockwise, from top right): broad beans; no-dig bed in a straw bale; pumpkin harvest; lilly pilly berries; tank beds.

All photographs are by Rodney Horsfall unless otherwise stated.

Set in 10.5/14 Adobe ITC New Baskerville
Edited by Janet Walker
Cover and text design by James Kelly
Typeset by Desktop Concepts Pty Ltd, Melbourne
Printed in China by 1010 Printing International Ltd

The paper this book is printed on is certified by the Forest Stewardship Council (FSC) © 1996 FSC A.C. The FSC promotes environmentally responsible, socially beneficial and economically viable management of the world's forests.

CSIRO PUBLISHING publishes and distributes scientific, technical and health science books, magazines and journals from Australia to a worldwide audience and conducts these activities autonomously from the research activities of the Commonwealth Scientific and Industrial Research Organisation (CSIRO).

The views expressed in this publication are those of the author(s) and do not necessarily represent those of, and should not be attributed to, the publisher or CSIRO.

CONTENTS

Acknowledgements   *vii*

Introduction   *ix*

Part One   All about the garden   1

1   **Why grow your own?**   3
10 good reasons

2   **Where and what?**   15
First thoughts

3   **High productivity from small spaces**   33
Some special techniques

4   **Creating super soil**   55
Soil biota and fertility

5   **Making the most of your space**   83
Plants for places

6   **Getting started with vegetables**   99
Seeds and seedlings

7   **Plant care**   109
Weeding, watering, controlling pests

Part Two   All about the plants   131

8   Vegetables   133

9   Fruits   165

10   Bush foods   187

11   Herbs and flowers   193

12   A taste for all seasons   207

     Final words   213

Appendix 1   *Suppliers and information*   *214*

Appendix 2   *Bibliography*   *216*

Index   *217*

ACKNOWLEDGEMENTS

Loving thanks to my husband Rodney Horsfall for always being ready with the camera, and for his support throughout the project. Unless otherwise stated, the photographs are his work.

A number of other people have helped generously at various stages and to all of them I extend sincere thanks:

Alison Mellor and Richard Walter for allowing me to use photographs of their wonderful permaculture garden 'Happy Earth' near Wollongong, NSW. To discover more about how this enterprising couple turned a suburban lawn into a permaculture paradise, see their website: www.happyearth.com.au.

Christopher Debek of EarthBox Australia for photographs of this productive system suitable for use in numerous small areas. See Appendix 1 for contact details.

Barb and Wane Cull for inviting Rodney to visit and photograph their Mornington Peninsula straw bale vegie garden.

Our neighbour David Cerini for access to his productive backyard food garden.

Sue Heggie for the photo of her bathtub vegie garden.

My gratitude also extends to the many contributors to *Grass Roots* magazine for their inspiration and shared knowledge over decades, which has contributed greatly to my own learning and to what I can share in my turn through this book. Little did I know when I started working at *Grass Roots* in 1989 where the journey would take me.

INTRODUCTION

This book is about empowerment, empowering you to take back a measure of control of your food supply. Australian Bureau of Statistics (ABS) figures indicate that about 35% of Australian households already grow some of the fruit and vegetables they consume. If you are one of the 35%, you are bound to find new ideas about how to increase your production. If you belong to the 65% who, according to ABS information, do not yet grow their own food, this is your starting point – a new adventure in taste, personal satisfaction, better health and money saving is about to begin.

Interestingly, a poll commissioned by the Nursery and Garden Industry of Australia (NGIA) in 2008 showed that 63% of those surveyed had a garden planted with herbs, vegies or fruit trees. Perhaps the large difference between the two sets of figures has to do with the amount of food grown and the higher figure on the NGIA survey included anyone surveyed who grew a pot of parsley. The NGIA survey reported that 80% of respondents were attracted to the idea of their garden being a mixture of decorative trees and plants intermingled with edible plants. This book will show how to achieve such a garden easily.

Just about anyone can grow some of their own food. You don't need a huge garden, though, of course, a large area gives you more options and allows you to grow a greater variety of vegies, herbs and fruit. Do not allow lack of space to hold you back; you'll be surprised at how much you can produce from a small patch of dirt. Even the patch of dirt is not essential, as long as you have space for some pots.

Through my work as editor of *Grass Roots* magazine I am fortunate enough to share the experiences of thousands of readers throughout Australia. If there is one thing above all others that never fails to amaze and impress me about this diverse readership, it is the amount of food that people with only small spaces at their disposal manage to produce in those small spaces. With a little resourcefulness, even a sunny balcony, courtyard or suitable rooftop can be made productive enough to supply you with salads and culinary herbs.

In 2003, I began a new garden from scratch on a double block in a country town. High on my list of priorities was a kitchen garden. I had been used to growing the majority of my family's vegies and herbs, and a fair amount of fruit as well, on a country acreage. There, I'd had plenty of space and a good supply of the fertiliser and mulch resources usually available on a small farm, but limited water. In the new location I had limited space and few free resources, but a reliable town water supply, or so I thought at first until an extended drought period led to severe restrictions.

Though not far in distance from the old garden, the new one was subject to significant climatic differences and had a different range of pests to identify and contend with, but the main difference was the space available. I had formed many ideas about gardening in small spaces, especially food growing, even written articles about it. Now was my chance to see how well those ideas translated to reality.

During this journey, changes in the world that had previously barely been noticed in the mainstream media escalated suddenly and came to prominence. A turning point in public consciousness of the vulnerability of our food supply occurred when Cyclone Larry struck northern Queensland on 20 March 2006. Just one of the devastating effects of the cyclone was the destruction of that year's banana crop. When the price of bananas rose to over $12 per kilogram many people who had previously never given the matter much thought suddenly became aware of the possible effects of climate change on the nation's food supply. Not long afterwards, extended drought conditions and higher fuel prices led to steep rises in the price of numerous food items. This is not a situation peculiar to Australia. A variety of climatic, political and environmental circumstances have coalesced to make food shortages and higher prices common worldwide. Alongside this scenario, higher interest rates on home loans in Australia added to the financial burden of many families.

By March 2008, just two years after Cyclone Larry thrust the spectre of food shortages into the national limelight, major Australian newspapers were running stories about rising food prices, citing drought, strong overseas demand for Australian-produced food and increased costs of energy, processing, packaging and interest rates as causes. At the same time, steep rises in food prices worldwide were claimed by the World Bank to be causing increased hunger and malnutrition in Third World nations.

Later that same year a worldwide financial crisis added to the woes of ordinary people trying to balance their budgets and care for their families. Interest rates began a downward spiral, but unemployment soared, as did anxiety about the future for our families, our world and our planet.

It has become obvious that the search for alternatives is no longer a fringe movement. Increasing numbers of people around the world are seeking ways to reduce their carbon emissions, ways to balance their household budgets while still eating well, and ways to maintain a healthier and more satisfying lifestyle for themselves and the small green planet we all ultimately depend upon. Growing our own food is one of those ways.

PART ONE
ALL ABOUT THE GARDEN

The motivations for wanting to grow food at home are many. Everyone will have their own special reasons and priorities. You might be intrigued by some of my top 10 good reasons, particularly if you have never before given the matter much thought.

Your excursion into the wonderful world of fresh homegrown food begins with an exploration of your own space, be it a backyard, front yard, courtyard, deck, verandah, rooftop or balcony. It could be the most rewarding journey of your life.

Having decided where you can grow some food plants and what you would like to try, you will find a plethora of exciting ideas about how to make the most of the space you have, how to improve your soil for maximum productivity, grow vegies from seeds or seedlings and care for your plants once they are in the ground.

Let the journey begin.

WHY GROW YOUR OWN?
10 good reasons

We have all grown used to having fresh produce readily available and reasonably priced throughout the year. This situation is changing rapidly and there are compelling reasons why it makes very good sense to learn how to grow our own.

A matter of taste

There is no question to my mind; supermarket fruits and vegies just do not taste as good as those you grow yourself.

Time lapse

One reason for this lack of taste is simply the time lapse between harvest and consumption. Commercially grown vegies are harvested, transported, kept in storage for unspecified lengths of time, packed on the shelves, picked over by fussy shoppers, transported again to your home, then kept refrigerated or otherwise stored until you need them. By this time the taste can be so bland you are lucky to be able to tell a carrot from a capsicum. Vegies and fruits grown in your own garden and taken straight from garden to kitchen retain maximum flavour and texture. Even after having been refrigerated or preserved, the sensational taste difference is obvious.

Bred to be tough

Another reason shop-bought produce tastes so bland is that, increasingly, varieties grown by farmers are selected for uniformity of size, fast and uniform maturation, ease of harvest, and ability to withstand rough handling during harvest and transportation without bruising. One commercial tomato developed to withstand rough treatment, for example, was undamaged after falling two metres to the floor. The same variety, when tested in a vehicle testing laboratory, did not split until subjected to an impact of 21 kilometres per hour. These qualities mean there is little waste from damaged stock in the supermarket, but whether it is worth eating is another matter.

Harvested unripe

Some produce, usually fruit, is picked too soon when it is still unripe. These finish their maturation, if they ripen properly at all, either in storage, on the supermarket shelf or in your fruit bowl, rather than on the tree or vine in the sunshine where the flavours can fully develop.

Unripe fruit contains salicylates that produce a bitter taste. This is an adaptation many plants have developed as a means of ensuring fruit is not eaten before the seed has matured sufficiently to grow a new generation. The bitterness is gradually replaced by sugars as the fruit ripens, making it palatable. It is during this last stage of maturation that the majority of the nutrients develop in both fruits and vegetables. Hence, foods left to mature on the plant before harvest not only taste better but have a higher vitamin and mineral content.

Put to the test

A Victorian seed company conducted a tomato taste test some years ago, comparing commercial varieties with traditional heirloom (open-pollinated) varieties. Not surprisingly, the commercial varieties scored worse than the heirlooms overall. The winner was the heirloom variety 'Tommy Toe'. When growing your own produce from seed you have the choice of scores of heirloom varieties, each with its own distinctive flavour. Good nurseries often have a choice of heirloom vegetable seedlings for anyone not wanting the extra trouble of growing from seeds.

Organic tastes better

In a survey conducted in 2005 by the Soil Association (the United Kingdom's organics organisation) 72% of respondents said organic fruits and vegetables tasted better than non-organic. When we grow food at home we have control over the products we use in the garden and can choose to use organic products and methods.

Does blandness cause obesity?

Rosemary Stanton, a well-known Australian nutritionist, posits that lack of taste in food might be linked with obesity. Her suggestion was based on the observation that in cultures where food is bland it is common for people to eat large quantities, whereas in cultures where food is strongly flavoured over-consumption is not seen as often. Maybe, the theory goes, people keep eating until their taste buds find satisfaction and when food has great taste this need is met by a smaller quantity.

Economy

The amount of money you can save by growing your own depends on many factors; the first of these is how much you grow. If you have the space and the time to grow a high percentage of your family's fruit and vegie requirements throughout the year, the savings will be substantial. Growing open-pollinated varieties and saving the seeds from season to season will reduce the cost of buying seedlings. Making your own compost or vermicompost for fertiliser will reduce costs further.

Nutritionists advise that we all need to eat more fresh fruit and vegetables to maintain good health. Seven serves per day, two of fruit and five of vegies, is the quantity often cited as being necessary. Some nutritionists go further and recommend up to 10 serves per day of fruits and vegies. With a greater proportion of our diet consisting of food we can grow at home, the potential for spending less money at the supermarket is obvious.

There will be initial costs involved in perhaps buying in good topsoil or improving your existing soil, edging the beds, installing a watering system and buying fertilisers until

> ### INCREASING FOOD PRICES
>
> There are several factors that are already leading to higher food prices and look likely to continue to do so into the future, the most obvious being the increasing cost of fuels needed to grow and transport food. A side effect of higher fuel costs is the increased cost of plastic packaging, a petroleum by-product.
>
> Unnoticed by the non-farming community, fertiliser prices have risen significantly, placing further cost increases onto food production.
>
> Another often-overlooked aspect of food production is pollination. Many food crops rely on bees and other insects for pollination. Globally, the number of pollinators has been diminishing as a result of pesticide use and habitat destruction. Fewer pollinators = smaller harvests = higher prices.
>
> The effect of climate change on food crops is a big unknown factor, but already in Australia we have experienced shortages and high prices of specific crops caused by extreme weather conditions – cyclones and floods as well as droughts.
>
> Growing demand from developing nations is another factor that could lead to higher prices at home.
>
> In many farming areas worldwide, increasingly large areas of former food-growing land is being used to grow biofuel crops, with one result being less food production and higher prices.
>
> If a carbon cost is imposed on agriculture, one result is sure to be increased food prices.
>
> Whatever happens to our climate and to world agricultural production in the medium to long term, growing some of your own food will cushion the impact.

your compost and other homemade fertiliser production systems are up and running. However, these costs are similar to those encountered in setting up a flower garden and will be offset by money saved in the long term and the numerous other advantages of homegrown produce.

Freshness

The freshness of fruits and vegetables is closely allied to taste and nutrition. Once harvested, all food gradually loses nutrients and often flavour as well. Fresh food retains maximum flavour and nutrients and the only guarantee you have that the food you eat is truly fresh is to grow it yourself. Think of the word 'fresh' as meaning 'retaining the original properties unimpaired'. Very often the produce we buy in the supermarket is labelled 'fresh' when in fact it has been in cold storage for an unknown length of time. When you grow it yourself, you are in charge. It might not always be possible to eat home-produced food picked straight from the garden, but your food will certainly be fresher than any you can buy.

Nutrition and health

Nutrients found in fresh vegetables and fruits are essential for maintaining good

> **SUPERFOODS**
>
> The 14 superfoods are: beans, blueberries, broccoli, oats, oranges, pumpkin, salmon, soy, spinach, green or black tea, tomatoes, turkey, walnuts and yoghurt.

health. In one published list of so-called 'superfoods' (those that are claimed to help slow the ageing process, reduce the incidence of cancer and diabetes and enable us all to live a longer, healthier life) fruits and vegetables figured strongly, making up half the list of recommended foods. Most of the listed fruits and vegies are suitable to grow in small home gardens, enabling us to have the freshest, most beneficial foods for the lowest cost. The recommendations are to eat each of the listed foods four times per week, remove refined foods such as sugar and salt from the diet and exercise regularly.

Nutrients in organic food

Some studies from around the world, including in Australia, show a higher level of nutrients in organically grown food compared with that grown commercially. It makes sense to either buy organic food or to grow as much of our own as we can to ensure our nutrient intake is optimal.

A study commissioned by the Organic Retailers and Growers Association Australia (ORGAA) some years ago found that organic vegetables showed up to eight times more calcium, 10 times more potassium and seven times more magnesium than their conventionally grown counterparts. Other studies have shown significantly more antioxidants, vitamins and trace elements in organically grown food. These nutritional differences do not only apply to vegetables; one American study, for example, found organically grown oranges contained as much as 30% more vitamin C by weight.

Studies around the world

A review of 41 studies from around the world found that, on average, organic food contained:

- 29.3% more magnesium
- 27% more vitamin C
- 21% more iron
- 13.6% more phosphorus
- 26% more calcium
- 11% more copper
- 42% more manganese
- 9% more potassium
- 15% fewer nitrates, which have been linked with birth defects, cancer, nausea, dizziness and miscarriage.

Organically grown spinach, lettuce, cabbage and potatoes showed even higher nutrient levels.

European Union study

In October 2007 results of a four-year study, believed to be the largest of its kind on organic food and funded by the European Union, were published. Some of the findings were that organic wheat, tomatoes, potatoes, cabbages and onions contain 20–40% more antioxidants (believed by many scientists to reduce the risk of cancer and heart disease) than their conventionally grown counterparts; and that organic spinach and cabbage contain

ORGAA ANALYSIS OF VEGETABLE PRODUCE

Nutrient	S/O	Beans	Tomatoes	Capsicum	Silverbeet
Calcium	S	40	6.7	4.7	65
	O	480	67	84	1600
Potassium	S	260	200	150	450
	O	1900	300	1600	2600
Magnesium	S	26	10	11	69
	O	240	89	700	1700
Sodium	S	<1	2.4	<1	180
	O	<10	26	20	1800
Iron	S	0.6	<0.5	0.5	1.4
	O	<5	<5	<5	9.4
Zinc	S	0.38	0.19	0.13	0.57
	O	3.4	1.2	2.5	130

S = Supermarket produce
O = Organic produce
Figures are in milligrams per kilogram

more iron, copper and zinc. In addition, this study found organic milk and dairy products contained significantly more nutrients than their conventional alternatives.

United States study

A recent report from scientists at two American universities has compared 11 key nutrients in organic and conventionally grown food and found that, on average, the organic food contained 25% more nutrients (see www.organic-center.org).

Why is it so?

Many reasons have been put forward to explain these results. One is that plants grown with artificial nitrogen-based fertilisers take up more water, thus diluting the nutrients. Another possible cause is that many chemical fertilisers and pesticides tend to make the soil more acidic, making some nutrients unavailable to the plants and thus to those who consume them. A widely held view is that modern farming methods have depleted the soil of a range of trace elements not usually supplied by chemical fertilisers.

No chemicals

Pesticides have been linked with a range of human health complaints, from allergies and skin disorders to cancers and reproductive and central nervous system disorders. A single example is research funded by the European Union that has linked the use of pesticides, including fly sprays and weed killers, to a significantly increased risk of developing Parkinson's disease.

Human health

Just how much pesticide residue might be in the food we eat has been hotly debated. It seems clear that much of our conventionally grown food contains minute pesticide residues, which government authorities assure us are within legal limits. Many of us, however, would rather our food contained no residues and the only way to be assured of this is to either grow or buy organic.

Babies and children are at most risk of health damage from pesticide exposure or ingestion, even at levels that might have been deemed 'safe' for adults. This is because of their smaller body weight and their immature immune systems. Babies are still being born with traces of long-banned pesticides in their blood. Who knows which of the dozens of crop chemicals in use today will be banned in the future and continue to take their toll in years to come?

One study in America found virtually no traces of the common pesticides malathion and chlorpyrifos in urine samples of a group of children who ate only organic food. When the children returned to eating conventionally grown food their urine samples showed pesticide metabolites at concerningly high levels.

A recent report claims that conventionally grown fruits are 3.6, and vegetables 8.6, times more likely to contain residues. Often the residues are multiple. Apples, for example, have shown 12 different chemical residues, grapes 10, lettuce 12, pears 10 and silverbeet 12. Even though each residue might be within the legal limit, there is no knowledge of how they might interact and multiply any harmful effects.

Environmental health

Humans are not the only creatures affected by chemicals. All creatures, from the beneficial soil micro-organisms to carnivores high in the food chain, are detrimentally affected.

Soil pollution and degradation, salinity, acidification, water contamination, atmospheric pollution and greenhouse gases are all by-products of modern farming methods and chemical use. Many large-scale food growers are reducing their chemical use and practising soil conservation farming methods and should be given credit for doing so. However, numerous studies continue to find that organic growing is better for the environment than conventional farming.

Organically managed soil is a wonderful carbon sink, with the capacity to store huge amounts of carbon dioxide. The decay of carboniferous organic matter forms humus which can remain in the soil for perhaps 1000

> ### WORDS OF WISDOM
>
> Former long-time ABC garden presenter Peter Cundall was quoted in the Sydney Morning Herald (21 July 2008):
>
> *'We've got a Depression coming. I've seen it coming for years but what I'm saying is . . . that we can survive by growing food in our own backyards . . . The best food you can eat. No poisons. No chemicals. Magnificent production.'*

> **GREENHOUSE GASES IN FOOD PRODUCTION**
>
> - About 20% of the world's greenhouse gas production comes from current agricultural practices.
> - Switching from conventional tillage (ploughing) to no-till agriculture reduces carbon dioxide emissions by anything from 50% to 90%.
> - Each tonne of nitrogen fertiliser used results in five tonnes of carbon dioxide being emitted into the atmosphere as well as significant amounts of nitrous oxide, which is a much more damaging greenhouse gas than carbon dioxide. Organic growing uses substantially less nitrogen-based fertiliser, so reduces emissions.
> - Organic growing methods sequester carbon dioxide in the soil.

years or more. Over time, as more organic matter decays, more carbon accumulates beneficially in the soil instead of being released as a gas that accumulates harmfully in the atmosphere, as it does when soil is regularly ploughed or dug over.

No matter how small your garden, organic methods can make a difference and help reduce greenhouse gas emissions worldwide. It has been estimated that a 1000-square-metre housing block can store as much as half a tonne of carbon, equivalent to about half the carbon emitted by an average car in a year.

Organic growing nurtures and replenishes soil, conserves water, reduces greenhouse gases and should emit no potential contaminants into the soil, water or atmosphere. Even on the small scale of your home garden these factors are important to environmental health.

Reducing ecological footprint

A lot has been spoken and written in recent years about the ecological footprint, a useful way of estimating the impact humanity is having on the planet. It refers to the area of the planet, in hectares, needed to produce everything humans use to sustain our lifestyles and to neutralise our wastes. Australians have, on average, one of the world's largest ecological footprints.

One of the major contributors to the ecological footprint is food production. The Victorian Environment Protection Authority (EPA) has found that food production

> **ECOLOGICAL FOOTPRINT IN HECTARES PER PERSON**
>
> | | |
> |---|---|
> | United States | 9.5 |
> | Australia | 7.7 |
> | New Zealand | 7.6 |
> | United Kingdom | 5.4 |
> | Japan | 4.3 |
> | Italy | 3.8 |
> | China | 1.5 |
> | Bangladesh | 0.5 |
>
> The amount of space per person available on the planet is 2.2 hectares.
>
> Note that different published 'footprint' charts differ slightly in their estimates. One recently published chart, for example, puts Australia's footprint at 6.6 ha.

(including its transportation) is responsible for 37% of the average Victorian's environmental footprint. Obviously, the more we can grow ourselves using planet-friendly organic methods, the more we can reduce our family's footprint.

Anyone interested in trying to calculate their own ecological footprint can visit the website: www.myfootprint.org.

Reducing our footprint in the garden

- Grow food without using artificial fertilisers and pesticides, whose manufacture and absorption strain natural resources.
- Recycle our own green wastes via compost and mulch, thus eliminating approximately 143 kg per person per year of food and garden waste that goes to landfill.
- Use our gardens as carbon sinks, with carbon being stored in both the biomass of the plants we grow and in the organic matter we return to the soil.
- Reduce the amount of fuel needed to grow and transport commercially grown food.
- Reduce our own fuel use through needing fewer trips to the supermarket.
- Reduce wasteful packaging.
- With more homegrown produce available to us we can reduce our meat consumption. The livestock industry produces a high percentage of the world's greenhouse emissions in the form of methane, which is at least 20 times as damaging as carbon dioxide, but which breaks down much more quickly. Thus, by reducing our meat consumption, we can have a quick and effective impact on reducing our environmental footprint.

MEAT AND METHANE

Global livestock production emits about 18% of the world's greenhouse gases. This is more than the total emissions produced by burning fossil fuels for all forms of transportation – about 13.5%. The methane produced by all the cattle and sheep in Australia has more environmental impact than the emissions from all the nation's coal-fired power stations.

Food miles

There is increasing attention being given worldwide to the distance food travels before it reaches the consumer's plate. In general, the further food travels the more fuel is used and the more greenhouse emissions are produced. A recent Melbourne-based study, believed to be the first of its kind in Australia, gives some fascinating insights into how far our food travels (go to www.ceres.org.au and follow the links: Projects & Research; Projects; Food Miles Report).

A selection of 29 food items chosen as being representative of a typical Victorian shopping basket was studied. The astonishing finding was that this average basket of food had travelled a total of over 70 000 kilometres from producer to consumer. The items had travelled by road within Australia and imported items had been transported by ship. Goods included fruit and vegetables, meat and dairy products, cereals and legumes, and miscellaneous items such as margarine, sugar, tea and chocolate.

Of the fruit and vegetables included, bananas had the highest food miles at 2746 and lettuce the lowest at 54. Overall, the five shortest travelling and lowest emission items were lettuce, apples, chicken, potatoes and beef, all of which require little or no processing and have no added ingredients.

Calculating the environmental effects of food production is immensely complicated and there is more to take into account than simply the distance food travels. Food grown in heated greenhouses, for example, uses more fuel and produces more carbon emissions than food grown out in the open. Fertilisers and pesticides used during a crop's growth will have their own associated travel and production impacts as well as other effects on the environment. Depending on economies of scale and routes travelled, large trucks could emit less carbon per tonne carried than smaller ones. Whether the truck is fully loaded or not and the type of fuel it uses are also factors to be considered. Air travel and packaging will add to the environmental effects of food production.

It has been estimated that the environmental benefits of buying conventionally grown food that is grown close to home outweigh the benefits of buying organically grown food that has been transported over long distances. By growing our food organically right where we live, or in community gardens nearby, we benefit the environment in every way.

Good exercise

One of the important ways we can maintain good health is to exercise more. Exercise prevents obesity with all its associated health problems, keeps our cardiovascular and circulatory systems in good condition and reduces osteoporosis. Gardening is an enjoyable and productive way of keeping fit. Do take care of your back by not lifting weights that are too heavy for you and match the duration and difficulty of the task to any physical limitations you might have.

Feel-good factor

The big intangible in growing your own food is how good you feel when you harvest, prepare and serve it to your family and yourself. Gardening is often recommended as therapy for those with mental or emotional health problems. How much more satisfying, when you can eat or share with friends the fruits of your labour.

Research into brain processes has shown that a particular frequency of brain waves (13 hertz) is the most beneficial and healing. This frequency is associated with relaxation states, some forms of exercise, deep sleep, or absorbing activities such as gardening.

Some interesting medical research has recently discovered that a bacterium (*Mycobacterium vaccae*) found in soil stimulates the production in humans of serotonin, a neurochemical associated with feelings of wellbeing. Perhaps this is another reason why gardening, involving frequent contact with the soil, has long been seen as a way of reducing stress. Do be aware, though, that there could be potentially harmful micro-organisms in soil, as well as spiders and other biting hazards or prickles that might be

> ### STRESS AND HEALTH
> Stress is frequently linked with many illnesses, including cancers, heart disease, chronic pain, infectious diseases, depression and immune dysfunction. Gardening lowers stress levels.

A variety of pumpkins on display at Heronswood, headquarters of Digger's Seeds.

lurking in garden detritus, so take appropriate care and always wear gloves when working in the garden.

Yet another example of the mental health benefits of gardening comes from the results of a long-term study into ways of preventing dementia. People who gardened regularly were found to have a 36% lower risk of developing dementia.

Variety adds spice to life

When you grow your own food, vast possibilities for culinary delights open up before you. If you grow vegies and decide to propagate them from seed, you can choose some of the more unusual varieties. There are red, purple, yellow or striped tomatoes; purple potatoes or the sausage-shaped Kipflers; yellow or striped beetroots; capsicums in all the colours of the rainbow; red cabbages and Brussels sprouts; multi-coloured silverbeet; an amazing diversity of lettuce and salad greens, pumpkins and squashes, or perhaps a watermelon with moon and star markings on its skin.

There are many fruits you can grow in your garden that are not often seen in shops. You might decide to plant a few of the more unusual species and to continue to buy the commonly available ones. Some to consider are feijoa, pomegranate, persimmon, guava, goji berry, pitaya and gooseberry.

You can grow a variety of herbs not usually available in shops. You can never have too many herbs around the garden for their culinary uses, aromatic scents, pest-repellent and beneficial-predator-attracting properties and pretty flowers. Many herbs also have medicinal properties and this is a whole new field to explore.

Another exciting field of interest to many is that of bush tucker. Many native plants have edible roots, seeds, fruits or leaves. They are usually hardy, low-maintenance plants and are often attractive garden dwellers in their own right, serving a multitude of purposes, from providing bird and insect habitat to producing pretty (though usually small) blooms in addition to their edible parts.

For the children

Gardening is a wonderful interest for children. It gets them involved in a productive

I grew all these delicious tomato varieties one summer.

> **ACTION PLAN**
>
> - Top 10 reasons to grow your own food:
>   - good taste
>   - economy
>   - freshness
>   - nutrition
>   - chemical free
>   - reduced ecological footprint
>   - exercise
>   - feel good
>   - variety
>   - for the children.

outdoor activity, teaches them about food production in the most practical way possible and is a pleasant way of bonding with and learning from an adult. Give a child his or her own patch to grow whatever they like to eat, keep adult interference subtle and discreet, and watch the pride when the crop is harvested and shared in the family meal.

Start with something that is quick to grow, maybe radishes or a punnet of mixed lettuce, or something fun and spectacular such as sunflowers. Most children like strawberries and they produce quite quickly and can be grown in a variety of small spaces or fun pots.

With the prevalent concern about childhood obesity and all its associated health ramifications, learning that growing food can be enjoyable and that homegrown food is so good to eat will be of inestimable value to children throughout their lives.

Under the leadership and inspiration of chef Stephanie Alexander, many schools have implemented the Stephanie Alexander Kitchen Garden Program. This involves children learning how to grow food at school, cooking it and eating together. In early 2009 the Federal Government committed funds to extend the program to 190 schools around Australia. The aim is to promote healthy eating habits for life and combat childhood obesity. Perhaps it will be the children in many cases teaching the adults how to do it.

WHERE AND WHAT?
First thoughts

You have decided to grow some of your own food. Now you need to decide what you would like or are able to grow, and where you can incorporate your new project into your existing garden. There are numerous options open to you, but what you can achieve will depend on both the time and the money you have available. Some projects are costlier to set up than others, some require more time. People with both time and money at their disposal will be able to try any of the options discussed in this book and grow a large amount of the family's fruit, vegetables and herbs, even in a relatively small space. Where time is available but money is short, some options will be restricted, but there is no reason a similarly large amount of food cannot be grown. Even if you are very busy and have little spare cash there are many possibilities open to you.

You can have a traditional dedicated vegie patch, orchard or herb garden or grow your food plants in a joyful productive mixture throughout the garden.

Location, location, location
Take a walk around the garden and see where you could plant some vegies, fruit trees or herbs. Ideally, vegies need a sunny spot sheltered from strong winds, facing north or north-east is preferable. Up to six hours a day of sun is required but morning sun is preferred, especially in Australian conditions, because afternoon sun can get too hot and burn plants. If your chosen spot faces the full force of the afternoon sun you will need to provide some summer shade.

Most fruiting plants need wind protection and sunshine as well, but berries will often thrive in dappled shade with just a couple of hours a day of sunshine. Blueberries and currants, for example, suit a cool, moist site sheltered from strong winds, with morning sun and afternoon shade. If you decide to grow some fruits, it is wise to ask for advice at a local nursery and to look at gardens in your area, noticing which plants are thriving and observing the microclimates they are growing in.

Avoid overhanging trees that will rob nutrients and cast too much shade, unless you want the afternoon shade for blueberries or currants. Steer clear of high fences and adjacent buildings that will cast shade in the mornings and early afternoons, though shelter from the late afternoon summer sun is a welcome feature in hotter locations.

Do you have pets and children? You don't want to site a vegie garden where it might be damaged by ball games, frisbees or frisky dogs; a dividing fence might be called for.

A flat site is easier to work with, but a sloping area can be terraced. You will need a tap nearby, and proximity to a shed to store tools and accessories in will make gardening more efficient.

You might have space for a designated vegie garden or mini orchard, but there are many other possibilities. Remember that as well as all the benefits of food growing discussed in Chapter 1, many food plants also look decorative so there is no need to hide your food garden in the backyard. Use your imagination to make it an attractive feature that enhances your home.

Food among the flowers

Do away with a flower bed and grow vegies there instead. Or grow vegies and herbs among the flowers. Alternate red cabbages or rainbow silverbeet with primulas, petunias or polyanthus. Grow broad beans at the back of a border, or in the centre of an island bed, with flowers in front and spreading around the base of the beans to attract pollinators and mulch the crop. The broad bean variety 'Crimson Flowered' is stunning in its own right. Grow sweet peas up the stalks of corn plants or climbing beans on a trellis behind the flower garden.

Other vegies that look attractive when incorporated in a flower bed include globe artichoke, purple broccoli, button squash, yellow zucchinis, miniature pumpkins, bush cucumbers, cherry tomatoes in a range of colours, hot peppers, capsicums, eggplant and decorative lettuce varieties.

Cheerful marigolds among the vegies.

Use thyme, oregano, marjoram, chives, dwarf lavender or strawberries as edging plants. Instead of a purely ornamental flowering cherry or plum, plant a fruiting variety. You might do away with the roses along the path and replace them with 'Ballerina' apples (in southern Australia) or a bush tucker hedge and plant strawberries or peppermint as an understorey. Can't bear to replace the roses? Keep them and plant an edible understorey crop. No doubt you can think of many other possibilities to suit your own situation.

Many herbs are attractive flowering plants in their own right. Use borage, calendula, nasturtium, violet, bergamot, sage, santolina, tansy, burnett and chamomile for their pretty flowers as well as their food and potential medicinal uses. Let them go to seed and they'll keep coming up year after year.

Flowers as food

Your flower beds themselves can be a source of food. Flowers are never going to be the basis of a sustaining meal, but many are edible and can add a unique flavour and

The marigolds deter soil nematodes as well as add colour to the bed.

Not only a beautiful focal point, the flowers can be eaten as well.

decorative appeal to a salad or garnish. Larger blooms such as zucchinis and nasturtiums make unusual appetisers when filled. Use flowers fresh and wash them under a gentle water spray to remove dust and insects. Tiny flowers are used whole, larger ones can be left whole for decorative impact or pulled apart into scattered petals. Never eat flowers from plants that have been sprayed with chemicals. Some flowers are poisonous, so if you are unsure of the correct identification of the plant, do not eat it. Some flowers are very mild in flavour, others quite strong. Try a little at a time if you are unsure.

Usually, flowers of the culinary herbs taste similar to the leaves. Try the blooms of borage, chives, sage, rosemary, mint,

Violas, hollyhocks and nasturtiums are just a few of the edible flowers you might already have growing in your garden.

bergamot, fennel, nasturtiums and rocket. Edible vegetable flowers include peas, broad beans and zucchinis.

Rose petals are edible, with the most highly perfumed being the most flavourful as well. Lavender flowers can be used in both sweet and savoury cooking and can be used dried as well as fresh. Violets, heartsease and dianthus all have edible flowers. Buds and flowers of daylily flowers can be eaten. See Chapter 11 for more details about a selection of herbs and edible flowers. The chart opposite names more edible flowers and some suggestions about what to eat them with.

Broad beans utilise the vertical space behind brassicas and youngberries are supported on leftover reinforcing mesh against the fence.

Go for height

Use any vertical support you might have around the garden. Attach lattice or wire trellis to fences or sheds. Metal fences that get the full force of the afternoon sun in summer become very hot and can reflect that heat onto plants and damage them, but they can still be utilised for peas that grow in early spring and crop before the heat of summer. Metal fences that get morning or early afternoon sun should be suitable to support a trellis to grow most fruiting plants.

Reinforcing mesh left from the house building or any concreting job can be cut to suit. I have seen the arms and wires from an old rotary clothesline used to make a trellis. If you have no suitable second-hand materials, you can

Fruit salad trees growing against recycled plastic lattice attached to the side of the deck.

This vertical trellis supports peas.

Flower	Good with
Angelica (*Angelica archangelica*)	salads, vegetables, fruit
Anise hyssop (*Agastache foeniculum*)	salads, vegetables, pasta, fruit
Basil (*Ocimum basilicum*)	tomatoes, vegetables, fish, chicken, pasta, rice
Bergamot petals (*Monarda didyma*)	salads, vegetables, pasta, fish
Borage (*Borago officinalis*)	salads, fruit
Calendula (*Calendula officinalis*)	salads, stews
Catmint (*Nepeta cataria*)	vegetables, pasta, rice
Chicory (*Cichorium intybus*)	salads
Chives (*Allium schoenoprasum*)	salads, vegetables, sauces
Coriander (*Coriandrum sativum*)	Asian dishes, salads, soups, vegetables
Daylily (*Hemerocallis* spp.)	Asian dishes, soups, salads
Dill (*Anethum graveolens*)	salads, fish, vegetables, dressings, pickles
Fennel (*Foeniculum vulgare*)	salads, fish, pork
Garland chrysanthemum (*Chrysanthemum coronarium*)	salads, vegetables, soups
Garlic chives (*Allium tuberosum*)	salads, vegetables, sauces
Heartsease (*Viola tricolor*)	salads, fruit
Hollyhock (*Alcea rosea*)	fruit, dessert
Honeysuckle (*Lonicera caprifolium*)	salads, desserts
Lavender (*Lavandula angustifolia*)	chicken, desserts, cakes, biscuits
Lemon (*Citrus limon*)	Asian dishes, desserts
Lemon verbena (*Aloysia triphylla*)	fruit
Mint (*Mentha* spp.)	salads, desserts, vegetables
Myrtle (*Myrtus communis*)	fruit, fish, pork
Nasturtium (*Trapaeolum majus*)	salads, vegetables
Orange (*Citrus sinensis*)	Asian dishes, desserts
Oregano (*Origanum vulgare*)	vegetables, fish, chicken
Phlox (*Phlox drummondii*)	salads, desserts
Pinks (*Dianthus* spp.)	fruit, desserts, cakes
Primrose (*Primula vulgaris*)	salads
Rocket (*Eruca sativa*)	Asian dishes, salads
Rosemary (*Rosmarinus officinalis*)	tomatoes, lamb
Rose petals (*Rosa* spp.)	jam or jelly, cake
Sage (*Salvia officinalis*)	Asian dishes, rice, meat
Sunflower petals (*Helianthus annus*)	Asian dishes, salads, pasta
Sweet cicely (*Myrrhis odorata*)	fruit
Sweet violet (*Viola odorata*)	salads, desserts
Yarrow (*Achillea millefolium*)	salads, vegetables
Zucchini (*Cucurbita pepo*)	usually battered and/or stuffed

Unless otherwise specified, the whole flower can be eaten.

Peas supported on reinforcing mesh behind baby corn plants.

buy plastic lattice (made from recycled material) to attach to a fence; plastic will keep its shape and last longer than timber.

Grow peas, climbing beans, cucumbers, passionfruit vines or berry canes up verandah posts, trellis or lattice, or espalier some fruit trees – it's easier than you might think.

Green walls

A commercial system, which so far has been mainly used for decorative effect in such places as shopping centres, could turn out to have useful applications for food growing in small spaces. Known as the Elmich Green Wall, this method consists of lightweight plastic Vertical Greening Modules (VGM^{TM}) made from recycled plastic and surrounded by metal support frames. The modules attach to each other with snap-on clips and are anchored onto structurally sound walls, which could be the walls of your house.

Each module has 16 spaced openings for plants and contains a geotextile bag, which is filled with a lightweight planting medium. Watering is via drip irrigation and any overflow can be collected in trays at the bottom of the wall to be reused. As well as being a vertical garden, the Green Wall insulates the wall it is attached to.

This system is not for everyone and will need some experimentation to be adapted to grow productive food plants, but anyone with the time, practical skills and curiosity might like to have a look at the website: www.elmich.com.

Climbing beans twine up the mesh behind cucumbers.

Go delightfully potty

Most food plants grow well in pots. Place large tubs on a sunny verandah or balcony, or in any otherwise wasted space. Long rectangular planters are space efficient. You can be very economical and reuse old containers such as broccoli boxes or even old bathtubs, or spend some money on attractive pots to enhance your garden theme. The pots will last for many years and you will be saving on food, so the money is well spent.

I recommend plastic pots over unglazed terracotta, concrete or glazed clay ones.

BE INVENTIVE

If the budget is tight or you prefer to source previously used items, look around you for suitable plant containers. Timber yards, scrap metal yards, garage sales and trash and treasure markets are all potential sources of numerous types of containers. A coat of paint might be all that is needed to transform them to suit your garden style.

My mother told me a story from her childhood in about 1939. Her family was very poor, lived at the time in a small cottage with little or no garden space and had a clutch of small children to feed. Her parents grew vegies in kerosene tins of ordinary dirt. The vegies were fertilised with poo from the babies' nappies and watered with the contents of the nappy bucket. I am not recommending this method, but it is a wonderful example of making the most of what is available to you.

Twenty years later, during my own childhood, I remember my grandparents' larger garden with fruit trees along one side of the house and a sizeable vegie garden taking up most of the backyard. They might still have been poor in monetary terms, but they seemed rich to me with that abundance of food on hand.

Capsicum surrounded by beets that have been grown for their edible, colourful leaves.

Unglazed terracotta and concrete are not water efficient. Glazed pots look wonderful, but often don't have enough drainage holes (resulting in boggy soil during wet times of the year) and they don't retain water as well as plastic during hot weather. In addition, large clay pots are very heavy even when empty, and virtually impossible to move once full of damp soil. They also break more readily if they do happen to get knocked over. Pots made from a composite of fibreglass and clay are lighter, but so far I have not come across much variety of shape or colour, although they can be painted to suit your colour scheme.

Pots full of soil, even plastic pots, are heavy. I recommend you buy a trolley and/or some wheeled pot supports to make moving them around easy on your back. The EarthBox® mentioned in Chapter 3 comes complete with castors for easy transportation around the garden or courtyard.

There are some systems of stackable plastic pots available, which are very compact and space efficient and suitable for growing herbs, strawberries or small vegies such as lettuce, Asian greens and radishes.

Grow strawberries in hanging pots to keep them out of reach of snails and grazing dogs (our Labrador ate any fruit within reach and especially loved strawberries). Culinary herbs can be grown in hanging pots accessible to the kitchen.

Tomato and basil, perfect companions. The wire frame supports the tomato as it grows.

Strawberries in hanging pots are out of reach of slugs, snails and the family dog.

Balconies, courtyards and rooftops

If your only space is a balcony, rooftop or courtyard, you can still grow some food in large pots or planter boxes made of a lightweight material such as Hebel blocks. The shape of your space will determine the shape of pot to choose. If the space is long and narrow, as these areas often are, rectangular pots are more space efficient than round ones.

In the case of a balcony, be aware of safety issues. Pots can be heavy. Soil and water make them heavier. Be sure your balcony structure is strong enough to support them and ensure they are well within the confines of the balcony so there is no chance they can fall over the edge. Consider a hydroponics system where the growing medium is lightweight vermiculite, rockwool or perlite, rather than heavy soil or potting mix.

Most plants will need to be in a spot that has sunshine for about six hours a day, though

Potted lettuce on the deck are handy to the kitchen.

An old bathtub has become a productive vegie garden. (Photo courtesy Sue Heggie)

mints, lettuces, strawberries and other berry plants will probably thrive in indirect sun or dappled shade. Where the spot is in full sun, perhaps with reflected and radiated heat from surrounding walls, you will need to provide some shade cover. A garden umbrella or shadecloth will do the job. Hot spots are suitable for many of the hardier herbs. Thyme, marjoram, oregano, rosemary, lavender or a bay tree should be ideal. Suitable vegies would be tomatoes, capsicums, globe artichokes and zucchinis.

The challenges for rooftop spaces are a little different. These are likely to be exposed, sunny, windy areas. If you have wing walls or other structures on the roof, place some pots where they will benefit from the shade and wind protection. Maybe it is possible to erect a lattice, a pergola structure or a gazebo. Alternatively use garden umbrellas, shadecloth or sails for shade.

Be aware that apartment block dwellers could need approval from the body corporate before making alterations that change the appearance of the building. Council approval might be needed for any construction on top of a house or garage. Waterproofing, drainage and the strength of the roof structure to take the added weight must be taken into consideration as well.

Herbs and bush tucker among the shrubs

Many herbs have similar growing requirements to native and other hardy shrubs. Try lavender, rosemary and sage throughout the shrubs, with thyme, marjoram, oregano and chamomile wandering at the base as living mulch. A lemon verbena bush or a bay tree would suit situations where a little more height is needed.

Incorporate bush tucker plants into your garden design. There are numerous shrubs, small trees and understorey plants that will suit a small garden. Find out where the plant originated and what its native habitat is to find an appropriate spot in the garden where it will thrive with little care. Planting a rainforest gully dweller in an exposed hot position is not a recipe for success.

Do away with the lawn

Lawns need lots of water and mowing and consume energy to keep them in order. I know they have their aesthetic appeal and often complement garden beds, but looked at from any logical perspective, lawns are a waste of valuable resources. Another downside of lawns is that the fertilisers used to keep them verdant too often make their way into our waterways, where they feed environmental weeds that proliferate and destroy native riparian ecosystems, and contribute to toxic algal blooms. Pesticides and weedicides used on lawns can also wash into waterways and leach into the ground water, with undesirable consequences for humans and aquatic wildlife. In addition, the lawn is usually located in the sunniest area of the garden, which would be ideal for a vegie and/or herb garden or for a copse of hardy bush tucker plants. Consider transforming your lawn into a productive and decorative food garden, such as the permaculture food forest shown being developed in Chapter 5.

You will find more great ideas to adapt to your own situation in Chapter 5 as well.

What to grow
After looking carefully around your garden you should have some ideas about how to best use the space available to you. Now you need to decide what you are going to grow.

How ambitious are you?
You need to be realistic about the available space, your time constraints and your physical ability. Do you want to have a variety of herbs and salad greens for the summer? Can you grow a good selection of your family's vegies and herbs and some fruit throughout the year? Are you more ambitious and think you have space and time enough to provide the bulk of your family's fresh produce? Perhaps you hate working outside in the winter and prefer to stick to warm season crops. Maybe incorporating a few herbs and bush tucker shrubs into the garden to spice up your meals appeals to you; this is a very easy and fun way to begin the adventure of growing your own food.

What do you like?
No matter how much space and time you have, there's no point growing anything you and your family don't like eating. Be realistic too, about how much you like certain foods. If zucchinis are only tolerated in moderation and heavily disguised by other flavours, either don't grow them at all or stick to one or two bushes.

Be selective
Some crops take up a lot of space or tie up a bed for a long time in relation to their productivity, so might not be best suited to gardens with space limitations. Onions, for example, can occupy their bed for five to six months. No matter how much you like homegrown onions, if space is a problem, you need to ask yourself whether another, more productive crop would be a better choice. Broccoli and celery will take up a bed for a similar length of time but produce more food, though most families would not use enough celery to make planting a bed of it worthwhile. Potatoes are usually very cheap to buy, so you might decide your space would be put to better use growing a higher dollar-value crop, though they offer one of the highest food-value crops for the space they take up. Pumpkins need lots of space to sprawl but they can be very productive and give you an easily stored vegie to enjoy over winter. Consider too that there are miniature varieties of pumpkins that might suit your needs better. You need to weigh up these choices carefully.

Fruitful concepts
Most conventional fruit trees grow too big for any but the largest gardens and large gardens are a luxury (or perhaps a burden, depending on your outlook) few people have these days. Plum trees, for example, are considered to be small trees, but they will grow to seven metres high and spread at least that much. Cherries can grow to 10 metres and apples from 10 to 15 metres, and let's not even think about pears as they grow so big.

However, there are many ways of enjoying fruit from the garden. You can continually prune your trees to keep them a manageable size – although this is too much work for me. Consider some of these ideas instead.

These multigrafted fruit trees are on dwarfing rootstock.

Grapevines utilise vertical space.

Dwarfing rootstock

Until recently the variety of fruit trees available on dwarfing rootstock was very limited. The trees are grafted onto dwarfing rootstock that will keep them to a much smaller size than their conventional counterparts, often down to about two metres, but this varies from plant to plant. Now, however, there is an extensive range, including tropical fruit trees, and even dwarfing avocados and macadamia nut trees. In general, nut trees grow far too large for a small garden (with the exception perhaps of hazelnuts, which grow to about six metres) so have not been discussed in this book. However, now anyone in a frost-free location can grow macadamia nuts. This development opens up exciting possibilities for home gardeners who can now grow an extensive range of fruit trees in pots or in the ground in their small gardens. Ask about these plants at your local nursery or see the suppliers listed in Appendix 1.

Citrus trees on dwarfing rootstock are widely available. Multi-grafted trees, with several varieties grafted onto the one trunk, known

Even mangos and avocados can now be grown in a small garden.

Pepinos take up little horizontal space.

as 'fruit salad trees', could be more difficult to source. Ask your nursery about this, or see details of my supplier in the Appendix.

Dwarf rootstock trees are perfect to grow in large tubs or espalier onto a lattice or trellis. I have eight different varieties of stone fruits on two plants, along with a four-graft and a two-graft citrus tree. The stone fruits are espaliered; the citrus are growing as central features in separate beds.

You can make a miniature food garden by having a multi-grafted tree in a large tub with salad greens or herbs growing around it.

Compact cultivars

A number of recent fruit cultivars have been especially bred to maintain a compact size, but still produce normal-size fruit. 'Ballerina' apples grow to a slender height of three to four metres and make an attractive and productive hedge. 'Nectazee' nectarine and 'Pixie' peach both grow to about 1.5 metres with a similar spread. All of these can be grown in the garden or in pots.

A tasty medley

Berry canes are easy to train up a trellis or lattice and take up little horizontal space. Kiwifruit can be grown over a strong pergola. Grapevines can be grown up a sturdy verandah post, espaliered on a strong trellis or grown over an arbour. Strawberries can be used as edging, planted into any sunny spots, or grown very successfully in pots. Feijoas are small, bushy, evergreen trees that can be successfully grown as a hedge or in a tub. Blueberries, black and red currants, gooseberries and pepinos are bushes that can be incorporated in many spots or grown in pots. Watermelons and cantaloupes can be grown in a vegie bed, perhaps as groundcover beneath corn plants, or trained onto a lattice.

Edible cacti and succulents

Many cacti and succulents have edible flowers or fruits; in fact, I have read that all cactus fruits are edible. Be sure, though, to only eat plant parts if you have positively identified them as safe to consume. Yucca flower petals and unopen buds, for example, can be eaten.

Some of the bush tucker plants fall into the succulent category. The fruits of pigface (*Carpobrutus modestus* and *C. rosii*), for example, were eaten by Aborigines and early settlers. Ruby saltbush (*Enchylaena tomentosa*) has edible berries which were a traditional indigenous food. Other saltbushes have edible berries, but most are very tiny.

The common pigweed *Portulaca oleracea* was a staple food of the Australian indigenous people, who used all parts of the plant, either raw or cooked, including the miniscule seeds, which were ground to a paste before being cooked. This plant is said to have been the most widely used indigenous vegetable by early settlers and explorers. It still grows profusely in some areas and is usually regarded as a weed. Other portulacas were also consumed.

A native plant called warrigal greens (*Tetragonia tetragonoides*) is still widely grown and eaten as a vegetable. The leaves are used in the same way as spinach. Once established in a spot it likes, this plant will spread and keep on producing greens for the table, but the succulents mentioned above, though hardy

Tree tomatoes are a good size for a small garden and taste nothing like tomatoes.

and water efficient, will not be a very productive resource in the small home garden.

One recent introduction that could prove to be both productive and popular is the pitaya or dragon fruit. The plant is available in three different types: red pitaya (*Hylocereus polyrhizus*), yellow pitaya (*Selenicereus megalanthus*) and white pitaya (*Hylocereus undatas*).

Fruits for the tropical backyard

Many tropical fruit trees grow far too large for an average or small backyard, but there are still numerous ones that are suitable. Guavas grow to a large, bushy shrub from three to 10 metres. Pineapples take up very little space. Pawpaws are slender plants, growing two to four metres and taking up little horizontal space. Bananas are quite space efficient if looked after and the unwanted suckers removed, otherwise they'll take over the garden. The tamarillo or tree tomato has delicious fruit, not tasting anything like a tomato, and grows to a large shrub about two to three metres high. Other tropical fruits to consider are acerola, babaco, black sapote, miracle fruit and Brazil cherry.

Most of these plants will thrive in a subtropical or tropical environment and many will even survive and fruit in a suitable frost-free microclimate in temperate areas, especially if there is radiated heat from a brick or stone wall.

Bush tucker

Maybe your preference is not for conventional fruits and vegies at all, or you might want to add a little variety by incorporating some bush tucker plants into your edible garden. There are many to choose from but they are not always readily available from nurseries, and some, of course, grow too large for most gardens. You will need to locate a specialist nursery in your area to advise you about what is suitable.

I consider that the fruit-producing plants are probably more suited for gardens than those with edible roots and tubers that need to be dug up or with seeds that need to be pounded into flour. Several small shrubs or prostrate plants should be suitable for garden situations in many areas of Australia. These include prickly currant bush, midgenberry, muntries, ruby saltbush and cranberry heath. Some fruiting bush tucker plants that grow to a large shrub/small tree size include finger limes and Davidson plum.

Some bush tucker plants are grown for their edible leaves. The leaves of warrigal greens, for example, are cooked and eaten in the same way as spinach. The leaves of plants such

> **BUSH TUCKER FRUITS HIGH IN ANTIOXIDANTS**
>
> Research carried out by CSIRO scientists has confirmed that many native fruits are much higher in antioxidants than blueberries, which are often cited for their rich antioxidant content. The finding applied to Kakadu plum, Illawarra plum, Burdekin plum, Davidson plum, riberry, finger limes, Tasmanian pepper, brush cherry, Cedar Bay cherry, muntries and Molucca raspberry. The most suitable of these for small to medium gardens are finger limes, muntries, Tasmanian pepper, Davidson plum and Molucca raspberries. Antioxidants have many health benefits, including reducing the risk of heart disease, diabetes, cancer, macular degeneration and Alzheimer's disease.

as broad-leaf palm lily, lemon myrtle and mountain pepper are used as flavouring. The berries of the mountain pepper can be used as a pepper substitute. Teas are made from lemon myrtle and lemon-scented tea tree.

Bush tucker plants suited to your area will be hardy and drought-tolerant, needing minimal watering and fertilising once established. However, like any productive plant, they will not produce good crops unless they are watered and fertilised appropriately. Maybe they need less care than our more conventional fruits to survive hard times, but if you expect plentiful crops you do need to look after them. If you choose not to water and fertilise them regularly, you will probably still be able to pluck a few berries as you walk around the garden.

There are bush tucker plants to suit every niche in the garden and every climate zone and soil type, naturally, because they originated here. If the small sample described later in this book excites your interest, I recommend you obtain one of the excellent books available and have a browse to find out what might suit your garden, or have a look at the website: www.goldfieldsrevegetation.com.au.

Rare and unusual

One of the joys of growing your own food is the ability to try some of the more unusual varieties of the commonly available species as well as some of the rare and unusual species. Remember though, most of the time if a food plant is not widely available, it is because there is a reason. It might be that the crop is not commercially viable because it does not transport and store without damage. Perhaps it only grows in a very limited climate and/or soil type, which will also limit commercial viability. These plants are ideal to try at home.

However, it might be that a plant is not widely known because it does not taste very good. There is a difference between being edible and being delicious.

By all means look for unusual varieties on the websites of specialist nurseries or at farmers' markets. Your local permaculture or seed savers group and community gardens are other sources of unusual edibles and, being sourced locally, are likely to be suited to the climate and soil in your garden. If your gardening space is restricted though, I recommend sticking with proven species and varieties or those recommended by other gardeners in the area.

Part of the picture

Your food plants are just part, or parts, of the whole garden picture of microclimates, mini ecosystems, plots, individual plants, hard surfaces, sheds, fences and other built structures. Consider how they fit into the picture; in particular, how they are influenced by other plants in the garden.

The importance of diversity

Other plants can be of inestimable value in maintaining the health of your food plants. Insect- and bird-attracting plants will help keep food plants free of pests. Many of the insects in a garden full of diverse plantings will prey on pests. Birds, frogs and lizards consume huge quantities of insects as well as slugs and snails.

You can attract beneficial insects to your garden by incorporating plants that provide nectar and pollen for them. Many of these same plants also attract birds that consume copious quantities of pests. A different range of plants will attract seed- or fruit-eating birds, which also eat insects.

A small garden pond will be a haven for frogs and at the same time provide water that is essential for birds and beneficial insects. Where there is no space for a pond, install a birdbath or bowl of water. Do make sure the water is not deep enough to drown any birds or lizards that fall in. Perhaps have a protruding rock or floating piece of wood in the water so any creatures that might fall in can easily escape.

Rocks and logs will shelter lizards and frogs. If you don't have access to rocks or logs, use substitutes such as lengths of pipe or upturned plant pots. Hide them in out-of-the-way spots and disguise them with mulch of leaf litter or prunings.

A small pond is an attractive garden feature and could be a home for frogs too.

Plants for birds and insects

You probably already have many of these plants in your garden; if not, consider where you can incorporate as many as possible for a variety of benefits. Those marked * are either suitable for small areas or have small forms that are easy to obtain. Those marked # are environmental weeds in some areas; avoid them if this applies to your location. Find out

Callistemons will attract birds and beneficial insects.

Many succulents have flowers loved by birds and bees.

Lilly pilly berries are loved by fruit-eating birds and are also edible for humans.

by visiting the Weeds Australia website at: www.weeds.org.au or the World Wildlife Fund at: www.wwf.org.au.

For nectar and pollen feeders
- aloes*
- alyssum*#
- austral indigo*
- banksias*
- bergamot*
- blue pincushion*
- borage*
- brachyscombe daisies*
- button everlasting*
- callistemons*
- camellias*
- carrots in flower*
- common Billy-buttons*
- common everlasting*
- correas*

A variety of native plants attract numerous birds and insects.

The nectar produced by banksias is an energy-rich food source for honeyeaters.

- epacris*
- ericas*
- erigeron*#
- flowering gums
- grevilleas*
- kangaroo paws*
- open daisy-like flowers
- paperbarks
- parsley in flower*
- penstemons*
- proteas
- red-hot pokers*
- salvias
- strelizias
- wattles*
- yuccas.

For seed eaters
- banksias*
- casuarinas
- conifers*
- crepe myrtles*
- eucalypts
- grasses (native types)
- silver birches
- tea trees*
- wattles.*

For fruit eaters
- bangalow palm
- blueberry ash

> **ACTION PLAN**
> - Decide where food plants will fit into the existing garden.
> - Consider what you would like to grow/eat and what is practical for your situation.
> - Incorporate non-food plants and garden infrastructure to support your food growing efforts.

- flax lilies*
- lilly pillies*
- wild cherry.

More uses for plants

The non-food plants in your garden, as well as providing food and habitat for a range of beneficial creatures, have many other uses that can benefit food plants.

- A hedge can be a windbreak for a vegie garden or orchard.
- A large tree can provide afternoon shade for black or red currants, blueberries and other shrubs that do not like extreme heat.
- Deciduous trees give free leaf mulch, shade in summer and let sunlight through in winter.
- Almost any tree or shrub can be pruned to give free mulch.

HIGH PRODUCTIVITY FROM SMALL SPACES
Some special techniques

There are some very smart ways of increasing productivity from any given area. Some of these techniques require a significant time or monetary commitment to set up, but will bring long-term benefits. Consider your own circumstances in deciding which methods could suit you.

Permaculture

Permaculture might be considered as a philosophy encompassing a multiplicity of techniques, rather than a single method. When the concept was launched by Bill Mollison and David Holmgren in 1978 it was described as a permanent system of agriculture based on 'self-perpetuating plant and animal species useful to man'. It was meant to be a system that worked with nature and not against it.

A large emphasis was placed on perennial species such as fruit and nut trees and vegetables that would not need to be replanted each year, such as Jerusalem artichokes, asparagus and warrigal greens, and preference was to be given to plants with multiple uses.

It was recommended that the land be divided into zones. The number of zones and what you do in them can be adapted to suit your situation. The most frequently visited area, perhaps the seasonal herb and salad garden and compost area, would be sited closest to the house in zone 1. Zone 2 might be an orchard of fruit and nut trees. Less frequently visited areas such as a perennial food and timber forest or a self-foraging system for large animals perhaps would be sited further from the house in zone 3 or 4. Furthest from the house in zone 5 could be an area of regenerated or natural bushland for biodiversity conservation. In a small to medium garden zone 5 might be a copse or border of native shrubs that screens your garden from the neighbours. In the early permaculture books there was detailed advice about how to calculate the number of times per year you would be likely to visit a given plant or animal and thereby decide where in relation to the house it should be planted or housed for maximum efficiency.

The idea has spread throughout the world and has expanded to include social and economic systems as well as food production.

This extremely brief introduction cannot begin to do justice to the comprehensive nature of permaculture and there are many excellent books giving great detail about it for anyone who needs to know more. I will describe just a few methods that can easily be adapted to any small garden.

Multiple uses

The concept of choosing plants (and other elements) with many uses makes very good sense and is especially relevant when space is at a premium. These few examples will set you thinking about your own plant choices.

The old vines are being mown to produce free mulch.

- Dwarf fruit trees can be grown espalier style on lattice placed so that it acts as a visual dividing element or privacy screen within the garden, shades a deck or verandah in summer and lets light through in winter and acts as a windbreak. The fruit itself is eaten and excess can be bartered or preserved. Damaged fruit can be fed to the earthworms or poultry or put in the compost bin. The fallen leaves act as mulch. When the trees are pruned, the prunings can be shredded to use as mulch.
- Pumpkin vines spread to act as living mulch and keep the soil beneath cool and moist. The pumpkins can be eaten or bartered and will store for many months. The peel and pithy centre are fed to earthworms or put in the compost. Seeds can be roasted and eaten or saved for the next season's crop. After the harvest, the

Take care where you plant them – pumpkins will spread.

The pumpkin vine mulch was used in several places around the garden.

> **IN THE PUMPKIN PATCH**
>
> On a sunny day in May I set out to clean up the pumpkin patch. The pumpkin vines had self-propagated from compost I'd spread over the area. Though I normally don't grow pumpkins in this small garden, I decided to let them go. Already I had harvested about 40 pumpkins and given many of them away. As I pulled out the old vines I discovered another 20 or so smaller pumpkins. The vines were spread out on the mulched walkway surrounding the vegie garden and mown over. Some of the material was used to replenish the walkway, some went into the compost bin and the remainder became mulch around a multi-grafted citrus tree. An added bonus was that the small carrots the vines had spread over were still growing underneath and had not suffered too much at all. So, as well as the intended carrot crop (somewhat delayed), I had a super-abundance of free pumpkins for using and sharing and a lot of mulch and compost material. How's that for multiple use?

This pot of clumping bamboo (*Bambusa gracilis*) screens the deck and will eventually produce edible shoots and plant stakes.

vines can be pulled out and shredded to go in the compost bin or used as mulch.

- Borage, once established in the garden, self-seeds readily. It can be used as mulch or a green manure alternative. Its flowers attract bees and other pollinating insects. Both flowers and leaves have culinary uses.
- Any fruit trees provide an edible crop, shade for other plants, leaves and prunings for mulch.
- Peas and beans produce an edible crop. They can be trained to grow vertically so are useful productive plants for small areas. They can be used as mulch or green manure. Seeds are easily saved for the next year.
- For most vegetables the edible crop is only the most obvious of the uses. Any excess or damaged produce can be fed to earthworms or poultry or put into the compost bin. The plant residue, unless it has become diseased, can be cut, chopped or shredded for the compost.
- The pretty French or African marigolds can be planted among vegetables to deter soil nematodes. The strong aroma of the flowers confuses insect pests including the cabbage white butterflies, and repels white flies, carrot flies and pumpkin beetles.
- Clumping bamboo planted as a privacy screen can also provide edible shoots and strong stems for staking other plants.
- The concept of multiple uses does not only apply to food plants. A native shrubbery can be a windbreak, give shade, provide cut flowers for the house and be a valuable source of food and habitat for birds and beneficial insects. In addition, the

prunings and natural leaf drop add to the mulch layer.

Zoning

Though you might never have a dedicated food and timber forest or large animal forage area, the concept of having frequently visited plants closer to the house is one that is sensible and easy to incorporate. Having a tub or two of herbs near the door makes it very easy to snip a few leaves to flavour your meals. A patch or pot of salad vegetables for summer use can be sited fairly close to the house as well. Vegetables that you harvest less frequently can be a little further away. Fruit trees that are harvested seasonally can be further away still. Remember that it is not only for harvesting that you visit plants; they need maintenance and watering as well.

The compost bin and/or worm farm will be visited often, but are not items you necessarily want in full view close to the house. Consider a compromise by putting them in a reasonably accessible spot behind a shed or lattice screen, then grow something on the lattice. In a small garden this is probably not an issue because nothing will be a long walk from the house anyway.

To conserve your own time and energy it is efficient to place the compost bin and worm farm close to the main vegetable growing area so crop residues can be quickly disposed of and finished compost, worm castings and worm liquid are close to where they will be most frequently used. A small storage shed for gardening tools and other necessities should be located conveniently close to the house and main vegie growing area.

There will, of course, be other plants in your garden. If there is a shrubbery of hardy native and indigenous plants, for example, it will require little watering or maintenance so can be sited furthest from the house.

If you keep poultry, consider where their housing is located in relation to the vegie garden and compost bin. You will want to be able to quickly throw them garden scraps and deposit their shed litter in the compost bin. It might be your intention to use them as a means of pest control and to cultivate the soil and scratch out weeds. This will influence where they are housed in relation to the garden. See below for ideas about incorporating poultry and other animals into your garden.

Incorporating animals

Animals have always been an integral component in permaculture practices, bringing many benefits to the system. Whether or not you keep animals in your small garden is entirely a matter of choice, but it can add a new dimension to your food production. Find out about the particular animal's husbandry needs and how keeping animals is regarded by your local government authority before making the decision.

Poultry

The most obvious animal to keep in a backyard is poultry. The romantic notion of having a few pretty hens clucking around the garden does have its drawbacks. Most breeds of hens are indiscriminate scratchers and will destroy any small unprotected plants. They are also indiscriminate fertilisers and will drop the smelly stuff everywhere, whether you want it there or not. You must devise a system that allows them access only to areas you want them to scratch and poo over. Ensure that any housing gives them shade in the summer and protection from rain, cold winds and predators such as dogs and foxes – yes, foxes are around, even in the suburbs. Remember, they will need to be fed grain and pellets as well as garden waste.

There are attractive small cages you can buy, or handymen can make their own. A small moveable cage housing a few hens has a number of uses.

- The hens will give you eggs, a source of protein not readily available from plants.
- The hens themselves can be eaten, if you have a pragmatic attitude.

The attractive poultry shed blends into the garden. (Photo courtesy Happy Earth)

- The manure can be processed through the compost bin to give you fertiliser.
- If you can design your system so that a portable cage fits neatly over a vegetable bed, the hens will scratch, weed, eat insect pests and fertilise the soil for free. Then they can be moved on to the next bed.
- The hens will turn any kitchen scraps and vegetable garden waste into fertiliser.

Other animals

Rabbits and guinea pigs can be kept for the fertiliser they produce and to eat the grass on the lawn and the vegetable waste from the garden. A couple of animals in a small cage moved around the lawn (if you still have a lawn) will keep the grass trimmed and fertilised at the same time. We are not very keen in Australia on eating cute, small, furry animals, but many other cultures are more pragmatic. I mention it only as a possibility to consider – who knows what changes in attitude we'll need to adopt in our changing world.

A pretty Silkie hen fossicks around the garden at Happy Earth. (Photo courtesy Happy Earth)

> ### POULTRY AND VEGETABLE DOME
>
> An idea that is popular among permaculture practitioners is to construct two or three domes from polypipe covered in bird netting and/or plastic. The dome houses poultry, which prepare and fertilise the soil in which vegetables are then grown. The poultry, meanwhile, are preparing the soil in the next dome. This is another good example of multiple uses. If trying this method, it is very important to ensure the poultry are safe from predators, cool enough in summer and warm enough in winter. The dome must be tightly secured to prevent wind damage.

Not many new gardens offer enough space for keeping a lamb or goat, but readers with a large garden or hobby farm will probably have room. Do make sure your council and your neighbours look on the enterprise favourably. Sheep make good lawnmowers, as long as they can be kept away from anything you don't want them to eat. They will happily eat any vegetable wastes and produce copious amounts of fertiliser. Goats will not thrive on a diet of grass and vegetable waste; they require more variety, including rough woody browse, which can be difficult to supply even in a large garden.

Both sheep and goats are herd animals and prefer company, so it is preferable to keep at least two animals. Both species can be dispatched and eaten and a nanny goat can be milked to give you another source of food. A neighbour of ours sometimes has a lamb in the garden to eat the grass. Eventually, the lamb disappears; we don't ask where it is.

A responsibility

Keeping animals is a responsibility. You must make sure their particular husbandry needs are met, even when you are away from home. Every animal has different needs, which are beyond the scope of this book. Do your research before venturing into animal keeping. If you like animals, it will be a rewarding experience in many ways and will complement your food production.

> ### MARY HAD A LITTLE LAMB
>
> When I was about six years old my father brought home a tiny lamb, which became my pet. I fed it from a bottle, and brushed it with my hairbrush until my mother found out and put a stop to that unhygienic practice. After a while the lamb was taken away. I was told it went to my aunt's house to eat the grass, but next time we visited there was no sign of the lamb. Perhaps someone had stolen it, the adults told me. For years after, every time we visited my aunt I would look over the neighbours' fences, hoping to discover the thief. It wasn't until I was an adult myself that I put together the lamb's disappearance with the knowing looks exchanged by my parents and the sudden arrival of roast lamb on our dinner table.

Swales

An idea popular in permaculture systems is the use of swales to make the most of rainfall and/or run-off that falls on the land. There are many adaptations of the idea. In essence, a swale is a mulch-filled trench that runs along the contour of the land. It traps rainfall

A swale running along the contour of the land has trapped rainwater to benefit nearby plants. (Photo courtesy Happy Earth)

or run-off, which gradually leaches into the soil to water nearby plants. This idea can readily be incorporated into most gardens, especially when the site is sloping.

Aquaponics

A food production system gaining in popularity is known as aquaponics. The basis of the system is a large fish tank, containing a species that will eventually be eaten. The fish excrete into the water, producing ammonia. The water is pumped through one or more grow beds containing a hydroponics medium such as hydroton or vermiculite. Bacteria in the grow bed convert the ammonia to nitrites, then nitrates (nitrogen), which is taken up by the plants. Vegetables or herbs grown in the medium extract the nitrogen from the water as it passes through the bed. The water, now cleaned and oxygenated, slowly drains back into the tank.

Once established, the system uses little water, with the tank only needing to be topped up to replace evaporation losses. In the early stages when the tiny fish are not producing enough fertiliser, some extra soluble fertiliser such as fish or seaweed emulsion is needed, but quite soon the fish are producing all that is needed to keep the system productive.

This method will not suit people with little time or a tight budget. It does take some work and is quite costly to set up. Commercial systems are available for anyone not wanting, or not able, to devise and set up their own tank and grow beds. However, the idea can be scaled up or down to suit individual needs, and it is possible to put a system together from recycled components to save on set-up costs.

It is possible to set up a system in a courtyard or even indoors, and grow beds can be placed at a convenient working height, making this method a viable option for elderly or

Aquaponics system with covered fish tank at front right.

Plants in the left-hand rear bed are well grown, those in the three smaller beds have been recently planted.

handicapped gardeners. It is an ideal system for anyone looking for an absorbing and productive hobby.

Practical tips

These are some suggestions arising from our own experience.

- The system should be under cover and on a firm surface such as a concrete slab.
- The water in the fish tank needs to be aerated to maintain oxygen levels.

The original system before the tank was covered and the extra beds installed.

- A cover over the tank itself, in addition to the roof over the system, will prevent algal growth caused by exposure to sunlight.
- Fish need to be obtained from a hatchery and are not available at all times of the year. To get a system going while you wait for your chosen species, put a few goldfish into the tank.
- Some species, such as the silver perch we started with, are not very active and do not eat or grow much during cold weather. In fact, they all eventually died during the worst of the winter. The trout we replaced them with, however, thrived during the winter. Next time, we will buy golden perch, which are more cold-tolerant. Another grower we know has his tanks set into the ground and the water temperature is quite stable. It is possible, too, to use a heater in the water.
- The pump that circulates the water is on a timer set to come on for 10 minutes every hour for 14 hours each day. It does not operate at night.
- A careful watch needs to be kept for pests on the vegies because even most of the organic pest control options can kill the fish if they get into the water. To date, the only real pest we have had to deal with is cabbage grubs. These are picked off by hand and fed to the fish.
- It takes some time in the beginning for the bacteria to build up in the grow bed medium and begin converting the ammonia in the water to plant fertiliser. I recommend not planting anything for at least a month to give the process time to work. The bacteria are naturally occurring, but the process can be speeded

Some of the trout were smoked over hickory chips in the barbecue.

up by adding some water from an established system.
- It is not uncommon for algal blooms to appear in the water when a system is new. If this happens, the water must be replaced. Pump it onto the garden so it is not wasted; it will also be a mild fertiliser for the plants it waters.

Feeding the fish

Of course, in order to grow and keep producing fertiliser for the plants in the grow beds, the fish must be fed. This is one of the few outside inputs to the system and the only ongoing one, apart from electricity to run the pump(s). We bought some bags of food from the hatchery that supplied our fish. This is the basis of their diet. In addition, we throw into the water things such as grubs picked off the brassicas, earwigs found under pots or trapped in cardboard tubes, mosquito larvae scooped from the top of other water sources and earthworms from the worm farm. Different species have different food requirements. Some are only meat eaters, others will eat shredded greens scattered onto the water.

Hydroponics

Many readers will be familiar with the concept of growing plants hydroponically, that is, in water to which nutrients have been added. There are a number of variations and you can devise a system to suit your own space. Balconies, verandahs, rooftops and courtyards are suitable areas for a hydroponics set-up. A system can be set up indoors in a well-lit area, or suspended from a fence. It is important to use no metal components because the nutrients will cause metal to corrode.

You need a channel (or several) for the water to flow through, which can be purpose-made hydroponics channel or simple PVC rectangular downpipe. The channel has holes cut out, in which sit blocks of rockwool or plastic plant pots filled with a medium such as vermiculite or perlite. The ends of the pipe or channel must be sealed with end-caps so water cannot escape. Channel is available in

Food doesn't get any better than a simple, fresh, homegrown meal.

various sizes to suit different sized plants. Tomatoes, for example, will need larger channel and bigger rockwool blocks or vermiculite-filled pots than lettuces.

The channel(s) can be supported on any type of stand you can devise, but should be angled so the nutrient solution flows back into a holding tank. Make the stand a convenient working height for you and about 20 cm higher than the tank.

The holding tank stores the water and nutrients; about 100 litres capacity will be needed for 50 plants. A small submersible pump in the tank circulates the nutrient solution throughout the channel(s). Premixed hydroponics nutrient in powdered or liquid form can be bought and is added to the water supply in the recommended dilution. It is not necessary to have the solution flowing all the time so a timer switch is needed on the pump. You should only need to pump the nutrient solution for an hour three times a day, during daylight hours.

The rockwool blocks or pots of vermiculite should be soaked in the nutrient solution before seeds or seedlings are planted. If planting seedlings, all traces of soil or potting mix must be gently washed from the roots before planting.

A very small system, such as one that can be suspended from a fence, can be made from a single length of channel or downpipe. Provided you can remember to pour in the nutrient solution manually often enough to keep the plants' roots well moistened, no pump or timer is needed.

If this all seems too hard or you want more information, there are numerous hydroponics kits available to suit all situations, from tabletop to balcony to commercial scale. Visit this website to have a look at some of the options: www.hydromasta.com.au or see the Appendix for a number of email contacts.

Verti-Gro® system

Though it is not available yet in Australia, a system worth looking at for small areas is called Verti-Gro®. It consists of stackable plastic pots that can be used in a variety of conformations, from tabletop models to large-scale commercial production. To have a look at this system, just type 'Verti-Gro' into your web search engine.

Nutrient strengths

Plants need varying strengths of nutrient and tomatoes will not thrive on the lower nutrient strength needed by lettuces. For this reason it is wise to plant in each channel, or stackable pot system, species with similar nutrient needs.

EarthBox®

An EarthBox® or two could be the perfect solution for small spaces, courtyards, decks, rooftops or verandahs. It consists of a rectangular plastic plant pot with a water reservoir at the bottom, separated from the growing medium by a plastic aeration screen. Water is added to the reservoir via a fill tube that projects through the top of the potting mix. Fertiliser is placed in a band on top of the potting mix, along the middle or on one side of the box, depending on the number and type of plants grown. A plastic mulch cover goes over this. Holes are cut in the cover

PLANT COMBINING FOR HYDROPONICS

The following is a guide to which plants can be successfully grown in the one channel with the same strength of nutrient.

- Beans, silverbeet, spinach, beetroot, broccoli, Brussels sprouts, cabbage, carrot, cauliflower, celery, chives, onion, tomato, turnip, parsnip.
- Parsley, peas, radish, rhubarb, cucumber, leek.
- Basil, lettuce, mint, thyme.

Eggplant growing in an EarthBox®, right, and begonias, left. (Photo courtesy EarthBox Australia)

for plants to be inserted. The comprehensive instructions include advice about how many of each different type of plants are best grown per pot, from two tomatoes to 16 beans.

The method claims double the yield of an in-ground garden with low water and fertiliser use, no weeding and no digging. The growing medium can be reused many times, with the addition of more fertiliser for each new crop.

It is similar to the wicking bed concept (see below) but contained within a pot. What is more, the pot sits on feet with castors attached so it is easy to move around as needed.

To find out more about this compact, productive method, see the website: www.earthboxaustralia.com.

Wicking beds

The ingenious, productive and water-saving gardening method of wicking beds was developed by some residents at an eco-village in Queensland. Many of the eco-villagers, and others they have shared the concept with, now use adaptations of the method with great success. The method relies on the bed being watered from the bottom so there is no loss through overspray and very little through evaporation, especially after mulch is applied to the surface.

The finished bed can be at ground level or built up within an edging as a raised bed. Begin by digging out an area the width and

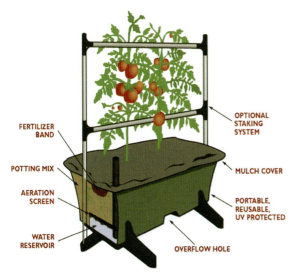

A simple, productive EarthBox® system could suit many small garden situations.

length of your proposed bed; the depth will depend on whether it is going to be a raised bed or a ground-level bed. If it is going to be level with the existing soil, then you might dig to a depth of 35 cm to 45 cm, making sure the bottom is perfectly level. A raised bed might be dug 10 cm into the soil with an edging 25 cm to 35 cm high, or be completely above ground with an edging to whatever height you choose.

Line the hole with heavy-duty black plastic, the sort used by builders, but only to a height of 10 cm to 15 cm, so the plastic looks like a bath within the hole. An option is to line the hole with sand before laying the plastic to prevent any bits of tree roots or stones in the soil from penetrating the plastic. Then lay along the centre of the plastic a length of slotted agricultural pipe, about 5 cm diameter and the same length as the bed.

At one end of the agi pipe insert a 4 cm diameter length of PVC pipe long enough to protrude about 10 cm above the finished depth of the bed. This is where the water goes in. At the other end, push the plastic down a few centimetres in one spot to allow overflow. An inspection pipe at the opposite end to the watering pipe is an option that allows you easily to check whether or not the bed needs watering.

Once the pipe is laid, it can be covered with charcoal, though this is not essential and should be avoided if the soil is alkaline. Then fill in the depth of the bed with a mixture of soil and either compost or worm castings. One person has used a 50:50 mix of soil and compost; another a 70:30 mix of black soil and worm castings. Incorporate worms into the soil mix to continuously fertilise and aerate the bed.

Another option would be to build up a no-dig bed of layers of different organic materials above the agi pipe, as described below. For this option, build up the bed at least twice as high as you want it to finally be because the material will decompose and reduce in height.

To water the bed, a hose is inserted into the protruding length of pipe and left running until the water begins to overflow from the low spot in the plastic. Plants in the bed are watered from the bottom, the soil absorbs the water from the plastic bath and holds it evenly. There is no water loss. A layer of mulch prevents evaporation and benefits the soil biota.

This method can be adapted to any size and height you need. In the eco-village one lady has a bed set up at waist height on a table so she does not need to bend and the rabbits cannot get to her crops.

Wicked adaptation

An alternative similar idea builds a raised bed starting from a perfectly flat surface.

- Level the site, perhaps by sand raked over a lawn area.
- Put edging in place around the bed.
- Line the bed with thick, builder's-quality black plastic so that the plastic comes up to the top of the edging. If building the bed over stony or twiggy soil, spread a layer of sand under the plastic to prevent holes.
- Make a drainage hole in the edging and plastic about 5 cm from the bottom and insert a length of 25 mm diameter PVC

pipe. This allows excess water to drain away. To use this excess efficiently, a length of hose or pipe can be directed onto another area.
- Spread sand over the plastic and level it.
- Lay shadecloth over the sand to help distribute the water evenly.
- Lay old woollen carpet or underlay over the shadecloth to prevent soil from clogging up the shadecloth or sand.
- Insert a length of 100 mm diameter PVC pipe vertically through the underlay and shadecloth into the sand layer, being careful not to pierce the plastic. The bed is watered via this pipe with either tap or recycled water.
- Fill up the bed with topsoil or your preferred growing medium.
- Plant bed and mulch well.

Raised no-dig beds

Gardeners can be broadly divided into diggers and non-diggers. Knowing no other way, I began my gardening life as a digger; however, as soon as I read about no-dig

Healthy leeks in a no-dig bed.

gardening I was converted. There are numerous advantages to the no-dig method.

- It is easier on the gardener's body.
- Some research has shown that plants grown in no-dig beds are healthier and stronger and crop and bloom more prolifically over a longer period than those in dug beds. My experience has found no-dig beds to be extremely productive.
- As the organic material used to make the bed decays it is incorporated into the soil, improving its structure.

No-dig bed in a straw bale surround.

Lettuce, silverbeet, broccoli and parsley in a no-dig bed.

- The bed retains water very well, thus less watering is needed.
- The rich organic material encourages beneficial soil biota.
- Much garden waste can be recycled via the no-dig bed.

A raised bed can be any size or shape. A sensible strategy is to decide on your watering method first and construct the bed to get the most efficient water use. Think about a convenient working width. If the bed is too wide, you will either be bending across and straining your back or standing on the garden and compacting the soil.

Beds can be made over an existing garden or lawn area and even on top of concrete. In the latter case you will need to provide drainage below the bed by means of scoria or screenings over the concrete. In wet areas slotted agricultural pipe in the screenings might be needed to direct water away from the bed. Set it up cleverly so the pipe directs any excess water to another area where it might be needed. A bed constructed on concrete will need to be built up considerably higher than one on soil.

What to use

There are numerous suitable materials and people adapt what they use to suit what they have available or can readily obtain. You can buy materials from a nursery supplier or gradually scrounge and recycle, depending on the amount of time and money at your disposal. Some materials can be bought in bulk by the cubic metre, and many are available in bags from any nursery. For most small gardens a variety of bagged products will do the job admirably, and if you buy a couple of bags at a time when you are doing other shopping, there are no extra 'food miles' to take into account.

Some recommended materials include hay, straw, any form of lucerne, compost and mushroom compost, any type of manure, fallen leaves, coir fibre and animal bedding. Just remember the carbon/nitrogen ratio (see Chapter 4) and aim for a reasonable mixture of nitrogenous and carboniferous materials. Generally, these materials are built up over a thick layer of newspaper or cardboard, so as soon as you decide to make a raised bed, start saving these. Thick cardboard from white goods boxes is very useful and usually retailers are happy to give it away.

There are garden writers who do not recommend no-dig beds on the grounds that plant roots are not able to access the nutrients in the soil beneath the bed. If this occurs, it is in the very short term during which time there are plenty of nutrients within the bed to enable plants to thrive. Even though the newspaper and cardboard in the bottom layer are very high in carbon and would normally take a long time to decompose, in the moist, nutrient-rich environment of a no-dig bed they decay quite rapidly and plants can then reach the soil beneath. The activities of all the soil biota that thrive in a no-dig bed help to incorporate the decaying materials in the bed into the soil, enriching and aerating it and increasing its water-holding capacity.

How to make a no-dig bed

The simplest, quickest method is to buy a load of topsoil from a supplier and build it up over the existing soil, either with or without newspaper or cardboard underneath it. I have used this method with great success. Do be aware, though, that if the imported soil is too different in texture from what is already there you could have drainage problems at the soil interface. Avoid this by loosening the original soil first. A few bags of bought compost or worm castings, or your own homemade variety if you have enough, will add organic matter and fertility to the bought soil.

To make a bed from a variety of materials here is a method to follow; adapt it to suit your needs. It is best to work on a wind-free day, otherwise you could be chasing newspaper and cardboard around the neighbourhood.

- Decide on your bed's location and mark it out with string or a hose.
- Closely cut any existing grass or other plants with a mower or brushcutter and leave the clippings in situ.
- In wet areas install any drainage that might be necessary.
- To lower the pH on acid soil sprinkle some dolomite or wood ash.
- A scattering of blood and bone, pelletised manure product or other fertiliser is optional at this stage.
- Cover the area thoroughly with overlapped newspaper and/or cardboard, wetting it as you go. The weeds and grass will die underneath this layer, decomposing and adding their nutrients and organic matter to the soil. A good strategy when using newspaper is to pile it into a wheelbarrow and fill the barrow with water.
- If the bed will be edged, now is a good time to lay it so the paper can be tucked beneath the edging.
- Begin building up your assembled organic materials with a coarse layer on top of the paper. Suitable materials include twiggy prunings, palm or fern fronds, autumn leaves, hay or straw.
- Keep building up the bed in layers, wetting each layer as you go. As well as bought materials, incorporate any garden waste such as grass clippings, fallen leaves, shredded prunings or weeds (before they go to seed).
- A couple of sprinkles of dolomite or wood ash throughout the layers will counteract acidity if necessary.
- If most of your materials are high in carbon, scatter blood and bone or pelletised manure over them.
- Build up layers until the bed is at least twice as high as the edging. For beds built on soil, 35 cm to 40 cm is a good depth; beds on concrete will need to be at least 50 cm to 60 cm deep. However, because the pile reduces in depth as it decomposes, if you have used a lot of bulky materials such as straw or shredded paper, the bed needs to be deeper than if compost, rotted manure and other mainly decomposed matter has been used.
- A layer of compost is good to finish.
- Release some earthworms into the pile. They will burrow and aerate, help to mix and decompose the material and add their own valuable vermicast to the bed. Though compost worms generally do not thrive in the garden, they will love the rich matter in a no-dig bed.

- If you have used hay or other matter containing weed seeds, you might get weeds growing in the bed. Just pull or tease them out and leave them to add to the mix. A biscuit of hay that starts to sprout can easily be turned over and the shoots will decay. If there are a lot of weeds, spread either newspaper or plastic over the top to smother them. You will need to put some straw or similar material over this to stop it from blowing away. Remove any plastic when it has done its job, shaking the straw back onto the bed; the newspaper can either be removed or left to decay.
- Keep the bed damp but not soggy.

Planting out the no-dig bed

It is usually recommended that a new bed be left for a month or two to settle and begin decaying before planting anything into it. Earthworms and myriad other beneficial organisms will be enthusiastically at work within the bed, releasing nutrients and transforming a pile of organic bits and pieces into a nutrient-rich, water-efficient growing medium.

I am usually impatient to get the bed planted. All I do is scrape a hole in the material, put a handful of topsoil and some compost and/or rotted manure into the hole, and plant directly into it. Small plants and large seeds can be planted this way. If you are more patient and leave the bed to decompose for a couple of months, they can be planted directly into the bed. It is best to wait until the bed is quite well decomposed before planting small seeds. However, an alternative is to spread a row of compost on top of the bed along where you want the seeds to grow and plant them into that.

BEST YET NO-DIG BED

I have been using this method for well over a quarter of a century, both in a large country garden and in my smaller town garden, and have incorporated numerous different materials. When we lived on a small property there was a range of materials available, including poultry litter, animal manures, animal bedding, hay and straw. The most productive bed came about almost by accident. We were going away for a few weeks and were worried about how to feed our small herd of cows while we were gone. We arranged for a neighbour to call by and check on them in case of any problems and left them with a large round bale of oaten hay to eat. When we returned we found that they really had not been very hungry. Most of the hay had been strewn around the bale. The cows had used it as a bed and a toilet facility. Most of it had been rendered unusable as fodder, but ever on the lookout for gardening supplies, I raked it up and used it as the basis for a no-dig bed. The cows' urine and faeces provided the nitrogen to break down the carboniferous straw. All I added to it was some compost and litter from the poultry sheds. The first crop into this bed was pumpkins. From an area of about four square metres I harvested over 100 large pumpkins.

I have used a variety of methods and materials to make no-dig beds and have never had a failure. Numerous readers of *Grass Roots* magazine have shared their own adaptations through stories and letters in the magazine. Everyone has adapted the method to suit their own circumstances. Now you can do the same to make a productive small food garden.

The new tank beds are ready to plant.

Beans and lettuce beginning to develop in the other bed.

No-dig tank bed

A no-dig bed with a difference can be made by filling a cut-down tank with whatever medium you choose to grow plants in. Tank suppliers can make a topless, bottomless round or oval shape from Colorbond® roofing iron to match your house roof, or you might have access to an old tank you can cut to suit.

The tank can be filled with bought soil to which you can add compost or rotted manures, or you can fill it with a mixture of organic materials in layers, as described above. Earthworms released into the bed will continue fertilising and aerating the growing medium.

The height of the tank can be varied to suit yourself. This technique reduces bending, so is very suitable for elderly or handicapped gardeners, or anyone with a bad back. It is rather like having a very big pot. In addition, it is a water-efficient method. You could combine it with the wicking bed idea, by lining the base of the tank with plastic.

Young corn plants in one of the tank beds.

Both tank beds in full production.

Square foot gardening

Square foot gardening, sometimes called grid gardening, is a very organised way of maximising production from a small area. The bed is marked out with string in 30 cm squares. One plant or a number of small plants (such as onions or radishes) can be planted into each square. As each plant or square of plants is harvested, it is replaced by another to keep production continuous.

The square foot gardening method is based on thorough preparation of the soil with generous amounts of organic matter before anything is planted. The area is thoroughly dug and layers of peat moss (coir fibre is an environmentally sustainable alternative), coarse vermiculite, manure and compost are added, followed by a small amount of blended organic fertiliser and lime for acid soil. After each cell is harvested a small amount of fertiliser is worked into the soil prior to the next plant(s) being sown. Apart from this there is no further digging required once the garden is established.

Planting can be by seeds or seedlings. Individual seeds are planted into a small hole with vermiculite in the bottom and are then covered by more vermiculite. Both seeds and seedlings are planted so as to be in a saucer-shaped depression that will hold water, allowing it to seep into the ground.

The recommended watering method is to leave a bucket of water in the sun to warm and use a cup to scoop out water from the bucket and into the saucer. This sounds very water-efficient but also time consuming, as each plant is individually watered. However, both leaving the bucket of water in the sun to warm and making do with only a cupful of water for each plant are possibly not appropriate for most Australian conditions, especially in the hotter months.

In this method, sprawling plants such as pumpkins and cucumbers are trained to grow up a trellis, otherwise they would ramble over everything else in the bed. Peas and climbing beans are also grown on a trellis. Larger plants such as tomatoes or zucchinis might need more than one square.

One possible design is to have a rectangular bed, no more than two squares wide for ease of access, and as many squares long as you have space for. Erect a trellis along the back and both sides of the bed so you have an open rectangle. It is best to have the open side facing north or east so plants get enough sunlight. Grow any sprawling or climbing plants on the trellis and smaller plants in the squares. Alternatively, if you decide to grow only smaller vegies and herbs this way, you could have a bed four squares by four squares that you can access from any side.

It is important never to compact the soil by standing on it to plant, harvest or water the garden. It is suggested that you work from planks or other forms of paving between blocks.

High productivity and low inputs are claimed for this method. However, as far as I can see, the high productivity is in comparison to space-hungry inefficient methods, in which no-one with a small garden can afford to indulge. There is much to recommend this method and it can certainly be adapted to suit many situations, even courtyards, balconies, rooftops and indoors. It can be used in conjunction with no-dig beds and/or wicking beds. However, its productivity is directly related to how efficiently the gardener manages each cell. If you are a very organised person, this could be the system for you.

Plant spacing

Here are some recommendations for how many plants of different vegetable types can be grown in each 30 cm square cell.

Plant	Per square
Beans	9
Beetroot	16
Broccoli	1
Cabbage	1
Capsicum	1
Carrots	16
Cauliflower	1
Corn	1
Cucumber	2
Eggplant	1
Lettuce	4
Onions	16
Peas	8
Radish	16
Silverbeet	4
Spinach	9
Tomatoes (bush)	1 plant per 2 cells
Tomatoes (vine)	1

Indoor productivity

There are several methods of growing food indoors, either as an addition to what is in the garden or as an alternative for people who literally have no space outside or are unable to work in the garden for reasons of age or disability. With regard to the latter, it is possible to set up wicking beds, square foot gardening beds or no-dig tank gardens to be at wheelchair height.

Sprouting

Sprouted seeds are very nutritious, tasty and easy to grow. Begin with a large jar, a piece of muslin or cheesecloth or similar fabric, and the seeds you want to sprout. If you have a lidded jar, perhaps one that held bottled fruit, you can punch or drill holes in the lid so you will not need the muslin.

Mung beans, alfalfa (lucerne), fenugreek and onion are popular sprouting choices, but others available (usually from health food stores) are broccoli, buckwheat, chickpea, lentil, oats, radish, soybean and wheat. Make sure the seeds you buy for sprouting from a health food store or supermarket are meant for human consumption. Seeds from nurseries, which are meant to be grown in the garden, have usually been treated with a fungicide and are not safe to eat.

Put about a tablespoon of seeds into the jar and cover them with water. Leave them for several hours or overnight. Place a muslin or cheesecloth cover over the jar and hold it in place with an elastic band. Alternatively, replace the lid you have drilled holes in. Turn the jar upside down and let the water drain out. Leave it upside down in the dish rack to drain well. Rinse and drain the seeds twice a day, more if necessary in hot weather. The seeds should remain damp, but should not sit in water or they will rot.

After about three to five days the seeds will have sprouted enough to be eaten. Give them a final rinse and drain and remove them from the jar. Sprouts can be stored in an airtight container in the fridge for a week or more. Wash the jar and lid or fabric cover before reusing to grow more sprouts.

Nutritious homegrown sprouts are very simple to produce.

> **ACTION PLAN**
> - Consider which of these techniques will suit your needs:
>   – permaculture
>   – aquaponics
>   – hydroponics
>   – EarthBox®
>   – wicking beds
>   – no-dig beds
>   – square foot gardening
>   – ideas for indoors.

There are commercial sprouting jars and kits available, but a simple DIY approach will produce sprouts that taste just as good and contain exactly the same nutrients.

Wheatgrass

Wheatgrass is a popular health supplement often added to juice mixtures. It can be sprouted as described above, or if you want the grass to grow longer, it can be grown on a tray. Obtain some organic untreated wheat seed. You need a tray such as a deep biscuit tray and some paper towel.

Soak about a half a cup of wheat overnight in a jug or bowl of water. Next day, line the bottom of the tray with several thicknesses of damp paper towel. Drain the wheat and spread it on the lined tray. Cover the tray with clear plastic and leave it until the wheat sprouts are pushing at the plastic. Remove the plastic and leave the tray in a well-lit spot, but not in direct sun or the shoots will dry out too quickly. Water the wheat once or twice a day, just enough to keep it moist. If it sits in water, it will rot. In hot weather a frequent misting from a spray bottle will be beneficial.

Depending on the weather and the amount of light the 'crop' receives, it will be ready to snip in one to two weeks. Snip the wheatgrass at any stage to either juice or chew it. You can chew the grass to extract the nutrients and then spit out the pulp. You will probably get two harvests from one crop of grass. If you have more than you can use straight away, snip it and store it in an airtight container in the fridge.

Mushrooms

Growing mushrooms is quite easy to do and is an interesting and inexpensive indoor gardening project. Several different brands of mushroom growing kits are available from nurseries or via the internet. A box of compost already impregnated with the mushroom spawn is provided, along with peat moss and instructions. The kit should be kept in a dim light so the contents do not dry out. If the instructions are followed, you should get two or three crops of mushrooms from one kit. Once the crops are finished, the compost can be used in the garden or as potting mix.

Aquaponics/hydroponics

The methods of hydroponics and aquaponics previously described can be scaled down to fit any available space in a well-lit room. If you already have a large fish tank, you can devise a system that pumps water from the tank through a grow bed such as a large rectangular pot and back into the tank. The nutrient-rich water will fertilise the vegies in the pot and return, cleaned and aerated, to the tank. To save space the grow bed could be mounted on a shelf above the tank, or on the floor beneath it if the tank is on a table.

CREATING SUPER SOIL
Soil biota and fertility

By now you have probably decided what you would like to grow and where you have, or can make, space. If you already have an established garden, you will know what your soil is like, but you might be asking yourself what you need to do to the soil to ensure your new food plants thrive. If you are new to gardening, soil might be just that mysterious dirt under your feet that, somehow, plants grow in. This chapter will show you how to improve your soil so you can grow fabulous food.

Know your soil

The soil in our gardens is a mixture of mineral particles derived from rock weathering over millennia, air, water, decomposed organic matter and living organisms. Though all soils are based on the same basic ingredients, they vary widely because of differences in the way the ingredients are combined.

Soils may vary in the size of their particles (texture), the way the particles stick together (structure), and the amount of space between the particles (porosity). They can be roughly grouped into three main types: sand, clay and loam. All soils are a mixture of characteristics and even within your garden you will have differing mixtures in various places.

Soil texture can range from coarse sand or even gravel at one extreme to pottery-quality clay on the other, with silt coming in the middle. Soils can be waterlogged or free-draining, have a hard crust or clay pan, have too few or too many of some minerals, be rich in organic matter and nutrients or deficient, be alkaline or acidic, and even be saline. To ensure our plants thrive and our gardening practices constantly nurture and replenish the soil instead of slowly degrading it, every gardener needs to know some simple soil science.

Texture

Soil texture refers to the size of the soil particles and is determined by the type of parent rock from which it originated.

Sandy soils are made up of coarse particles with a lot of air between them. Both wet and dry sand feels gritty between the fingers. Such soils allow water and nutrients to dissipate very quickly.

Clay soils are made up of very fine particles with not much air between them. The particles cling together and can retain water too well, resulting in waterlogging. Nutrients can be tightly bound to the fine particles, to the extent that they might be unavailable to plants. Clay is hard when dry, and greasy, rubbery or sticky when wet.

Silt is finer than sand and coarser than clay and may feel powdery when dry. Wet silt may feel slightly sticky or plastic; this is because of a film of clay adhering to the silt particles.

Loamy soil has a good balance of sand, silt and clay and adequate humus content from decomposed organic matter. Loam is usually considered to be the best type of soil for gardening, but there are myriad gradations and varying amounts of organic matter, air and water. Clay loam might have too many fine particles and still become waterlogged, whereas sandy loam could have enough of the larger particles to remain too porous.

What texture is your soil?
A simple way to determine the texture of your soil is to mould it between your hands. Take about a heaped tablespoon of soil, discard gravel and small pebbles, add water a little at a time and knead it into the soil until it is moistened evenly through. Squeeze the wet soil. Sandy soil will feel gritty as you work it and will not hold together when squeezed. Clay soil will feel smooth and elastic and will hold together in a firm lump when squeezed. Loam will hold together in a spongy lump.

Now pull the lump of soil between thumb and fingers to form a ribbon. The longer and more elastic the ribbon, the higher the clay content.

Structure
Soil structure is the way the soil particles are held or grouped together to form aggregates. Aggregates are clusters of minerals and humus that are held together tightly enough that they will not come apart when it rains or when the soil is lightly dug. An individual aggregate is called a ped.

Ideally, aggregates are from 0.2 mm to 0.3 mm in diameter. Soil with good aggregate structure is friable or spongy so it is well aerated and drains well and plant roots can travel through it freely to find nutrients.

Soil with poor structure may have particles that are joined together to form large clods (clusters of peds) or dense sheets. Water has difficulty penetrating this aggregate structure so the soil might remain waterlogged for long periods. Plant roots cannot travel freely through the clods in search of nutrients. Over time, especially if overwatering, frequent cultivation or compaction by heavy machinery take place, a hard crust or clay pan can form.

Improving soil structure
Both sandy and clay soil structures can be improved by the addition of organic matter: compost, manures or any other once-living plant material. An ideal way of making garden beds on very clayey or sandy soils is to build up raised no-dig beds, which have many additional benefits (see below).

Sandy soil can be improved by adding a volume of clay soil at a ratio of about one part clay to four parts sand in the area being treated. Water-holding granules or crystals will help sandy soil retain moisture.

Depending on the relative amounts of sand and clay in your particular soil, adding sand to clay soil, especially if organic matter is

> ### WILL GYPSUM HELP?
>
> There is a simple test to find out if gypsum will improve the structure of your clay soil.
>
> - Drop a pinch of dry soil into a glass of rainwater.
> - Leave it undisturbed for 24 hours.
> - If the soil is surrounded by a halo of clay particles or if the halo spreads to a general cloudiness of the water, gypsum will be effective.

deficient, might not do a lot to improve its structure unless a very large amount of sand is used. It is only practical to do this in very small areas or for individual plants. Very waterlogged clay might need to have drainage installed beneath garden beds. Gypsum added to clay soil at about 0.5 kg to 1 kg per square metre will often improve its structure. Gypsum is particularly effective in clay soil that is high in sodium.

Acid or alkaline?

The soil's level of acidity or alkalinity is referred to as its pH value. The pH scale ranges from 1 to 14, with pH 1 being the extreme of acidity, pH 14 the extreme of alkalinity and pH 7 being neutral. To put this into an everyday context, a well-known cola drink has a pH of 2 and washing soda has a pH of 10. The scale increases and decreases in multiples of 10, so pH 6 is 10 times more acidic than pH 7, and pH 5 is 10 times more acidic than pH 6 and 100 more than pH 7.

The importance of pH to our gardens is that many plants have a preferred pH range and will not thrive, if they grow at all, outside that range. In addition, changes in pH affect the availability of soil nutrients. Below about pH 5.5, nitrogen, phosphorus, potassium, sulphur, calcium, magnesium and molybdenum become increasingly unavailable. Above about pH 7.5, iron, manganese, boron, copper and zinc become unavailable.

Most garden plants will survive at pH levels from 5.5 to 7.5, but many grow best in slightly acid soil from 6 to 6.5. Plants adapted to acid soils, such as rhododendrons, azaleas, camellias and blueberries, are likely to suffer nutrient deficiencies, particularly iron, at a pH level greater than 6 and to grow very poorly in alkaline soil.

Plants growing in potting mix will thrive at a slightly lower pH (5 to 6.5) than in garden soil. Potting mixes are mostly made up of organic materials, from which nutrients are most readily available from pH 5 to pH 6.5. This also indicates that plants will thrive in garden soil that is very rich in organic matter at a lower pH than would be the case where the soil is deficient in organic matter. If your soil is not full of luscious organic matter, you are about to change that situation.

Managing soil pH

It is relatively easy to raise soil pH, but more difficult to lower it. The simplest strategy is to choose plants that are best suited to the pH of the soil you have. You might need to adjust the pH of vegie gardens or soil where you intend to grow fruit trees. The constant addition of a variety of organic matter to the soil will help to stabilise the pH.

Buy a colour-coded pH test kit from a nursery and test the soil in areas where you want to grow food plants. Sprinkle any necessary amendments over the bare soil and rake them in, then water the area well.

Lowering pH
If the pH is above 7.5, this is too high. To lower it use agricultural or dusting sulphur or iron sulphate. For a one unit change in the top 10 cm of soil, use about 25 g of sulphur or 50 g of iron sulphate per square metre in sandy soil and 100 g of sulphur or 200 g of iron sulphate per square metre in clay soil.

Raising pH
Where soil pH is lower than 5.5, you can raise it by adding lime, dolomite or wood ash. The amount to use will depend on the texture of your soil and the amount of change that is needed. To change pH by one unit in sandy soil, add about 100 g of lime per square metre. For the same amount of change in clay soil you are likely to need 400 g per metre.

Mulch and pH
The pH of various mulches can differ remarkably. By using acidic mulches on alkaline soil and vice versa you can gradually adjust and stabilise the soil pH. For example, I found that composted manure and stable bedding were both quite alkaline, while sugar cane and a packaged soil improver and mulch were both acidic. Peat is another acidic product that can be used to acidify a small area such as a planting hole.

Test your preferred mulches with the colour-coded kit. You might need to pulverise some products to a powder before testing. Try to obtain a sample of mulches you intend to use, or buy a small quantity to start with. You don't want to use acidic mulch on acid soil, or alkaline mulch on alkaline soil. To do so would only compound the existing problem.

Improving soil fertility
Nutrient rich soil, containing a generous helping of organic matter and teeming with life, both visible and microscopic, is the basis of all life in the garden. If your soil is lacking in nutrients and organic matter, your food crops will fail to thrive. Fortunately, it is usually quite easy to rectify any problems and create superior soil that will grow super-tasty, super-nutritious food for your family.

Soil biota working for you
Micro-organisms, as the name implies, are life forms which can only be seen with the aid of a microscope. They include algae, protozoa, nematodes, viruses, fungi, bacteria and actinomycetes – a group intermediate between the bacteria and the fungi. So what does this have to do with your garden soil? Simply that a gram of fertile soil (think of the mass of a 1000 mg vitamin C tablet) can contain as many as one hundred million bacteria, as well as millions of other micro-organisms, making approximately a billion in all. Add to these the visible life forms such as earthworms (up to 40 000 per cubic metre), soil mites, slugs, termites, millipedes, ants, springtails, and both the larval and adult stages of insects and beetles, and we begin to realise the magnitude of the resource beneath our feet.

The soil biota is responsible for processing nitrogen into nitrates (essential for plant growth), recycling phosphorus and other nutrients, and the decomposition of dead plants and animals to produce nutrients for the plants we grow. They also aerate the soil and allow water to seep below the surface to plant roots. Estimates range from two to five tonnes of soil organisms per hectare of healthy soil.

We have all heard or read how beneficial earthworms are in enhancing soil structure and increasing fertility, but they are only the most publicised and widely recognised part of the vast biodiversity of the soil. All the soil biota are composed of proteins, minerals, amino acids, nitrogen and other essential elements. When the organisms die, they enrich the soil and their nutrients become available to our plants.

Earthworm casts concentrate all these nutrients and are extremely important to soil (and hence plant) health. Just as important a role, however, is played by some of those millions of bacteria that we do not even see. They break down organic matter, help maintain a plant-friendly pH, dissolve nutrients into a form plants can absorb and help produce nitrogen. They even break down soil pollutants.

Soil organisms are sensitive to temperature and moisture. In tropical and subtropical areas with fairly constant warmth and moisture they are active constantly so mulch is recycled quickly and continuously. In areas where it becomes very hot and dry, or very cold at different times of the year, soil organisms slow down or cease activity for a period of time and nutrient recycling is more periodic.

Healthy soil needs to be damp but not soggy. Overwet soil will prevent the entry of air and the escape of unwanted gases, so the plant roots will 'drown' and rot. Many soil organisms will also either die or depart to deeper levels or drier areas. It is essential to drain around wet areas and add large amounts of organic matter, which will increase the soil's water-holding capacity, enable sandy soils to hold more water and clay soils to drain more freely. In addition, decomposing organic matter provides favourable conditions for the soil biota that will work so generously at enhancing your soil.

All this fantastic soil life that plays such an important role in keeping our gardens thriving and healthy can be destroyed by overuse of artificial fertilisers, which increase soil acidity and make trace elements unavailable, and by pesticides that affect soil life and beneficial above-ground organisms as well as the targeted pests. Look after the soil and surface biota. Keep it healthy, keep it organic.

Diet for active micro-organisms

All organic matter contains varying proportions of carbon and nitrogen. The soil micro-organisms largely responsible for the decomposition of organic matter in compost, mulch and no-dig beds need carbon for growth and nitrogen to synthesise protein. Ideally, the ratio is 25 to 30 parts of carbon to one of nitrogen.

Too much carbon will slow down decomposition, which might be desirable in some areas where you do want mulch to be long-lasting. Too much nitrogen causes the excess to be converted to ammonia and dissipated wastefully and odorously into the atmosphere. This is what often happens if a pile of damp green grass clippings is left in a pile to decompose.

> ### MYCORRHIZAL FUNGI
>
> High on the list of beneficial soil organisms, and deserving of special mention, are the mycorrhizal fungi. These fungi invade plant roots in a mutually beneficial (symbiotic) relationship in which the plant provides the fungus with sugars and the fungus spreads out a network of hyphae (filaments that extend the reach of, and act as, roots). The hyphae increase the roots' ability to extract nutrients from the soil.
>
> Most plants have these symbiotic mycorrhizal associations with specific fungi. Exceptions in the food plants are brassicas, horseradish and saltbush.
>
> The fungi also play a role in increasing the plant's heat and drought tolerance, produce antibiotics that can suppress some pathogens, and increase disease resistance.
>
> You can encourage the proliferation of mycorrhizae by digging as little as possible and maintaining a layer of decomposing mulch. Avoid using fungicides and soil fumigants as they will destroy the beneficial mycorrhizae as well as the pest fungi. Mycorrhizae do not grow on plants in soils with high levels of soluble phosphorus, such as that caused by overuse of superphosphate.

The following table is a guide to the carbon/nitrogen ratio of some commonly used mulching and fertilising materials. The ratio is likely to vary for any material according to the conditions it was grown under and the stage of maturity at which it was harvested or collected.

Observe what happens in the compost you make and the mulch you use. If it breaks down more slowly than you want, add more of the materials with a lower C/N ratio, such as manures, blood and bone or chopped lucerne. Materials that break down more quickly than you require need to have others with a higher ratio added, such as wood chips, sawdust, shredded paper, coir, straw or leaves.

Mulch or fertiliser	Carbon/nitrogen ratio
Wood	700:1
Sawdust	500:1 to 250:1
Paper	170:1
Coir	110:1
Pine needles	110:1 to 60:1
Straw	100:1
Palm peat (also called coir fibre pith)	80:1
Oaten straw	80:1
Leaves (will vary with type used)	80:1 to 40:1
Bagasse (sugar cane waste)	50:1
Fruit waste	35:1
Seaweed	25:1
Horse manure	25:1
Legume/grass hay	25:1
Rotted manure	20:1
Grass clippings	20:1
Leafy green weeds	19:1
Grape marc	18:1
Mixed food waste	15:1
Lucerne	13:1
Cow manure	12:1
Poultry manure	7:1
Blood and bone	7:1
Fish waste	5:1
Feathers	4:1
Hair	4:1
Bone meal	2:1

Beware nitrogen drawdown

Remember that the micro-organisms that help decompose your compost and mulch need nitrogen for their own life processes. When high-carbon materials such as wood chips, sawdust or straw are used as mulch, there is not enough nitrogen for them so they use some of the nitrogen that is stored in the soil, the same nitrogen that your plants need to grow well and produce bountiful crops. This process is known as 'nitrogen drawdown' and must be considered as a cause if symptoms of nitrogen deficiency become obvious (see section on nutrient deficiency symptoms).

To avoid nitrogen drawdown:

- Limit the use of undecomposed materials with a carbon/nitrogen ratio of higher than 100:1 around plants, food plants in particular. However, they are perfectly fine for paths or for use around areas of native trees and shrubs.
- Mix high-nitrogen materials with high-carbon materials, or sprinkle blood and bone over high-carbon materials and water it in.
- Leave high-carbon materials to decay, or compost them, before use.
- Do not dig undecomposed high-carbon materials into the soil.
- Continually add a wide variety of mulches and fertilisers to ensure there is always plenty of nitrogen (and other nutrients) to feed your crops.

Soil nutrient content

The major nutrients necessary for plant growth are nitrogen, potassium and phosphorus. Secondary nutrients are calcium, magnesium and sulphur. Trace elements include iron, zinc, copper, boron, manganese and a few dozen others. For optimum growth and productivity food plants need a constant supply of nutrients, though not all plants need the same nutrients. Different plants extract differing amounts of nutrients from the soil.

In addition, plants need carbon, hydrogen and oxygen, which they obtain from air and water. As long as plants have air circulating around them and we remember to water them when necessary, there will be ample supplies of these elements available and we don't need to worry about applying them.

We need to add organic fertilisers and mulches to our soil to make it more fertile and friable. No special knowledge of soil chemistry is needed, as long as a wide variety of organic materials is added it will be decomposed by the soil biota to make the necessary minerals and trace elements available to our plants. It will also encourage more diversity of soil organisms all carrying out their predator/prey life cycles and adding to the health and vitality of the soil.

Manufactured chemical fertilisers such as superphosphate can acidify the soil and inhibit plants' uptake of minerals. Superphosphate has been claimed to significantly inhibit copper uptake and also to lock up magnesium, sulphur, selenium, cobalt, boron, zinc and phosphorus, all vital plant nutrients. In addition, chemical additives do nothing to increase the organic content of soil that is so important for fertility and moisture retention.

Soil nutrients and pH

In acid (low pH) soils, below about pH 5.5, phosphorus becomes bound to other elements and is unavailable to plants. On the other hand, zinc, cobalt, copper and manganese become more soluble and can increase to the extent of causing plant toxicity. This very low pH is also detrimental to beneficial bacteria while encouraging harmful fungi. Strictly speaking, low pH does not 'encourage' harmful fungi. It is rather that fungi are present at all pH levels, but the lower number of beneficial bacteria at low pH levels means that the less-fussy fungi are present in disproportionate numbers and more likely to have detrimental effects.

If the soil is too alkaline (above pH 7), elements such as magnesium, iron, manganese, copper and boron can become increasingly locked in the soil and unavailable to plants, with detrimental effects on the soil biota.

The effects of acidity and alkalinity are very variable and depend in part on whether the soil is sandy, clay or loam, and on its humus content. However, it is clear that both high and low pH levels are detrimental to the nutrient status of the soil, to the soil biota and ultimately to our plants.

Be careful about applying trace elements to correct a diagnosed deficiency as the trace elements are possibly already in the soil, just not available because of incorrect pH. Once the pH is corrected they are usually available to the plants in a form they can use. If your plants show signs of nutrient deficiencies (usually indicated by weird malformations and odd leaf colours), test the pH first and correct this before trying other options.

Keep mulching, adding organic matter to your soil, and use rock dust, seaweed, compost, decomposed manures, vermicompost and fish-based fertilisers, and in time the problem will probably be rectified.

If, having taking measures to correct the pH of your soil and given them time to work, you are still concerned about a possible nutrient deficiency, you can have a soil test carried out by a laboratory. It is recommended that you collect soil from different parts of the garden and mix them well. However, the problem could be confined to one area, in which case only collect soil from the relevant area. You then send a sample of the mixture to the laboratory, which will send you a detailed analysis.

Where the analysis indicates a lack of a particular nutrient or trace element, you can safely apply this at the recommended rate. In the vast majority of cases, however, no soil analysis will be necessary. A pH level between about 5.5 and 7.5, combined with the addition of a variety of mulches and organic fertilisers, will keep your plants thriving.

Organic fertilisers

There is a wide range of acceptable organic fertilisers available from nurseries. When buying fertilisers, look carefully at the packaging. The word 'organic' only means that the product contains once-living material, not necessarily that it is chemical free. If you want to buy only chemical-free products look for an accredited organic logo such as Biological Farmers Australia (BFA) or National Association for Sustainable Agriculture Australia (NASAA). Make sure, too, that products have an Australian Standards logo on the packaging.

Some of the bought fertilisers I like to use are blood and bone, blood and bone with potassium (both of which will be licked up by

NUTRIENT DEFICIENCIES – WHAT TO LOOK FOR

Nitrogen: yellowing, appearing first in oldest leaves, often with reddening as well. Stunted growth. Leaf fall. Plant matures prematurely.

Magnesium: patchy yellowing between the leaf veins, appearing first in oldest leaves. Reddening, particularly on the edges of yellow areas.

Potassium: scorched leaf edges on the oldest leaves, with spots encircled by paler outlines. Possibly red pigmentation in young leaves.

Phosphorus: erect but slow growth. Blue-green or purple colour showing in older leaves first.

Molybdenum: older leaves become mottled over the entire surface. Leaves form a cup shape and stems are distorted.

Cobalt: only in legumes, the same symptoms as for nitrogen.

Manganese: yellowing between pale green veins may appear in any leaves, but often in the middle of the plant first. Watery spots, more prevalent in dull weather.

Calcium: beginning with the youngest leaves, tips of leaves become hook-shaped, blacken and die.

Sulphur: the whole plant often yellows. Leaves are smaller than usual with turned-down edges.

Iron: yellowing between bright green veins, beginning with the youngest leaves which can turn white in severe cases.

Copper: leaves yellow and tips die, beginning with the youngest leaves. Young growth is distorted. Flowering is much reduced.

Zinc: leaves are smaller than usual. Young leaves form bunches. Yellow or white mottling, beginning with the youngest leaves.

Boron: leaf edges yellow. Growing tips die. Leaves crumple, blacken and become distorted, beginning with the youngest leaves.

---

the family pet if left uncovered), seaweed emulsion, fish emulsion and Dynamic Lifter.

Fish emulsion

There is a product made from carp, an introduced fish that is taking over many Australian waterways and destroying native biodiversity, which I find particularly satisfying to use. It is very high in nitrogen and potassium, so take care to use it diluted as instructed on the bottle.

Fish emulsion should be washed off food before it is eaten. No human health risks are known, but it does not taste pleasant.

Seaweed emulsion

As seaweed emulsion contains little nitrogen or phosphorus, it is referred to as a soil

Seaweed and fish-based liquid fertilisers are good choices.

> ### NUTRIENTS IN FISH EMULSION
>
> Typically, a fish emulsion could contain the following nutrients:
>
> - Nitrogen, 9%
> - Phosphorus, 2%
> - Potassium, 6%
> - Trace elements: calcium, sulphur, magnesium, iron, zinc, manganese, copper and boron.

> ### NUTRIENTS IN SEAWEED EMULSION
>
> The following is a typical nutrient composition of seaweed emulsion:
>
> - Nitrogen, 0.10%
> - Phosphorus, 0.05%
> - Potassium, 2%
> - Trace elements: calcium, magnesium, sodium, sulphur, boron, cobalt, copper, iron, iodine, manganese and zinc.

conditioner rather than a true fertiliser. However, it contains potassium (see Chapter 5 for the role of potassium) and a variety of trace elements.

Seaweed has numerous benefits for plants. It:

- promotes flowering and fruiting
- stimulates root growth
- encourages beneficial micro-organisms
- increases plants' resistance to diseases and insect damage
- might increase plants' tolerance to frost and extreme heat.

Seaweed has no known damaging effects on humans but tastes unpleasant, so food sprayed with it should be washed before consumption. The concentrate typically has a pH of 10.5 which is very alkaline. If your soil is alkaline, I suggest you test the pH of an area on which you intend to use the emulsion before and after use and monitor it carefully.

Manures

The most commonly available bagged manures are from cattle or poultry. They are usually sold as decomposed manures, which are safe to use around food plants straight away. If you have a source of fresh farm manure or buy bagged manure from the roadside when travelling in the country, these are not decomposed. You will need to put them through your compost bin or leave them in an out-of-the-way pile, kept damp, until they have decomposed before using them on food crops. There will probably be weed seeds germinating from the manure. Just pull them out and add them to the compost.

Manure is available also as a pelletised product, Dynamic Lifter made from chicken manure being the most well known in Australia. This can be sprinkled around plants and covered with mulch. Dogs love to eat it if it is left exposed.

Nutrients in manures

The amount of major nutrients found in the manure of different animals will vary considerably depending on a range of factors. The following are some typical analyses of nitrogen (N), phosphorus (P) and potassium (K) content.

Animal	N%	P%	K%
Horse	0.7	0.3	0.6
Cow	0.6	0.2	0.5
Sheep	0.7	0.3	0.9
Pig	0.5	0.3	0.5
Hen	1.5	1	0.5
Duck	0.6	1.4	0.5
Pigeon	5	2.4	2.32
Turkey	1.3	0.7	0.5
Rabbit	2.4	1.4	10.5

Avoid fertiliser overuse

Fertiliser application increases the concentration of nutrients in the soil around a plant's root zone. Too strong a concentration of nutrients will cause the plant to draw moisture down from the stems and leaves to the roots in an attempt to dilute the nutrients, thus damaging the above-ground growing parts, a condition sometimes known as 'fertiliser burn'. Apply fertilisers a little at a time and water the area before and after application to prevent damage. Fertiliser burn is more likely to occur in warm weather because nutrients are released faster when the temperature is higher.

Free homemade products

There are several ways you can recycle your own household waste to produce free fertiliser. You will be doing the environment a favour at the same time. Remember that you are dealing with living organisms, including moulds and potentially harmful micro-organisms, so always wear gloves when working in the garden and a face mask when handling material that might contain mould spores.

Compost

Making compost at home from kitchen and garden wastes is generally held to reduce greenhouse emissions when compared with emissions produced by those same wastes going to landfill. A big environmental concern of landfill is the methane gas it produces, methane being a much more damaging greenhouse gas than carbon dioxide. No methane should be produced when compost is made with good aeration. However, compost made in soggy anaerobic (without air) conditions will produce methane gas.

According to information from the Australian Greenhouse Office, the carbon dioxide that

> **ORGANIC FERTILISERS AND SOIL CONDITIONERS**
>
> Use any combination of these products to enrich your soil and ensure good nutrient availability:
>
> - Compost
> - Mushroom compost
> - Well-decomposed manures
> - Blood and bone, and blood and bone with potassium
> - Pelletised manures
> - Fish meal or liquid
> - Seaweed products
> - Worm castings, also known as vermicompost or vermicast
> - Rock dusts, including rock phosphate and dolomite
> - Wood ash
> - Bokashi solids and liquid
> - Compost, manure or herbal 'teas'.

might be produced by composting garden and kitchen wastes at home in an aerated compost bin will be less harmful to the environment than the methane that would be produced from the same waste going to landfill. The same source confirms that food or garden waste that breaks down in anaerobic conditions generates three to four times more greenhouse gas than it would if it decomposed in aerobic conditions. Thus, composting our wastes at home is an easy way to reduce our household's greenhouse emissions, as long as we compost aerobically. At the same time we are producing free fertiliser and soil conditioner. How good is that?

There are a variety of ways to make compost, not all of them suitable for a small garden. To work properly, an open heap needs to be about a cubic metre in volume and you need at least two of them, one to be decomposing while the other is in use or being built up. There might not be space for such large open heaps, and the neighbours probably won't appreciate having to look at, and possibly smell, them either. Open heaps do tend to attract flies and rodents as well, no matter how careful you are.

> ### NUTRIENTS IN COMPOST
>
> The benefit of compost as a fertiliser depends on what has gone into it. A typical analysis of the major nutrients is: nitrogen 1.4% to 3.5%, phosphorus 0.3% to 1%, potassium 0.4% to 2%. In addition there will be trace elements and beneficial micro-organisms, which themselves contribute to soil health and fertility.
>
> The nutrients in compost are slowly released and thus less likely to be lost by leaching from the soil.

Most gardens will have space for an enclosed bin, maybe positioned behind the shed or garage, or you can erect a small dividing wall to screen it from view. There are several styles available, but I recommend you choose one with plenty of ventilation holes as a good supply of air assists decomposition and reduces greenhouse gas emissions. If your compost smells bad, it does not have enough air in it and is producing greenhouse gases.

Rodents can easily enter a bin at the base if it is just sitting loosely on top of the soil. To minimise this possibility, dig a trench in the soil about 10 cm deep and the circumference of the bin. Settle the bin into the trench and backfill it, firming the soil down.

No doubt, the quickest way of making compost is to fill the bin at one time, with a variety of kitchen and garden waste, keep the contents damp and turn it often. In reality, our kitchen and garden wastes accumulate a little at a time, and most of us will fill our bins

Homemade compost is a free fertiliser that plants will love.

> ### DISADVANTAGES OF HOT COMPOST
>
> Quick or hot composting made by building the heap all at once and turning it frequently probably conserves less nitrogen than compost made by the slow, gradual method described below. The bacteria in a hot heap grow and multiply (and inevitably die) more quickly, using more nitrogen in the process. Some of the nitrogen is inevitably released into the atmosphere in the form of ammonia.
>
> As well, the high temperature kills off the beneficial bacteria and fungi that attack plant pathogens. This suggests that hot compost has less ability to counteract soil-borne diseases than compost made by the slow, cool method.
>
> ### DISADVANTAGES OF COOL COMPOST
>
> The main downside to the cool composting method is simply the time it takes to obtain a usable product. As well, weed seeds and plant pathogens will not be killed in the cool method as they probably would be by the high temperatures generated in the hot quick method.

more gradually, perhaps over several months. Many of us, too, do not have time or strength for all that turning. We can still make compost; it just takes longer. It might even be better.

Easy compost making
Here is a simple procedure to follow:

- Wet the soil at the base of the bin.
- To assist aeration, put a layer of coarse material such as twiggy prunings at the bottom. Two or three lengths of slotted pipe vertically through the centre of the bin will assist aeration as well.
- Empty your kitchen vegetable and fruit scraps into the bin each day.
- Add any garden waste from light prunings, spent annuals, residues from the vegie garden or grass clippings.
- The smaller the scraps the more quickly they will decompose, so chop, cut or break material first. We have a mulching mower that efficiently shreds most garden waste, then we can use it as mulch, put it in the compost or top up pathways with it.
- Remember the carbon/nitrogen ratio and if you add high-carbon materials that take a long time to decompose, balance this by adding some manure or blood and bone. If the bulk of your scraps consist of kitchen food wastes, these will be high in nitrogen, so add some chopped straw, sawdust, leaves, shredded newspaper or coir from time to time.
- Keep the whole damp but not soggy. You will need to water the compost during dry hot weather.
- From time to time I like to water the compost with a solution made up of a mixture of fish and seaweed emulsions.
- Many people add molasses, comfrey or yarrow to speed decomposition.
- You can turn the contents at any stage, but I usually do it only once.
- Some people buy a device (sometimes called a 'compost lung') similar to an elongated corkscrew to mix up the contents of the bin with and assist aeration.
- If you do not have aeration pipes in place, once the bin is about half-full, you can

drive two or three garden stakes into the contents. Leave them there and give them a wobble from time to time to encourage air flow.
- When the bin is full, cover the contents with straw, hay or grass clippings, perhaps having turned it first, water it and leave it to decompose, making sure you keep it damp.
- Start a second bin while the first is decomposing.

This method is not quick, but it is easy and it does recycle your wastes into free organic fertiliser. It is unlikely that the contents will have reached a high enough temperature to kill weed seeds and plant diseases. For this reason it is best to avoid including diseased plants or weeds that have gone to seed. If weeds do grow in the compost, they are easily pulled out and added to the next bin. On the plus side, you will probably have free pumpkins and tomatoes from seeds you have put in the compost.

Rotating bins
Rotating bins are completely enclosed and above the ground so there is no possibility of rodent entry. They make compost very quickly. However, they are costly to buy and they must be filled all at once. One possibility is to fill your ordinary bin gradually and then transfer the contents to a rotating bin to complete the process quickly.

Lime, dolomite and wood ash
There is disagreement about the addition of lime, dolomite or wood ash to the compost bin, with some authorities recommending their use and others cautioning against it. Composting occurs more rapidly at a pH of about 7 to 8, so adding one of the materials that will raise the pH can hasten the process. The pH will naturally lower again as the compost is 'cooked'. However, the addition of liming materials when the heap is at what is known as the 'thermophilic' stage (above 40°C), when it is alkaline anyway, can result in loss of nitrogen to the atmosphere in the form of ammonia. In bins with limited air movement, and consequently anaerobic and acidic compost, the addition of some form of lime will be beneficial. If you do add any of these three ingredients, most benefit and least loss of nitrogen will result from sprinkling only small amounts at a time.

> **LESS WORK, BETTER COMPOST**
>
> A study in Canada some years ago found that incorporating straw or similar coarse material throughout an unturned compost pile resulted in compost that was ready almost as quickly as if the pile was turned twice a week. In addition, the no-turn compost made with straw incorporated contained about 13% more nitrogen than the frequently turned pile.

Millions of micro-organisms
There are millions of micro-organisms at work in compost. They include many different bacteria and fungi and the fine branching filaments of actinomycetes, which are somewhere between the two. The types of micro-organisms and visible soil biota will vary at different stages of the composting process and even in different parts of the mixture. Anaerobic bacteria might be present

WHAT CAN I PUT IN THE COMPOST BIN?

- Any kitchen vegetable and fruit scraps
- Leaves
- Straw
- Manures
- Weeds, preferably before they seed
- Chopped prunings
- Leaves
- Grass clippings
- Seaweed, fresh or emulsion
- Fish emulsion
- Molasses
- Spent annuals
- Excess from the vegie garden
- Cut flowers
- Blood and bone
- Wood ash
- Tea bags
- Coffee grounds
- Egg shells
- Vacuum cleaner detritus from woollen carpet
- Hair
- Shredded paper and cardboard
- Scraps of wool, cotton or other natural fibres
- Rock dust
- Lime, only if your soil is very acidic or you add a lot of acidic material such as fruit wastes.

Do not use

- Meat
- Fish, other than as a diluted emulsion
- Cheese
- Fats and oils
- Anything that might contain chemical residues
- Diseased plant material
- Human and cat or dog faeces
- Disposable nappies
- Glossy magazine paper
- Plastic
- Glass
- Metal.

---

in the centre and bottom of the heap. Aerobic bacteria will be living around the top and sides.

After compost is turned (if you are a compost turner) and oxygen incorporated, the aerobic bacteria will spread throughout and speed up decomposition. Once the heap packs down again and the oxygen in the centre is used up, more anaerobic bacteria will be present. If compost is made in a bin with very little oxygen present, there will be mainly anaerobic bacteria, decomposition will be slower and there will probably be a very unpleasant odour as ammonia (and probably methane) is emitted.

Of course, if you don't want to make your own compost, it is available from nurseries.

Mini compost heaps/bins

A simple alternative if you don't want to make compost in a normal bin, or to use as an adjunct to your bin, is to place mini bins throughout the garden. This could be convenient in a vegie garden or at the base of fruit trees.

- Take some lidded buckets or large food containers, about 20 litres is a good size.
- Cut off the bottom of the containers. Place them wherever you like around the garden, base down, working the base into

> ### SPEEDING UP THE PROCESS
>
> If you are not a compost turner and your heap is taking a while to decompose, you can speed matters up by trying some of these tricks.
>
> - Make a manure tea by soaking manure in a bucket of water for a few days. Empty the liquid over the contents of the bin and pour the sludge into a hole in the centre.
> - Add green grass clippings to a hole in the centre of the mixture.
> - Vitamise comfrey, yarrow, borage, stinging nettles, dandelions, or any combination of them, with some seaweed emulsion and molasses. Pour the slurry into a bucket or watering can and fill the container with water. Pour the liquid all over the contents and into the holes.
> - Cover the contents with a layer of green grass clippings and water well with seaweed emulsion diluted in water.

- Either rake the contents around nearby plants, or plant straight into the decomposing pile.

Bury waste

A very simple idea for anyone who does not want to make compost or have a worm farm is simply to bury kitchen waste. You can bury it in a trench or beside a plant. Some proponents of this method have a system that starts at one end of the garden and works its way back and forth or around.

To ensure the waste breaks down more quickly, you can vitamise kitchen scraps in water and even add seaweed or fish emulsion to the slurry before burying it.

Dog owners will want to cover recent burial spots with a stone, garden statue or similar to prevent it from being dug up again.

Vermicompost and worm juice

Many people like to keep a worm farm and feed their scraps to the earthworms. Worm farms do not take up much space and there are several commercial models to choose from. Instructions for feeding the worms come with the kit. Handymen can easily make their own; just go to any retailer of worm farms and have a look at the general principles of how they go together.

If you decide to make your own, ensure that liquid can drain away and does not build up in the worm container, or the worms will drown. You need at least one tray or large bucket with holes for the worm liquid to run through. This should have a lid to prevent the worms from escaping and rodents from entering, and sit tightly over a container that

the soil for a few centimetres to prevent rodent entry.
- Fill each small container with chopped up kitchen and garden waste. Use the same ingredients as you would in a normal bin, but chop them finely so they decompose quickly.
- Always replace the lid after adding material to the bucket.
- Add some decomposed or pelletised manure or blood and bone as you go.
- Keep the contents damp.
- When the bucket is nearly full, cover the contents with any mulch you have available and leave it to decompose for a few weeks or as long as necessary.
- Remove the bucket when you are ready.

will catch the juice. A tap in the bottom container allows easy removal of the liquid. Before adding worms to the container, put a layer of bedding about 6 to 8 cm deep in the bottom. You can use coir fibre, hardwood sawdust (definitely no treated timber) compost, decomposed manure or shredded cardboard or newspaper. A mixture of bedding can be used. The bedding should be damp but not soggy.

Do position your worm farm in a shady spot, otherwise they might cook in the summer. We found the best place was under a bench in the garage. Worms are likely to cease activities in very cold weather unless they are kept somewhere a bit warmer than the chilly outdoor conditions. Remember, in the ground worms can burrow to deeper levels of the soil to escape from excessive heat or cold, which they cannot do in a small worm farm.

The worms you put into a worm farm are different from worms that live in garden soil so you need to buy some to get the farm started. Many commercial kits come with worms and starter bedding included. The species to put in a worm farm are known as 'tigers', 'reds' and 'blues'.

In general you can feed your worms with the same sort of materials you put in the compost, and avoid the same things you avoid putting in the compost. However, do not include coarse garden waste; worms prefer a soft diet. In addition, avoid or use very small amounts of onion, citrus peel and coffee grounds. Worms can be given pet faeces, but not if the animal has been recently wormed. Chop worm food finely so they can eat it more easily. One recommendation is to lightly cook it in the microwave oven first.

Keep the worms' environment damp, but overwatering will cause them to crawl up onto the back of the lid to escape the water and could cause their food to go mouldy. Keep a sheet of damp cardboard on top of the bedding and worms. They will eventually eat this, so it will need to be replaced from time to time. When you feed the worms, lift the cardboard and spread the food underneath.

To prevent or treat acidic conditions in the worm farm, sprinkle a handful of lime over their food and bedding from time to time. Acid conditions might be indicated by mouldy food, the presence of ants, the presence of tiny white worms called entrachyadids or by an unpleasant odour.

Your worms will convert food scraps and other wastes into vermicompost (worm castings) and worm juice. To harvest the vermicompost, remove the cardboard from half of the bedding and leave the worms exposed for a couple of hours. They will move into the covered half and you can harvest the castings from the uncovered section.

The vermicompost can be used in the same way as compost, but you don't need much. A generous double handful per plant worked loosely into the surface of the soil or scattered under the mulch will give plants a boost. The liquid that seeps into the bottom tray of the bin can be diluted with an equal amount of water and used as a foliar spray or watered over the soil. It is possible that the liquid will contain potential human pathogens, so do not spray onto foods which are eaten raw and always wash food before eating it.

This commercial worm farm is only one of several options available.

In addition to your worm farm, encourage earthworm activity throughout the garden by using mulch everywhere and replacing it often as it decomposes. Avoid using chemical sprays as they can kill the worms. The worms that live in garden soil are different species from the compost worms, but they are still very beneficial to the soil. You do not have to buy them. They will be there naturally if you provide conditions they like. However, compost worms can live in no-dig beds, manure piles and other rich organic sources.

Bokashi bucket

There is a wonderful way of producing fertiliser from kitchen scraps for those people with a very small garden, or apartment dwellers with a balcony, courtyard or rooftop garden, or those who are unable to turn and otherwise handle compost. It is called a Bokashi bucket. The domestic-size bucket has a capacity of 20 litres and can be kept on a kitchen bench or in a cupboard or out-of-the-way corner.

The system is made up of a bucket with an airtight lid. Inside is a plastic drainage grill. Below the drainage grill is the bottom section of the bucket, where liquid accumulates; there is a tap in this section. Food scraps are put in the bucket, on top of the drainage grill, and pushed down tightly to remove air. Scraps are sprinkled with a beneficial bacterium in granulated form, which ferments the waste. The scraps are not decomposed or composted, but rather preserved in anaerobic conditions.

No odour is emitted from the lidded bucket, so no insects or vermin are attracted. There is almost no odour when the lid is opened to add more scraps and press them down. However, the liquid extracted via the tap does smell somewhat cheesey, and the solids, once exposed to air while you are in the process of burying it, smell even stronger.

All food scraps can be included, even meat, small amounts of milk, stews and other leftovers. The only exceptions the manufacturers give are bones and liquids, apart from the small amounts that might be incorporated in leftover soups and stews. If a leftover dish is a bit wet, it is best added to the bucket after there is a layer of vegetable or fruit scraps.

You do need to buy Bokashi bacterium to keep the system going, but it is not expensive.

> ### WONDERFUL WORM CASTINGS
>
> Worm castings (vermicompost) contain five times more nitrogen, seven times more phosphorus, 11 times more potassium, three times more magnesium, twice the amount of calcium and 35% more organic matter than are usually found in topsoil. Castings are pH neutral and have very good water-holding capacity.

The manufacturers claim that the running cost is about $1 per week and users can expect to obtain about 20 kg of fertiliser a month. This seems very reasonable, especially when you are solving a kitchen waste disposal problem at the same time. I have found it somewhat cheaper than this because I feed a good proportion of the kitchen scraps to the earthworms, so the Bokashi bucket takes longer to fill.

In addition, the liquid produced during fermentation is drained off each time scraps are added by a tap in the bottom of the bucket. The liquid is diluted with water and used as fertiliser.

When the bucket is full it is left to ferment from seven to 10 days, after which it can be used as fertiliser by burying it in the soil where needed. It is not broken down at this stage, but quickly decomposes once buried. Two or three weeks after having buried Bokashi waste the only traces of it I am likely to find are eggshells, avocado seeds and peach pips.

Scraps inside the bucket are sprinkled with granules containing a beneficial bacterium.

To use the waste for fertilising pot plants, fill a plant pot to about one-third with potting mix, add a third Bokashi waste, then top up with more potting mix to fill the pot. Leave for a week before planting into the mixture. Alternatively, in a wheelbarrow or large container, mix one part Bokashi waste to two parts potting mix. Leave for a week before using the mixture for repotting or topping up pots.

Compost tea

Compost tea has numerous benefits when used as a foliar spray or a soil drench. As a foliar spray, so long as at least 70% of the leaf

The Bokashi bucket recycles your kitchen scraps into garden fertiliser.

MORE USES FOR BOKASHI

The Bokashi bacteria (also known as Effective Micro-organisms or EM) have been used to reduce odour from sewage treatment plants and from piggeries and other animal production. It has been sprayed on pasture and crops to increase production.

surface is covered, it can prevent a range of fungal diseases. As a soil drench, it encourages beneficial soil biota and leads to improved nutrient availability. Both methods will introduce a range of nutrients to the leaf surface and the soil.

Many farmers wishing to avoid or minimise the use of chemical fertilisers, pesticides and fungicides are using compost teas on a large scale to improve the health and productivity of their crops. Research has shown that compost made from specific ingredients is most effective for preventing particular fungal infections. The effectiveness of any compost tea depends on its ingredients, its age, the method used to make it, the frequency of application and the weather conditions at time of application.

The small-scale home gardener can use compost tea for its general beneficial effects throughout the garden without being too concerned about prevention of specific diseases. It is very simple to make.

- Put some well-decomposed compost in a large bucket or well-sealed rubbish bin.
- Cover it with water. You need a volume of about one part compost to five parts water.
- Stir the mixture.
- Put the covered bucket in a warm spot and allow the mixture to steep for one to three weeks.
- Pour liquid through a fine strainer such as cheesecloth or pantyhose and spray the desired plants or beds.
- The mixture should be the colour of weak tea. If it is darker, dilute it with more water.
- To more effectively drench the soil, pour the mixture from a watering can rather than using a sprayer.
- The residue can be applied to the garden, or put back into the compost bin.

Compost tea, made from well-decomposed compost, is said not to contain any potential human pathogens, but it is always wisest to wash food before eating it. Even organically grown food will probably have dust on it, especially if watered with drippers or soaker hoses, and could very well have been crawled over by slugs and snails, which can cause illness in humans.

Manure tea

Manure tea is made in the same way as compost tea. It contains a range of nutrients, but does not have either the disease prevention potential of compost tea or the same range of beneficial micro-organisms. Raw manure can contain potential human pathogens, so tea made from it should not be sprayed on foods such as leafy greens that are eaten raw. However, fruit trees can be sprayed either before fruit formation or after harvest and any food plants can be sprayed before the edible part begins to form.

Green weed tea

Green plant matter such as weeds or herbs contains a variety of nutrients. You can take advantage of this fact by making a green tea from any variety of greens you have available. Many gardeners find it especially satisfying to make liquid fertiliser from weeds like dandelion, cat's ear and couch grass, but prunings from any herbs you have in abundance can be used as well.

Push as much of the weed as you can into a bucket. Cover it with water and put a lid on the bucket. Leave it in a warm spot for two or three weeks. Remove the plant matter from the liquid and put it into the compost bin. Dilute the liquid to the colour of weak tea before using it.

Green manures

Green manuring is a technique widely used by organic farmers and can easily be adapted by home gardeners. It is especially beneficial in vegie gardens. It involves growing a crop which is either dug into the soil or slashed and left on the surface as mulch just prior to its flowering. The many benefits of green manure include:

- increasing organic matter in the soil
- encouraging earthworms and many beneficial soil micro-organisms
- increasing the available nitrogen in the soil
- improving the soil's water retention
- bringing up minerals from deep levels of the soil and making them available to plants
- aerating the soil so water, air and plant roots can more easily penetrate
- preventing weed growth which could occur when a bed is left vacant for a time
- as part of a crop rotation technique, even on a small scale in pots, a green manure crop can break the cycle of pests and diseases.

Many of the plants recognised as green manure plants are those which have the ability to obtain nitrogen from the air in the soil and fix or store it in nodules on their roots. When the green manure plant dies, the nitrogen from the root nodules, as well as that in the plant's leaves, becomes available to subsequent crops. Some of the nitrogen in the root nodules can be released into the soil while the green manure crop is growing and be of benefit to other plants nearby. Nitrogen-fixing green manure plants include clover, lucerne, peas, beans, medic, chick peas and vetch, all of which are legumes.

For nitrogen fixation to occur a particular type of bacterium called *Rhizobium* needs to be present in the soil. Each green manure plant needs a particular *Rhizobium* bacterium, which might not necessarily be naturally present in the soil. So when the green manure seed is bought you need to obtain the correct type of bacterium to coat the seed with. This is called inoculation. The seed supplier should know what is needed.

Often, grasses such as oats or Japanese millet are grown along with the legume. The grasses provide additional organic matter from both their leaves and their large root mass. The grass seed does not need to be inoculated.

Green manure seed mixtures are available from nurseries or organic gardening suppliers (see Appendix) and should come with the correct bacterium. To grow the green manure crop, simply scatter the inoculated seed over bare soil, rake it in and keep it watered.

Green manures to grow in the warm spring and summer seasons include buckwheat, cowpea, Japanese millet, lablab (in tropical and subtropical areas) and sorghum.

Green manures to grow in autumn and winter include fenugreek, woolly pod vetch, rapeseed, subclover, lupins, rye and oats.

Simple alternatives

If the concept of inoculation sounds too complicated for your small patch, the following are some alternatives you can use.

If the correct bacterium is in the soil, broad beans like these will fix nitrogen in nodules on their roots.

- Ordinary pea and bean crops either dug in or used as mulch after the crop is finished will have a similar effect. Even if their roots have not stored nitrogen because the correct bacterium was not in your soil, their leaves will supply organic matter and nitrogen.
- In a very weedy patch, use the weeds as green manure. Mow, slash or dig them in before they flower and go to seed.

Borage does not have root nodules, but is a good alternative green manure.

> ### RECOGNISING NITROGEN-FIXING NODULES
>
> To check whether your peas, beans or other legumes are fixing nitrogen, pull one up and examine the root nodules. Cut a nodule open. If it is pink inside, nitrogen fixation is occurring.

- Borage is quick to grow from seed. Use it instead of a recognised green manure seed mixture. It does not fix nitrogen in root nodules, but its lush leaves add plenty of organic matter and nitrogen to the soil when dug in or used as mulch. Let it flower and seed for a constant supply.

Growing in potting mixes

Perhaps you have a small area and most of your food garden will be in pots. Buy the best quality potting mix with added slow-release fertiliser and a water-saving product.

Adjusting pH in potting mix before planting

Test the pH of the potting mix before use and make any adjustments needed. To raise the

> ### MAKE YOUR OWN POTTING MIX
>
> Many people prefer to make their own potting mix. A simple recipe is to begin with one bucket each of compost, coarse sand and peat moss or cocopeat. Add to this about half a bucket of vermicompost. Some people like to add silica. You can also add compost and/or vermicompost to commercial potting mix.

pH by one unit, mix in three heaped teaspoons of lime per 10 litres. A recommended lime mixture is equal quantities, by weight, of agricultural limestone and dolomite.

If the mixture is too alkaline, lower it by about one unit by adding a slightly heaped teaspoon of sulphur per 10 litres.

Adjusting pH in potting mix after planting

It is a good idea to retest the pH of potting mixes every few months as it does change over time because of the effects of added fertilisers, mulches and water. If you test the pH of products you add to the mix as well, you are likely to find that a slightly acidic compost and an alkaline manure will balance each other out and no further treatment will be needed.

If it becomes necessary to adjust the pH while there are plants growing in the pot, you can scatter a little of the required lime or sulphur over the top of the mixture and water it in. Alternatively, mix the amendment with water and pour the solution into the pot.

For example, if the pH of the mix is too acid (about 5), for every 10 litres of potting mix scatter over the surface two or three heaped teaspoons of a 1:1 mixture of hydrated lime and dolomite (I usually use only dolomite). Water it in. If the pH is less than 5, use another one or two teaspoons of the lime mixture. The lime can be mixed with two litres of water and watered in.

To lower the pH of an alkaline potting mixture, make up a solution of 2 g of iron sulphate per litre of water and use about 500 ml for each litre of mix. You would need 10 g of iron sulphate in 5 litres of water for each 10 litres of potting mix. Immediately wash off any of the solution that might be on the leaves. A few minutes after this treatment thoroughly soak the pot with water.

Fertilising pots

Food-producing plants in general need more fertiliser than do purely decorative plants. Let your plants become established for a month or so, during which time they will be using the slow-release fertiliser in the potting mix. There are various ways of fertilising pots. Use any of the following methods or combinations that are practical for you.

- Scatter more slow-release fertiliser over the top and water it in.
- Use a weak solution of worm juice from your worm farm as a foliar spray or watered in.
- Use liquid seaweed, fish emulsion or other organic liquid fertiliser, either watered in or applied as a foliar spray, at the rate recommended on the bottle.
- Mulch with compost, well-decomposed manure or vermicompost, covered with straw, sugar cane mulch or similar.

Fertiliser timing

How frequently you fertilise your potted food plants will depend on the type of plant and the fertility of the original mixture. In all cases your own observation will guide you as to when a plant needs to be fed. If plants are not thriving, leaves look yellow, or flowers and fruit are small or fail to form, it is time for a feed. Take care always not to overfertilise; a little at a time is a good policy for all potted plants.

Fast-growing lettuce are planted into top-quality potting mix with extra compost worked in.

Fast-maturing plants

For quick-growing plants such as lettuce, I probably would only fertilise them once during the growing season, but I plant them in the best quality potting mix with some added compost and decomposed manure. Once the lettuce, for example, is harvested, I add more fertiliser, maybe blood and bone or manure, before planting the next crop in the same mixture.

Most vegetables

Plants that have a longer growing season and higher nutrient requirements, such as tomatoes and many other vegetables, need more frequent fertiliser applications, maybe as often as every few weeks. However, use a different fertiliser each time and only a little at a time. Too much fertiliser in the confined space of a pot can damage the plant's roots.

Herbs

Herbs in pots need less fertiliser than most other plants. A fast-maturing herb such as rocket or coriander will probably not need any more fertiliser than what is in the mixture to begin with. A herb that will be in the pot for some time might need a very little fertiliser every two months, or even less frequently if it is growing well.

Fruit trees

The main fertilising time for fruit trees is in autumn and spring; this is when you add compost, manures, vermicompost or blood and bone. A weak liquid fertiliser can be used in addition, perhaps every month or two.

Practicalities of potting

Apartment dwellers will need to go to some effort to bring bags of potting mix up in the lift and will, understandably, not want to have to repeat the procedure more often than necessary. There is also the issue of the disposal of used mixture. To minimise this problem, in most cases potting mix can be reused for several different seasonal crops. Always start with the best quality potting mix you can find and look for the Australian Standards logo.

Avoid growing the same crop season after season as diseases could carry over in the mix. Each plant has different nutritional requirements as well, and will deplete the nutrients in the mix as it grows, For example, if you grow tomatoes year after year, they will be extracting the same minerals and trace elements until nutritional deficiencies result.

After each seasonal crop, check the pH of the mix, adjust it if necessary, and rejuvenate it by planting a green manure or tipping it into a barrow and working in some decomposed manure, compost, worm castings, blood and bone, or blood and bone with potash. Work the fertiliser into the mix well so you are aerating it at the same time. It is a good idea to thoroughly clean the pot while it is empty so pathogens are not transferred to the new crop. Alternatively, leave the mix in the pot and work the fertiliser into it with a trowel.

If growing fruit trees or perennial herbs that will be in the pot for a number of years, scrape away the top few centimetres of mix every year or two and top it up with compost and decomposed manure.

Mulch

An important way of increasing the organic matter and nutrient availability of your soil is to use mulch. As the mulch decomposes, through weathering and the activities of myriad creatures that live in and under it, nutrients and organic matter are incorporated into the soil as humus. In addition, many of the soil biota burrow into the earth, opening up channels through which air and water can enter. The soil biota themselves defecate and die, adding their own nutrient content and becoming part of the soil's organic matter.

Mulch has numerous other benefits for your garden, including conserving water by reducing evaporation, reducing erosion from wind, rain and foot traffic, stabilising soil pH, reducing temperature extremes in the soil by insulating it, improving soil structure, reducing weeds and reusing garden wastes.

Some suitable mulches for food plants include compost; decomposed manures; pea straw; lucerne hay, straw or pellets; shredded sugar cane and grass clippings. When using compost or decayed manure, cover it with a more fibrous mulch to prevent it from drying out and losing nutrients before your plants can access them. Refer back to the section about the carbon/nitrogen ratio. Food plants usually will benefit from materials higher in nitrogen, but will not suffer if occasionally mulched with a higher carbon material such as straw, especially if you have previously been generous with manure, blood and bone or lucerne.

When growing food plants in pots, remember that the potting mix will dry out much more quickly in hot weather than will soil in the rest of the garden. To reduce evaporation, keep a good covering of mulch over the top of the mix and replace it as it decomposes. Be careful not to let fine mulch build up against plant stems as a fungal disease called collar rot could be the result.

Have a look at the earlier information about nitrogen drawdown. It is very important that you not dig high carbon materials into the soil as their decomposition will deplete the soil of nutrients that your plants need to grow and be productive.

For much more information about mulch see my earlier books, *The Miracle of Mulch*, or the relevant section in *Creating Your Eco-Friendly Garden*.

The humus connection

Humus is produced by the breakdown of mulch and organic matter added to the soil as it is acted upon by the soil biota. These myriad creatures, mainly micro-organisms, produce sticky secretions that bind the decomposed organic matter to the soil mineral particles, so the humus acts as a binding agent or glue that sticks the soil particles together into crumbs or aggregates. The air spaces between the soil aggregates ensure good drainage as well as good water-holding capacity. The humus itself can hold several times its own weight in water and helps prevent nutrients from leaching out of the soil during heavy rainfall.

Humus is often described as the end result of decomposition when the organic matter, after being broken down by micro-organisms, is dark and earthy smelling and fully incorporated into the soil. It is regarded as stable and long-lived, storing nutrients for future generations of plants. However, humus is not the end of the decomposition cycle; it breaks down very slowly, releasing its store of nutrients.

To have good, stable soil humus that decomposes slowly, gradually releasing nutrients, it is important that it be based on a range of organic materials, from quickly decomposing nitrogenous materials to slowly decomposing more woody or carboniferous materials. Nitrogenous materials will decay quickly and give plants a fast nutrient boost, but for a more even, gradual release of nutrients materials higher in carbon should be used as well. This can be achieved by sprinkling decayed manure around plants (for quick decomposition and nutrient release) and covering it with straw (for slower decomposition).

In addition, the lignins and cellulose in woody materials encourage beneficial mycorrhizal fungi. These special fungi grow in association with plant roots, extending their reach into the soil and helping them access more nutrients.

Digging exposes humus to air and speeds its decomposition, so it is important to replace mulch every time the soil is turned over to ensure the continuous wonderful process of decay, humus formation and nutrient release.

Drainage

Plants can often develop root diseases and die as a result of the soil being waterlogged for an extended period. Make sure your garden beds and plant pots are well drained, especially if your soil is heavy clay. The plant might not look stressed or die immediately after waterlogging, but damage could become apparent the next time there is hot weather and the damaged root system cannot supply enough water for the plant.

One of the simplest ways of coping with very clayey soil that is prone to waterlogging is to build up raised beds. It might be necessary, depending on the severity of the problem, to lay drainage pipes beneath and around the bed to direct water away from it and/or have a base of coarse gravel or fine pebbles.

Compaction is your enemy

Waterlogged soils are often compacted soils. Compaction reduces the amount of air and nutrients (and water in dry times) that can enter the soil and makes it harder for roots to

> **ACTION PLAN**
>
> - Learn about soil and pH.
> - Improve soil fertility.
> - Use organic fertilisers.
> - Make your own:
>   – compost
>   – vermicompost
>   – Bokashi fertiliser
>   – liquid fertilisers
>   – green manure.
> - Grow successfully in pots.
> - Mulch.

penetrate. The result is poor growth and weak, shallow-rooted, disease-prone plants. If your garden soil is compacted, use a long garden fork to lift and fracture the soil without digging it over. You only need to loosen the soil enough so the natural processes can begin. Your additions of organic matter will encourage soil biota to do the rest for you.

Some people prefer to dig the soil to break up the compaction. This is not my preferred option, but if you decide to dig, do it once only and when the soil is damp, not saturated.

To prevent compaction, have designated paths or walkways so garden beds are never walked on. Design you garden so that all work can be done from a path.

MAKING THE MOST OF YOUR SPACE

Plants for places

Everyone's situation will be different. The size of the area at your disposal as well as the shapes, orientation, climatic conditions and microclimates within each garden will vary enormously. In Chapter 2 I provided some suggestions about edible plants you could grow and where to grow them. By now you might have carefully examined your own situation and come to some decisions. Now is the time to put plans into action.

Perhaps you have drawn up a plan showing where you intend to build new beds, change existing ones or position some pots. Maybe your approach is more casual and you want to feel your way gradually, trying one idea at a time. There is no right or wrong way to go about this; it depends on your own situation and preferences. Use this chapter to gather ideas about how to put the spaces in your garden to the most productive use.

Replacing a tree or shrub

One of the simplest and lowest cost ways to begin your food production program is to replace an existing tree or shrub with a fruit tree or shrubby herb. Late autumn, winter or early spring are all good times to do this.

Perhaps a shrub has died in the drought or come to the end of its attractive life, or maybe you have never really liked it. Remove the existing plant and as much of the root system as you can. As long as there was no root disease in the plant, there is no need to remove all the scraps of root material; they will decay and add to the organic matter in the soil. You will be left with a nice planting hole with soil already loosened by the previous root system and by your digging or levering to remove it.

Depending on your soil type, add whatever improvements might be needed. I like to add some compost and decayed manure to the hole and work it into the existing soil. However, when planting bare-rooted fruit trees, do not add fertiliser when you plant them. Wait until the tree has some leaves appearing and fertilise in spring and autumn. It's a good idea to test the pH and make any adjustments necessary. See Chapter 4 for details. Wet the soil in the hole and allow the water to drain away before placing your new plant into the hole and back-filling the soil. Water again and mulch the plant.

You probably have an existing watering system. If not, see Chapter 7 for some ideas about efficient watering. An effective method for individual plants where there is no watering system in place is what I call the mound, moat and mulch method. Position your plant so it is on a slightly raised mound and make a moat around the perimeter. Then mulch over the whole mound and moat. The plant can now be watered by hand without the water running off. The mound aids drainage and prevents the roots from becoming waterlogged in wet weather. The mulch absorbs water, slows down evaporation from the moat and gradually decomposes to enrich the soil.

Any of the dwarfing rootstock fruit trees or specially bred cultivars are suitable. You might have to order what you want from your local nursery. Use this opportunity to talk to your nursery about what you want to do. You might get some good advice about fruits suitable for your area.

Shrubby perennial herbs suitable to replace an existing shrub or small tree include rosemary, lemon verbena, bay or sage. Bush tucker plants to consider are Australian finger lime, Davidson plum, kangaroo apple, lemon myrtle, native ginger, mountain pepper or prickly currant bush.

Wherever possible, chop up or mow over the plant you removed and either put it in the compost bin or spread it as mulch. A mulching mower will chop up most fresh prunings up to about 2 cm diameter.

Frost protection

Young plants might need frost protection for the first winter or two. A simple plastic guard is cheap and easily installed with the help of a

The simplest frost protection for young plants is a plastic sleeve supported by bamboo stakes.

few bamboo stakes. Alternatively, there is a product available called Hydronurture, which is a plastic guard with built-in tubes into which water is poured. The water insulates and helps keep an even temperature.

Fertiliser for fruit trees

Briefly, fruit trees need nitrogen, phosphorus and potassium in addition to a range of other minerals and trace elements. Nitrogen is needed for leaf growth and efficient photosynthesis; phosphorus for root growth, flower bud, fruit and seed formation and fruit quality; potassium for transporting carbohydrates throughout the tree (apples and some berries require high potassium), strengthening cell walls, protecting plants from disease and for improved flavour, colour and keeping quality. If too much nitrogen is used on fruit trees, there will be strong leaf growth and little fruit; it also predisposes the tree to pest and fungal problems.

Blood and bone, worm castings and manure (especially poultry manure) will supply nitrogen. Potash (potassium) is sourced from compost, wood ash, fish emulsion, worm castings, seaweed emulsion, manures and blood and bone with potash. Phosphorus will be supplied by worm castings, fish emulsion, compost and manures. Thus, a mixture of manures, compost, wood ash, worm castings, seaweed and fish emulsions and blood and bone will provide the major nutrients needed by fruiting trees, as well as a variety of minor nutrients and trace elements. A sprinkle of dolomite or agricultural lime occasionally will be beneficial on acidic soil and ensure nutrients in the soil are available for plants to access.

Organic fertilisers release their nutrients slowly with little or no leaching into waterways and improve the soil structure by adding humus and encouraging soil biota.

As long as the holes for newly planted fruit trees were prepared well, the trees won't need any additional fertiliser during the first growing season (usually spring for deciduous trees). Bare-rooted trees that have been planted with no fertiliser in the hole should have a little sprinkled around the base when the first leaves appear. During late autumn sprinkle about half a kilogram of compost, manure or vermicompost (or a combination) around the drip line and water it in well. Double this amount each year until a large tree is receiving 3 to 4 kg per year, half in autumn and half in spring. Smaller trees or trees planted close together will need about half this amount. Citrus, passionfruit, peaches and bananas have a higher nitrogen requirement than most fruit trees, so will need a greater percentage of manure in the fertiliser mixture applied in spring.

Best benefits will be achieved from fertilisers when mulch is applied on top of them. Fruit trees, vines and berries grown in a no-dig bed that is constantly being replenished with a variety of materials are likely to produce well with very little extra fertiliser.

> ### FERTILISER IN THE PLANTING HOLE?
>
> Expert advice is usually not to add fertiliser to the planting hole. The reason for this is that strong fertiliser such as blood and bone and pelletised or fresh manure can damage the roots of young plants and can also cause fertiliser burn in the leaves (see Chapter 4). However, I nearly always do add fertiliser to the planting hole and have not had a problem in over 30 years of gardening. But my last two gardens have had very poor soil to begin with and I always try to dig a very large hole (about four times the diameter of the pot) and work the fertiliser well into the existing soil, at least a month before planting when I can be that organised. I use compost or well-decomposed manure in the hole and later sprinkle blood and bone over the surface, watering it in well. The secret is not to overdo it and to mix the fertiliser well into the soil. It helps if you can prepare the hole four to six weeks before planting. You need to use your judgement and knowledge of your own soil and garden conditions and the needs of the plant. If the soil is friable and has been fertilised for previous plants, there is no need to add anything to the hole at planting time.

Fertiliser from poultry

Anyone who keeps poultry and has an enclosed run for them can plant a fruit tree or two within the run that will be automatically fertilised by the poultry. This is in keeping with the permaculture concept of multiple uses. The danger could be that excess nitrogen from the poultry manure might encourage lush leaf growth to the detriment of fruit. Compensate for this by mulching the tree(s) with straw, autumn leaves or other high-carbon materials. Wire netting, either as a guard around the tree or laid over the mulch, is necessary to prevent it from being scratched away. A further benefit of this system is that any fruit that falls to the ground will be eaten by the poultry and not left lying around to attract fruit flies or other pests.

Replacing flowering annuals

Another simple and economical way to start growing a few food plants is to remove spent annuals at the end of the season and replace them with vegetables, herbs or small fruiting plants such as strawberries. Pull out the annuals, sprinkle some fertiliser over the area and work it in with a trowel. Now you are ready to plant some edible seedlings.

Many vegetables are very decorative, so don't think you can only do this in the back garden. See Chapter 2 for some suggestions of attractive vegetable combinations. If you don't want to go the whole way in replacing your annuals, scatter food plants among, behind or in front of them. Use your imagination to create designs that are pleasing as well as productive. Tall broad beans, for example,

Red cabbage is one of the most decorative vegies.

might look great with nasturtiums, violas or marigolds meandering around them.

Many herbs are suitable to replace small- to medium-sized annuals. They include basil, borage, caraway, chamomile, chervil, chives, comfrey, coriander, dill, marjoram, oregano, parsley, savoury, salad burnett, tarragon and thyme. You need to decide whether you want a plant that is there all the time because many of these herbs are perennials, but die back leaving bare spots during the winter.

Alternate red cabbages and broccoli to paint a picture.

You might prefer to replace annuals with some of the smaller bush tucker plants such as warrigal greens, broad-leaf palm lily, muntries, native ginger, yam daisy, cranberry heath or ruby saltbush.

Tiny spots

Most gardens have small spots vacant where a herb, vegetable or bush tucker plant would grow. These areas could be perfect to plant a few decorative and edible flowers such as violas, calendulas, violets, dianthus or nasturtiums. They are also suitable for any of the plants previously mentioned to replace annuals. In tropical areas, try pineapples.

As these spots have been vacant, the soil could need some improvement. Dig a hole and work in whatever fertiliser or additives are needed. Mulch around the new plant and devise a way of watering it.

Alternatively, a not-too-tiny spot could be a good area to place a large pot in which to plant a fruit tree or small herb garden; maybe a bay tree surrounded by marjoram, basil and thyme, or by strawberries spilling over the lip of the pot.

Narrow strips

Very many gardens, especially those in newer subdivisions, have one or more long narrow areas. It might be along the space between the house or the shed and a fence, or between neighbouring houses. This could be a good spot to erect some trellis or other support for climbing plants.

There are numerous interesting varieties of climbing beans and peas. Some suitable fruiting plants include passionfruit, berries, kiwifruit, grape vine, sweet apple berry (a bush tucker plant), cantaloupe and watermelon. Ensure that your supporting structure is strong enough to support the weight of the chosen plant and its fruit.

The type of plant you can grow in a narrow area will depend largely on whether it is in sun or shade. For shadier spots, try kiwifruit or berries. Grapes, passionfruit, watermelon, cantaloupe and sweet apple berry need more sun, but will benefit from some shade in the hottest part of the day.

In the tropics such an area could be ideal for banana plants, pawpaws or pitayas.

Any of the smaller herbs and bush tucker plants mentioned above can be grown at the base of the climbing plants, depending on just how narrow your space is.

Be careful when trying to grow plants on a lattice attached to a metal fence on the west side of the house. This side bears the full force of the sun in summer afternoons and the heat reflected from the metal can be fierce. Unless you are able to provide some shade, most plants will wither. Use your ingenuity to work around this. Maybe you can get in an early crop of peas before the summer really kicks in. Perhaps a shade sail over the area will look attractive and give the human occupants as well as the plants some shelter.

A narrow area along a pathway could be ideal to grow a row of small fruit trees with herbs, vegetables, strawberries or edible flowers

Pansies and alpine strawberries combine to make a pretty and productive bed along a pathway.

below them. A hedge of sage or rosemary is another possibility. Many people plant roses along the path. Rose petals are edible. You might like to leave the roses and grow other edible plants beneath them, or remove the roses and replace them with small fruit trees.

Bush tucker plants suitable to grow beneath roses or fruit trees in narrow spots include cranberry heath, muntries, midgenberry, broad-leaf palm lily and warrigal greens.

Replacing a lawn

The lawn area could be the largest space many gardeners have available to convert to food production. Once you have decided to replace an unproductive lawn area with edible plants, you are faced with a variety of choices about what to do and how to go about it.

Lawn herbs

You might want to retain the look and feel of a lawn and still keep an open area of ground-covering plants, but have edible plants rather than grass. There are many herbs that will spread to become lawn-like, but be aware, they will never have the smooth, uniformly green look we are used to. The herb lawn plants are most likely to be used as salad greens or to make teas, some have medicinal uses and some can be used to make pest repellent sprays.

Some suitable low-growing and spreading herbs that can be mown from time to time and will take light foot traffic include yarrow, lady's mantle, peppermint (and other mints), pennyroyal, chamomile, chicory, pennywort, self-heal, salad burnet, dandelion, white clover, coltsfoot and thyme. Some of these will spread from a creeping root system, others will grow a bit taller and self-seed after flowering. If you choose this option, you will have a flowering meadow of food, flavour and medicine, which will attract bees and many other beneficial insects to your garden.

Prepare the ground by digging up the lawn, by hand or rotary hoe. Make sure all grass and weeds are removed, rake the surface smooth and level, then plant your chosen lawn herbs. Alternatively, you can lay down sheet mulch of thick cardboard boxes or commercial weed mat over the lawn. Cover the cardboard or weed mat generously with mulch such as shredded sugar cane or pea straw. Leave the sheet mulch in place for long enough to allow the lawn to die underneath, then cut holes in it and plant your herbs into the soil beneath. Scatter some compost or rotted manure over a dug lawn area or incorporate it into each planting hole if necessary. However, often a lawn area will have been fertilised more than is really

A lawn area about to become more productive. (Photo courtesy Happy Earth)

The area is now a biodiversity-friendly food forest. (Photo courtesy Happy Earth)

needed and no additives will be required. It depends on your own situation, soil type and previous fertiliser use.

More productive possibilities

If keeping an open lawn-like area is not important to you, there are more productive uses for that area. You can plant an orchard of small fruit trees, a bush tucker garden, a dedicated vegetable garden, or even a clever combination such as a permaculture food forest.

There are several ways to go about it.

- Dig up the lawn, as described above.
- Lay sheet mulch (also above) and plant through holes cut in it.
- Build a raised bed, wicking bed or aquaponics system over the area (see Chapter 3 for details about these).

The grass is being removed. (Photo courtesy Happy Earth)

A path meanders through the food forest. (Photo courtesy Happy Earth)

A herb lawn planted instead of grass, with a fruit tree in the centre.

- Plant a herb lawn, as described, and place large pots among the herbs. In the pots you can grow any edible plants you like.

Design ideas

You might be thinking that, as the lawn is in the front garden, you don't want an ugly vegetable garden in that location. Think again. There is no need for a food garden to look unattractive. With a little imagination your new food garden will be the envy of the neighbourhood, and not just for the fabulous fresh food it produces. Here are some ideas to adapt to your own situation. Your strategy will depend on the type and quantity of food you have decided to grow, the climate of your geographical area and the particular microclimate within the garden. You can really have some fun with this.

- For a square- or rectangular-shaped lawn, plan a circular, oval or hexagonal shape in the centre of it. This can be a dedicated vegetable garden. Divide it into segments, like the spokes of a wheel, for separate beds. In the centre, plant a fruit tree, maybe a multi-grafted one or a pitaya. Perhaps an obelisk with a sweet apple berry clambering up it appeals to you. The four curved triangular shapes in the corners can have fruit trees or bush tucker plants planted in them, either in the ground or in large pots. Alternatively, make tepees from long lengths of bamboo and grow climbing beans and peas on them.
- Make a small inner circular, oval or hexagonal bed and surround it by a larger outer ring. Plant a single fruiting tree or a bamboo bean tepee in the inner bed, surrounded by a herb lawn or a strawberry patch, and a vegetable garden in the outer ring. Stepping stones at intervals in the outer ring will give you access to the inner circle and something to stand or kneel on while working in the bed, and will conveniently divide the ring into separate beds.
- Have a diamond shape within a circle so that each tip of the diamond touches the circle. Put a fruit tree in the centre of the diamond, surrounded by self-seeding herbs such as parsley, rocket, nasturtiums and borage. Plant strawberries in the tips of the diamond, either in the ground or in strawberry pots. You are left with four curved shapes around the diamond. These are your vegie beds.
- Plant a hedge of rosemary, lavender, sage or small fruit trees around the perimeter of the area to give wind protection and some shade to a vegie garden in the middle.
- Erect a pergola or other structure and grow grapevines or a passionfruit over it.

A hexagonal vegie garden ready to plant.

A productive backyard vegie garden with rectangular beds all the same size.

Have a herb lawn as the ground cover beneath the pergola and pots of red or black currants, blueberries and strawberries scattered around it.
- Divide your area into two sections by a lattice fence. Grow raspberries, youngberries, loganberries, native raspberries or a passionfruit vine on the lattice. Behind the lattice keep your compost bins and/or a small garden storage shed. Use any of the ideas above in front of the lattice.
- On a sloping site make stepped terraces. Plant to keep the stepped look by having taller fruiting plants or bean tepees on the highest terrace, grading down to ground-covering herbs or bush tucker plants, strawberries or small vegies on the lowest.

A dedicated vegie patch

As discussed above, you might want to create a vegie garden over the whole or part of what

Hexagon planted and mulched.

A different garden uses rectangular vegie beds surrounded by gravel paths.

was previously a lawn area. Maybe you have decided to replace a flower garden or copse of shrubs with vegies. Many older suburban gardens have a lawn area in front with narrow beds of roses or other shrubs on the fence line, along the front path and in front of the house. These narrow beds can be made into vegie beds. Leave some of the shrubs if you want to and plant vegies around them or get rid of the lot and dedicate the beds to producing fresh, nutritious and flavourful food.

Existing beds will need very little preparation other than removing the old plants and improving the soil in whatever way is necessary with organic fertilisers. If your home production of compost, vermicompost or Bokashi is not ready yet, you will need to buy some products to get you started. See Chapter 4 for details of what to look for at the nursery or garden centre and how to make your own organic fertilisers from kitchen and garden waste.

A new bed can be made by digging over the designated area, removing all weeds and raking in necessary soil improvements, or by building raised no-dig beds. Raised beds can be created either from imported topsoil or by building up layers of a variety of organic materials which will gradually decompose. See Chapter 3 for how to do this. The soil should be well aerated and fertile.

Planting vegetables

What you can grow in your vegie beds will depend on the time of year and where you live. It is always a good idea to talk to experienced vegetable growers or nursery staff in your area to find out what they recommend for different times of year. A good guide to go by is what seedlings are available in the nurseries. There are so many regional differences and variations of microclimate that any published advice can only be very general.

It is important to remember that vegetable gardens need planning. It is not like going to the shops and immediately buying what you need. You must get into the habit of thinking ahead. A tomato planted in October, for example, will not begin to produce fruit until December or January, but will continue for several months. Broccoli planted in February will be producing in April or May and after the main heads are harvested will keep producing edible side shoots for many months, sometimes even years. Broad beans planted in May or June will begin cropping in October or November. Asian greens such as buk choy are quick growers, but will still take four to six weeks before you can be eating them.

Some seed packets and seed catalogues give an estimate of the time you can expect from planting to harvesting. Note that these are in

You can grow a variety of nutritious vegies for your family.

ideal conditions and it will often take longer than the time given.

Let's assume you have your bed prepared and ready to plant in spring. Wait until the soil feels warm to the touch. One old saying is not to plant spring vegetables until the soil feels warm to a bare bottom. In much of Australia this is the time to plant beans, capsicums, sweet corn, cucumbers, eggplants, potatoes, pumpkins and squash, tomatoes, cantaloupes, zucchinis and watermelons. In some tropical areas, however, most of these vegetables are planted in the autumn because summer temperatures are too scorching for them. Know your area.

As these vegies mature, are harvested and begin to die, they are removed and replaced by crops that will grow in cooler conditions. These include Asian greens, broad beans, broccoli, Brussels sprouts, Chinese cabbage, leeks, onions, peas, radishes, spinach, turnip, beetroot, silverbeet, spring onions, cabbages, celery and lettuces. In some areas carrots will grow in the cooler season, in other places they do better when planted in spring.

Some vegies are fast-maturing and relatively small in size and can be planted to give a quick crop either between seasons or between bigger, longer-maturing vegies when they are first planted and well spaced. These include radish, lettuce, rocket, spinach, Asian greens, coriander and peas.

Crop rotation

Vary what you grow in any vegetable bed, or pot, from season to season to prevent the possible build-up of diseases in the soil and to avoid depleting the soil of the same nutrients year after year.

TOLERANCE TO ACIDITY

Most vegies prefer a pH from 6 to 7, but there are a few that will tolerate more acidity. Asparagus, celery, brassicas, leek, lettuce, okra, onion, parsnip, pea and spinach should grow well at pH 6 to 6.8. More tolerant of acidity are beans, beetroot, capsicum, carrot, cucurbits, eggplant, radish, tomato and turnip, which will grow at pH 5.5 to 6. Potatoes are possibly the most acid loving vegetables, preferring a pH of 5 to 5.5.

Plant families

Vegetables are divided into groups or families of plants that are related to each other and, generally speaking, related plants are prone to the same pests and diseases and need the same nutrients. Some of the relations in the lists below might surprise you.

Brassicaceae family

Referred to as brassicas, this family includes cabbage, cauliflower, broccoli, Brussels sprouts, kohlrabi, radish, swede and turnip.

Solonaceae family

These plants are referred to as solonaceous or solanums and include tomato, capsicum, eggplant and potato.

Fabaceae family

Commonly known as legumes, these plants include all the peas and beans, including broad beans.

Cucurbitaceae family
All the pumpkins, squashes, melons, cucumbers and zucchinis belong to this family and are referred to as cucurbits.

Apiaceae family
The root vegetables carrot and parsnip and the leafy celery and parsley belong to this group.

Chenopodiaceae family
Vegetables in this family include silverbeet, beetroot and spinach.

Asteraceae family
This group includes lettuce, globe artichoke and Jerusalem artichoke.

Amaryllidaceae family
Members of this family are onion, garlic, shallot, leek and chive.

How to rotate
There are different recommendations for specific crop rotations, but the most important thing to remember for the home garden is not to plant members of the same family in subsequent years. For example, to plant Brussels sprouts one year, cabbages the next and broccoli the next in the same patch is asking for problems.

In an ideal situation, with plenty of space and numerous beds available, a solanum bed should not have more solanums planted in it for four or five years, brassicas need a gap of three or four years and legumes a three-year gap. In a small garden it is not always possible to work to this time frame. Most problems can be avoided by using the following strategy.

- Leave as long as you can between crops, perhaps avoid planting a particular family for two or three years or grow some in pots instead of in the ground.
- Replace nutrients with compost, manures and other organic products.
- Plant and dig in (or slash and decompose) a green manure crop between seasons or whenever a bed is vacant. Do this even in pots used for vegie growing. The addition of the organic material from the green manure crop will rejuvenate and aerate the potting mix.
- Use mulch to encourage beneficial soil biota.

Balcony/verandah/patio/rooftop/courtyard
In most cases your food will have to be grown in pots. Choose pots to suit the shape available. Big pots can look fabulous and are

Dwarfing rootstock citrus tree on the left, avocado on the right, both underplanted with strawberries.

CROP ROTATION HINTS AND OPTIONS

- Plant root vegetables, which do not require a lot of fertiliser, after a heavy feeding crop such as tomatoes or sweet corn.
- Alternate shallow-rooted crops such as lettuce with deep-rooted plants like potatoes.
- Leafy green vegetables need a lot of nitrogen and root crops need more phosphorus.
- Follow a brassica or solanum crop with a legume, then a leafy crop such as lettuce, then a root crop such as carrot.
- Keep a garden diary that includes crop rotations so you won't forget from year to year.
- Potatoes (or sweet potatoes in frost-free tropical areas) are a good first crop to break up the soil. Follow them by brassicas or other leafy greens, then a legume, then tomatoes, root crops other than potatoes, and, after generous fertilising, sweet corn and/or pumpkins. Then you are back to potatoes.
- I often plant tomatoes, followed by broad beans and brassicas (broad beans at the back and brassicas in front), followed by carrots. The carrots do not receive any extra fertiliser, there will be enough for their needs left from the previous crops. Quick-growing crops such as lettuce, rocket, Asian greens and radishes can be grown between the tomatoes or brassicas.

Strawberries thrive in pots of all sorts; this one is a dedicated strawberry pot.

other foods, a pot of herbs near the door will add interest to a courtyard and give zest to your meals. In fact, this is an ideal, simple and cheap way to make a start.

Pot care

Make sure pots have plenty of drainage holes so there is no waterlogging, which will cause root rot. Remember that the plants' roots are

very good for growing fruit trees, but they are almost impossible to move, so make sure they are in their permanent spot. Smaller pots can be moved around as needed, either to make the most of the sun, or to give plants some shade in the heat of summer. If you grow no

The strawberries are beginning to drape over the side of the pot.

> **FRUIT TREES FOR POTS**
>
> Any of the trees on dwarfing rootstock and the small cultivars are suitable to grow in pots. Other good choices are blueberry, black and red currants, pepino, dragonfruit, gooseberry, cumquat, banana, pawpaw, babaco, miracle fruit, pineapple and strawberry. Many of the normal taller fruit trees will naturally miniaturise if grown in a pot, but might not be very productive.

fully contained within the pot and totally dependent on your input for water and fertiliser. In particular, ensure an adequate water supply in hot weather. Small pots will dry out quickly in summer and the mix in them, along with plant roots, will get very hot. Bigger pots need less frequent attention and will grow more food.

A medium-sized pot inside a larger decorative pot has some advantages. You can fill the outer pot with mulch such as coir fibre or bark and nestle the smaller pot into it. This will keep the plants' roots cooler and moister in hot weather. It also allows you to more easily remove and replace the inner pot when it comes time to replace the plant growing in it.

A saucer under the pot to catch the excess water and fertiliser prevents your tiles or decking from becoming stained, creates a humid atmosphere around the plant and conserves the water so plants can access it for longer. However, it can cause root rot if plant roots are sitting in water for extended periods. In hot weather the water in the saucer will evaporate quite quickly so root rot is not likely to be a problem. A workable system is to leave saucers in place during hot weather and remove them during wet and/or humid weather. To prevent staining of your hard surface, stand pots on feet made especially for the purpose (or on a wheeled pot plant holder) and sit a plastic bowl under the drainage hole(s) to catch the drips.

The frequent watering pot plants need can remove nutrients from the mix, so apply regular small amounts of compost, manure, manure tea, seaweed or fish emulsions or worm juice. Use a variety of fertilisers to ensure a wide range of nutrients.

Exposed hot areas are most suited to growing herbs and the vegies that like a lot of sun, including tomatoes, capsicums and zucchinis. Even these, though, might need some sun protection during the hottest weather. A garden umbrella is ideal; it can be wound up or down or moved from place to place according to need. Do make sure it is either wound down or securely fastened during strong winds. Shady areas are good for

Potted vegies have got off to a good start along a north-facing wall. As the weather heats up, they can be moved to a less hot spot.

> **VEGETABLES FOR POTS**
>
> Though you can grow most vegies in pots, the size of the pot is a limiting factor and it makes sense to choose some of the smaller varieties. Try silverbeet, baby carrot, bush bean, capsicum, lettuce, radish, potato, kale, mini cabbage, mini cauliflower, Chinese cabbage, bush cucumber, squash, celery, mini tomato, beetroot, spring onion, garlic, eggplant, mini pumpkin, warrigal greens and Asian greens. Obtain some seed catalogues to find varieties of mini vegies that are great to grow in pots.

lettuce, Asian greens, cabbage, spinach, berries and mints.

Those who want to make maximum use of their small courtyard or similar can look at ways to fit in a number of pots and erect more permanent protection for areas that are too exposed.

Tall plants

Plants that grow tall, including tomatoes and broad beans, need a sturdy stake or wire frame. Useful wire frames are available from nurseries and are a neat way of containing tomatoes, which can tend to straggle and fall everywhere if not tied to supports. The frames are good for peas and climbing beans too. Simply jiggle the legs into the potting mix in the centre of the pot and either plant a tomato seedling in the middle or some bean or peas seeds around the outside. Another option to grow beans, peas or cucumbers on is to make a bamboo tepee from long stakes. Tie the stakes together at one end, spread them apart so the other end fits within the circumference of the pot and push them into the mix. Then you can push the vegetable seeds into the mix so the plants will twine up the tepee.

Climbers

Anyone with verandah posts or strong railing on a balcony or deck can place pots in the appropriate places and grow climbing vine-type plants. A passionfruit vine will live for a number of years and be very productive. There are passionfruit varieties to suit most climates. Sweet apple berry is a suitable bush food plant. Climbing beans, peas, cucumbers, cantaloupes and watermelons are suitable seasonal plants. There are small-fruited watermelon varieties available that would be more suitable for this use than the gigantic ones we are probably most familiar with.

Hydroponics or aquaponics

A courtyard, balcony, rooftop or verandah could be a good spot to try small-scale hydroponics or aquaponics. Even inside in a well-ventilated room can be used for these techniques. Some sun and wind protection will probably be needed. Aquaponics, in particular, once established can provide an almost endless supply of food and an enduring interest for someone with time on their hands. You don't need to raise fish to eat. If you have an existing large fish tank and keep goldfish as a hobby, this can easily be used as a water and nutrient source for food growing. See Chapter 3 for details of these methods.

The challenge of shade

It might seem odd in hot, sunny Australia, but too much shade can be a challenge for many would-be food growers. In cities and suburbs where buildings are close together garden space can be in deep shade for much of the day. Likewise, in established gardens with large shady trees the required hours of sunshine for many crops is not available.

Depending on your situation, there are some strategies to overcome this situation. If nearby fences or other structures allow, paint them white or another light colour to reflect light onto the garden patch. Alternatively, use cleverly placed mirrors to direct sunlight into dark corners.

Some plants will do very well in areas of dappled shade, especially if there is morning sun and afternoon shade for sun protection in summer. For these areas try kiwi fruit, black and red currants, blueberries and gooseberries for fruit, and salad greens and Asian greens for vegies. Most herbs like full sun, but mints will thrive in shade, basil and borage will be fine in semi-shade, parsley will thrive with filtered shade or morning sun and afternoon shade.

If shade is your problem, save your rare sunny patches for sun-loving plants like tomatoes, capsicums, thyme, rosemary, marjoram and coriander and choose plants from those listed above for shady spots.

> **ACTION PLAN**
> - Replace a tree or shrub.
> - Replace flowering annuals.
> - Fill a tiny spot.
> - Plant out a narrow strip.
> - Replace the lawn.
> - Consider design variety.
> - Plan a vegie patch.
> - Select plants for balcony, verandah, rooftop, courtyard.
> - Consider strategies for shade.

GETTING STARTED WITH VEGETABLES
Seeds and seedlings

The easiest way to grow vegies is to start with seedlings bought from a nursery and plant them into a compost-enriched hole in a no-dig bed. Each year good nurseries seem to have a wider range of seedlings available. On the other hand, most of these will be hybrids and you won't be able to save the seeds for next season. The varieties available from nurseries still represent just a fraction of those it is possible to grow from seed.

If you want to obtain seed that you will be able to save season after season to grow your own vegies from scratch, or if you simply want to try some less common varieties and play a part in preserving them, open-pollinated seed is available from specialist suppliers and seed saving groups.

Preserving the past

The varieties of fruits and vegetables generally available in our supermarkets are few compared with the rich diversity once widely grown by orchardists, market gardeners and backyard enthusiasts. Modern hybrid food plants have been bred to:

- ripen within a short time period for economical harvesting
- have a long shelf life
- be of uniform size and colour
- withstand transportation and handling without bruising.

All of these are, no doubt, viable economic reasons. Unfortunately, along the way, many of the new varieties (and even many old varieties selected for economic reasons) have lost much of their distinctive taste. Consumers have become conditioned to expect their food to be cosmetically perfect and gastronomically insipid. If you grow vegies from seed, you have access to a much broader range of food you can really taste.

Hybrid or open-pollinated?

Most commercially available vegie seeds and seedlings are hybrid varieties which, while giving gardeners a reasonable choice, will not reproduce true to type. This means that if you want to save seeds from your crop to use for next year, you don't know what, if anything, you will end up with.

The old-fashioned open-pollinated varieties, however, will reproduce true to type so you can save and reuse your own seeds. Not only is this a very economical way of gardening but you are helping conserve a valuable seed heritage. Many open-pollinated plants will self-seed without much effort on your part at all, apart from leaving them in place long enough to allow this to happen.

Anyone with a small garden intending to let plants pollinate and set seed is wise to only grow a single variety of any vegetable; one type of tomato, one of corn, one of pumpkin and so on. The reason for this is that many of these varieties will readily cross-pollinate and you will no longer have the variety you intended.

Some plants, too, will take up a large amount of space for the long period of time it takes for flowers to form and seeds to set. Those with limited space might want to avoid letting silverbeet, broccoli or parsley, for example, self-sow. Having said that, I do think parsley is one of the best beneficial-insect-attracting plants while it is in flower and is one of the most versatile herbs. I always let a few plants go to seed and scatter the seeds around the garden. When the seeds germinate in late autumn, they often make a thick mat of seedlings. I leave in place, or transplant to where I want them, some of the seedlings and rake over the rest so they act as a green manure.

Plants that will not take up any extra space or time for the seed-setting process include those in which the seed is a part normally eaten: tomato, corn, peas and beans, for example. Pumpkin, cucumber and the cucurbit family also lend themselves to seed collection without tying up the bed for a longer period of time than that taken in the production of the crop.

Home vegetable growers play an important role in maintaining the genetic diversity of our food heritage. This diversity within the gene pool enables plants to adapt to changing circumstances and resist pests and diseases, and is likely to be increasingly important as our climate changes. Because of commercial imperatives like convenience, economy and uniformity, diversity is being eroded. It is a sobering thought that today's society relies on only about 150 food plants from a possible range of approximately 80 000.

How do you know if it is open-pollinated?

When buying seed for the purpose of growing a crop you can later save the seeds from,

> ### SELECTING SEED TO SAVE
> Always save seed from the best produce or that which has the characteristics you want. If you want small pumpkins, for example, do not save seed from giant-sized specimens, and vice versa. If you want produce that matures earlier or later in the season, select seed from plants that show this characteristic. If you eat beans or peas that are especially sweet, save some of the remaining crop of that bush or vine for seed. It is a good idea to have a marker such as a ribbon tied around the plant or particular vegetable you want to save for seed; you can easily forget and harvest it to eat by mistake, or someone else in the family could unknowingly harvest it. Try to save seeds from several different plants so you maintain diversity and vigour in your garden gene pool. Leave the vegetable until it is perfectly ripe and let the seed dry out before storing it in a vermin-proof container in a cool, dry, dark place. Some seed savers in tropical areas store their seeds in the refrigerator to avoid problems with mould and insects.

> **LIFE SPAN OF SEEDS**
>
> Different seeds will remain viable (capable of germinating and producing) during storage for varying lengths of time. Sometimes seeds will keep for many years if properly stored, but the longer they are stored the fewer will eventually germinate, or they might germinate but not be productive.
>
> **Under 1 year:** parsnip seed is not a good keeper; buy it fresh every year or sow your saved seed in the following season.
>
> **1 to 3 years:** carrots, French and runner beans, onions, peas, sweet corn.
>
> **5 years:** beetroot, broad beans, brassicas, tomatoes.
>
> **Over 5 years:** pumpkin, squash.

> **F1 HYBRIDS**
>
> F1 stands for 'first filial'. An F1 hybrid seed or plant is the result of a lengthy breeding program. Plants are selected for specific properties such as early maturing, maturing within a limited time frame or high productivity. Two separate plants, each showing one of the desired traits, are bred together to produce a plant that possesses both of the traits. There are two main problems with this process. One is that selection for desired traits reduces the plant's ability to adapt to a range of conditions. The second problem is that the next generation, F2, will be very variable; plants will probably not have the selected traits, possibly revert to undesirable characteristics and might not germinate at all. These concerns make F1 hybrids unsuitable for home gardeners who wish to save seed for future propagation.

bypass any that are labelled 'F1 Hybrid'. The lack of such a label on the packet, however, does not necessarily mean that the contents are open-pollinated and you will only know this from experience. Fortunately, there are seed suppliers who specialise in open-pollinated (often called 'heirloom') varieties and you can send for their catalogues. In addition, there are seed saving groups around the country dedicated to preserving as many as possible of the heirloom varieties. Members list the varieties they have available and exchange seed between them. The main coordinating body is the Seedsavers' Network based in Byron Bay. Contact them to find a group near you (see Appendix).

Activities of seed saving groups are increasingly important in preserving the diversity and genetic integrity of our food heritage as commercial seeds become increasingly subject to hybridising, patenting and genetic manipulation. Even gardeners who grow vegetables on a small scale in their backyards can be involved and this adds another interesting dimension to the food garden.

Outdoor or indoor sowing?

Some seeds can be sown directly into the ground; usually these are larger and fast-growing seeds such as beans, peas, corn, pumpkin, zucchini and cucumbers. Root crops such as carrots, beetroot and parsnips are generally also sown directly into the soil.

Some seeds need to be sown into seed punnets indoors and then transplanted into the ground when the soil has warmed up. This is the part that is already done for you when you buy seedlings from a nursery, but it is not too difficult to do at home. These seeds include tomatoes, capsicums, eggplant, silverbeet, cabbage, broccoli, cauliflower, celery, lettuce, spinach, onions and leeks; in general, the smaller and slower-growing seeds.

Of course, it is possible to grow the direct-sown seeds in punnets indoors, or in a suitable protected environment. This is a good strategy to follow if you are in an area where the soil can be slow warming up in spring and late frosts are possible. Some of the punnet-grown seeds can also be direct-sown if the soil is warm enough.

Soil temperature is crucial to seed germination. If the soil is too cold for a particular seed's needs, germination could be delayed or the seed might rot in the ground. Hot season crops such as tomatoes, as well as needing warm soil in which to germinate, need to have up to four months with an air temperature from 18°C to 30°C to form fruit. Cool season crops such as silverbeet need enough time to mature with an air temperature between 12°C and 25°C, otherwise they might not produce a good flavour and will quickly go to seed.

You will soon learn the seasonal constraints of your area. If there is a vegie grower nearby you can ask, all the better.

Direct sowing

The bed must be prepared before seeds are sown. The soil should be well aerated and a fine tilth, especially for small seeds. Test the

> ### SOIL TEMPERATURE FOR GERMINATION
>
> This is a rough guide to how warm the soil needs to be for germination of a variety of seeds.
>
> The following are considered to be cool weather vegetables and will germinate at a soil temperature of 12°C to 24°C: beetroot, broad bean, broccoli, Brussels sprouts, carrot, cabbage, cauliflower, celery, leek, lettuce, onion, parsnip, pea, radish, silverbeet, spinach, turnip.
>
> The following are considered to be hot weather vegetables, they are frost tender and need a soil temperature of 18°C to 24°C to germinate: bean, capsicum, cucumber, eggplant, pumpkin, tomato, zucchini.

pH and adjust it if necessary. Scatter compost, rotted manure or other organic fertiliser and rake it over the bed. There are a couple of different ways to go about seed planting, but whichever way you choose you need to know how deep in the soil the seeds should be.

As a general rule, plant seeds to a depth of about twice their diameter. Large seeds such as broad beans can be covered by 5 to 7 cm of soil, while tiny lettuce seeds need only a sprinkling of less than a centimetre. Plant seeds more shallowly in clay soil and more deeply in sandy soil. Seeds of the cucurbit family (cucumber, marrow, pumpkin, squash and zucchini) are best planted with the pointy end down.

Dug beds

If digging is your preferred gardening practice, dig the bed over to at least a spade's depth, breaking up clods and removing weeds. Rake the surface smooth and level and add any fertiliser. Make a furrow in the soil and drop the seeds in at intervals. Most packets will tell you how closely to space seeds. I usually plant them at closer intervals than recommended to allow for a few casualties. Any excess seedlings can be carefully transplanted elsewhere or simply uprooted to join the mulch layer; you can afford to do this if you save your own seeds and have plenty, but it is wasteful if you have bought the seed.

You might want to grow peas, climbing beans, cucumbers and other climbing or vine-type plants on a tepee or wire frame and not in rows at all. Simply position your plant supports where you want them, poke holes at the base of the support with a trowel or stick, drop the seeds in and backfill the holes.

Small seeds such as carrot or lettuce can be mixed with sand and sprinkled from a shaker. Use a jar with a lid in which you can punch holes of the appropriate size. It is easier and more economical of seed to sprinkle it thinly at sowing time than to be down on your hands and knees thinning out young plants after they germinate.

No-dig beds

In a no-dig bed large seeds can be planted directly into holes scraped into the bed. For a new bed that has not fully decomposed, put a handful of topsoil and compost mixture into each hole. If the bed is already established and rotting down well, seeds can be planted in rows as for dug beds.

Small seeds will need a finer seed bed. They can be planted as normal into a decomposed no-dig bed, but if the bed is still mainly organic matter, cover it with compost or good weed-free topsoil, or a mixture of the two, and plant as normal.

All my vegie beds are raised no-dig beds and are never dug over. Once decomposed, they have a good texture and structure. I simply pull up the old plants, which loosens and aerates the soil, scatter fresh fertiliser and rake it over the bed. Once the new plants are growing well, I mulch them so new organic material is constantly being incorporated into the soil.

Care of seed bed

If the prepared bed was weed-free, there should be few weeds and those that do germinate are easily removed. Check beds and remove stray weeds frequently so a major weeding job never has to be done. For energy and time efficiency, combine this with watering.

The seed bed should be kept damp, but not boggy. If it dries out, seeds are unlikely to germinate, especially small seeds that are closer to the surface of the soil and will dry out very quickly in hot weather. Seeds planted in cool damp weather (peas and broad beans, for example) might never need to be watered until after they germinate, but check frequently.

In hot weather the bed could need to be watered lightly at least twice a day until the seeds germinate, then daily until roots develop further. Gradually increase the time between waterings and water more deeply to encourage strong root growth. When seedlings are growing strongly, start mulching the bed to conserve moisture.

It is difficult when you are out at work all day to keep the seed bed damp. Try this trick. I have a two-metre length of shadecloth that can be used to cover an area of seeds. The bed can be watered once a day or every second day, depending on weather conditions, and the soil will stay damp. The shadecloth can be left in place, weighted down with garden stakes to prevent it from blowing away, until a few days after the seeds have germinated. It is removed at dusk so the tiny shoots are not immediately exposed to strong sunlight, then can be used to cover the next seed bed. If extra shade is needed to protect seedlings in hot weather, either rig up a system that uses the shadecloth as a roof suspended over the bed, or use a garden umbrella that can be moved around as needed.

Fertilise and mulch the bed as needed. A good practice is to scatter your preferred organic fertiliser around plants about once a month and cover it with straw. I just fertilise with whatever I have available when it is ready to be used rather than sticking to a regular routine. If the previous mulch has not decomposed, lift it and spread the fertiliser underneath.

Growing your own seedlings

Buy seeds from a specialist supplier of open-pollinated seeds and you will be able to save seeds from your own garden to use in future years. It is fiddly and time consuming to do this, so if you don't want to be bothered, stick with planting bought seedlings. However, once you have raised your own seedlings and get to know the routine, it will seem quite simple.

There are several methods you can use, but remember that cleanliness is of prime importance. The most common problem encountered when growing seeds inside or in a controlled environment such as a greenhouse or propagating box is a fungal disease called damping off, which can cause a high loss rate. For maximum success:

- Scrub all pre-used punnets or trays to remove any soil remaining from previous uses.
- Wash them in hot water with a little non-chlorine bleach added.
- Rinse well by pouring boiling water over them.

Propagating mix

Homemade propagating mixes could contain pathogenic fungi that multiply rapidly in the warm humid conditions and can decimate your seedlings. Use bought, sterilised seed-raising mixture or sterilise your homemade brew in the oven or microwave. A temperature of 60°C or more should be maintained in an oven for at least 30 minutes to kill most pathogens. To achieve this in a microwave oven, cook a four litre ice cream container of propagating mix on full power for seven to eight minutes. Leave the mix to cool before using.

Planting the seeds

When I first started growing from seed I had many losses caused by damping off, so I

> **HOMEMADE SEED RAISING MIXTURES**
>
> Any of these should give you a good propagating medium.
>
> - mature sifted compost
> - 50:50 sand and compost
> - 50:50 sand and vermiculite.

A good strike of young seedlings.

developed this procedure, which has worked successfully for me ever since.

- Put the sterilised mix into sterilised punnets. Margarine containers with drainage holes poked through the bottom are ideal if you have no 'proper' seed punnets. The mix should come up to about a centimetre from the top of the container.
- Gently place the seeds at well-spaced intervals. Ten to 12 tomato or capsicum seeds are ample for a normal-sized punnet. Cucumbers, pumpkins and other large seeds can be placed four to six in a punnet, or can be planted in individual small pots.
- Sprinkle mixture to cover the seeds. Firm down evenly by pressing the bottom of an empty punnet into the top of a full one.
- Place punnets into a large flat tray such as a baking tray and pour cool boiled water into it to a depth of about a centimetre. To be extra sure of deterring fungi, you can make a jug of strong chamomile tea and use it instead of water.
- Leave the punnets in the tray until the water has been absorbed. If the mixture still looks dry, add a little more water.

The propagator

Plastic propagating boxes are available from nurseries and many department stores and supermarkets with a garden section. For many years I used a polystyrene box with a sheet of clear plastic over the top held down by drawing pins. There are miniature plastic greenhouses available quite cheaply from nurseries, which are worth trying if you intend to grow many pots of seedlings.

These seedlings are being hardened outside before transplanting. Note the Jiffy Pots® at the back.

Whatever you use should be cleaned well before use.

- Place watered punnets into the propagator and leave it in a warm spot, either inside or outside against a protected north-facing brick wall.
- Check every few days. When more water is needed, again use cool boiled water or chamomile tea and water from the bottom. If you use a polystyrene box or kitty litter tray, water can be poured directly into it. Do not overwater. The mixture should be damp only, not swimming. Depending on where you keep the propagator, it might be that no extra water is needed.
- Once seedlings emerge, remove the lid of the propagator, or open up the mini greenhouse.
- When watering seedlings, I like to add a small amount of seaweed emulsion to the boiled water as a fertiliser and fungicide.
- When the seedlings are at the four-leaf stage, gradually expose them to outside temperatures for a week or two before planting them in their final position in the ground. A good strategy is to first move the lidless box onto a protected verandah for a few days before placing it right outside.
- If seedling stems are growing long and sappy and leaves are yellowish rather than a vibrant green, they need more sun and less water.

Transplanting

Transplanting of seedlings into the garden should be done quickly and on a cloudy day or at dusk if at all possible. Leaving tender

These tomato seedlings are ready to be planted in the garden.

seedlings in the sun while you answer the phone or attend to children's demands will result in a quick death and be a waste of all your previous time.

- Water the seedlings and the bed they are to go into before you begin.
- Use a small trowel to make a hole in the bed and half-fill it with compost or vermicompost.
- Invert the punnet into one hand and gently break off a seedling.
- Place the remainder of the seedlings into a suitable container while you work, only

Protect new seedlings from pests.

A seedling once the protective bottle has been removed.

breaking each one apart from the propagating mixture just before you plant it.
- Holding the seedling by the leaves, place it gently into the compost-enriched hole.
- Firm more compost or garden soil around the seedling to the original level of the propagating mix (tomatoes can go a little deeper).
- Protect individual seedlings with juice bottles or coffee tins to keep pests off them until they become established and begin to grow vigorously.

More super seed growing ideas

Transplanting seedlings can set back their growth and the tiny seedlings are easily damaged during the process. To overcome this there are a couple of alternative methods you can try. With both methods mentioned below it is still necessary to keep the pot in a protected environment until seedlings are at the four-leaf stage and harden them off for about a week before planting into the garden.

Egg cartons or newspaper

Try planting single seeds into seed-raising mixture in the sections of an egg carton. When the seedling is ready to go out into the garden simply detach each section and plant it in the ground. The cardboard will soon decompose and the plant will not be damaged. Alternatively, make tubes of the size you desire from several layers of newspaper.

An established seedling growing strongly.

Jiffy Pots® before and after being soaked in water.

Jiffy Pots®

You can sow single seeds directly into a block of compressed peat and wood pulp known as a Jiffy Pot®. Soak the pot in water for 10 minutes to allow it to expand before inserting the seed. When the seedling is ready to plant, the whole block goes in the soil. Take care that all of the pot is in the soil.

ACTION PLAN

- Choose open-pollinated seed.
- Grow your own seedlings.
- Sow seeds indoors.
- Sow seeds outdoors.

PLANT CARE
Weeding, watering, controlling pests

There is no doubt that keeping your garden productive and healthy requires some care and attention, some might even describe it as work, though others think of it as 'therapy' or 'sanity time'. Most of us are so busy with all we try to fit into our lives that the time involved in caring for an edible garden might seem like a good reason not to get started in food production at all. The good news is that steps taken in the setting up stage can minimise ongoing maintenance. Once you become involved in the fascinating cycle of seasonal changes and the satisfaction of cooking and eating food you have produced yourself, garden maintenance will seem like an innate part of life, a reconnection with the natural world that will bring many far-reaching benefits, as discussed in Chapter 1.

Weed control

Some gardeners regard weeds with loathing. I am not one of them. Weeds are free mulch as long as you don't let them go to seed. Many weeds have long been used as food and folk medicine. Even if you never use them as such, the knowledge that cultures around the world have benefited, and continue to benefit, from these humble plants might help to change your mind-set.

> **EDIBLE WEEDS**
>
> Weeds you can eat include chickweed, clover, dandelion, dock, plantain and stinging nettle. The young leaves can be used in salad mixes or added to soup. Teas can be made from the leaves of blackberry, cleavers and fennel; use them alone or mixed with more well-known herbal teas such as lemon balm, mint, sage, marjoram and thyme. Never consume weeds in any form unless you are sure of their identification and are also sure they have not been contaminated in any way, such as by agricultural chemicals or by vehicle emissions if they were growing near a busy road. Stinging nettles do sting, so wear gloves to harvest them.

Always begin with a weed-free bed or planting hole and future weed problems will be vastly reduced. Any that do grow can be easily removed by some simple techniques; there is no need to let weeding become a daunting back-breaking task. Some weeds have deep roots that aerate the soil and bring up nutrients from lower levels in the soil that might not otherwise be available to plants. Letting them decompose under newspaper or cardboard sheet mulch, or solarising them, will feed the earthworms and other soil biota and enrich your soil with organic matter and nutrients.

Pot plants

There is very little weeding needed with a potted garden, only the occasional blow-in that is easily removed on your regular rounds of the garden, balcony, deck or courtyard. Tuck the plucked weed under the mulch or put it in the compost bin or worm farm.

No-dig beds

No-dig beds have very few weeds, unless you have used old hay or other seed-bearing material in their construction. Most weeds are easily tickled out and added to the bed. Sprouting hay biscuits can be turned over so the shoots decompose underneath. A more persistent weed problem is very unlikely to occur, but can be dealt with in several ways. The first method is to hoe or rake the weeds so they become part of the organic matter of the bed. Alternatively, you can cover the bed with newspaper or cardboard then place a layer of straw or similar material on top. Cut or tear holes in the newspaper to plant into the bed beneath. The final method is the traditional weed pulling option, which could be physically harder and more time consuming, depending on the particular situation.

Solarising

Solarising is a handy technique to use when converting an existing area, such as a lawn or very weedy border, to a vegie garden or orchard. It must be done at the hottest time of year.

- Cut or slash the area.
- Water it.
- Cover it with heavy duty clear or black plastic.
- Weight the edges of the plastic with bricks or soil.
- Leave in place for about six weeks.
- The heat under the plastic should have killed all weeds and most seeds.

The effectiveness of solarisation depends on the heat generated and the time the area is left. If the temperature is too low, all weeds and seeds might not be destroyed. Either repeat the process, sheet mulch the area (see below), or resort to digging the weeds out. If the heat is too intense, beneficial soil biota will have been destroyed. Replace them by spreading compost or worm castings onto the now weed-free bed.

An adaptation of solarisation can be used to destroy seedy weeds before adding them to the compost or mulch. Pull or dig out the weeds as normal. Put them into a black plastic bag and leave the bag in the sun for a few weeks. Weeds and seeds will cook inside the bag and are then safe to use without the risk of spreading seeds around the garden.

Sheet mulch

If you are too impatient to wait for solarisation to work and have a weedy patch to redevelop, sheet mulching could be for you.

- Mow or brush cut the area.
- Water it.
- A sprinkle of fertiliser is optional at this stage, as is gypsum if you need it to break up clay soil.
- Cover with a thick layer of newspaper or thick cardboard.

Sheet mulch preparation for a new bed over a section of lawn.

The bed is planted, mainly with bush tucker plants, and mulched.

- Spread a cosmetic layer of mulch over the newspaper or cardboard. Straw, sugar cane, autumn leaves and many other natural materials are suitable.
- Leave the sheet mulch for as long as you can to let the weeds die underneath.
- When you are ready to plant, cut a hole in the bottom later, and dig out any remaining weeds.
- Dig a hole as big as needed for your plant, adding any fertiliser or organic matter required.
- Plant as normal.

A watering system can be installed under the newspaper or cardboard, or on top of it beneath the cosmetic layer. Ensure water can get to the root zone. The bottom layer can take from a month to a year to decompose, depending on weather and soil conditions and the composition of the cosmetic layer. The weeds will decompose under the sheet mulch to add organic matter and enrich the soil. Replace the cosmetic layer as it decomposes.

In this case topsoil was spread over the sheet mulch.

Overview of the same bed showing how it fits into the garden.

Watering

With many areas of Australia on more or less permanent water restrictions, keeping your food garden adequately watered can be a challenge. There is no doubt that to be productive, food plants for the most part need more water than do many other plants in the garden. You need to plan how you intend to water the plants before you begin. There are many water-efficient options to consider.

Install tanks

Install as many tanks of as large a capacity as your space can accommodate. New houses now are likely to have tanks installed, but it is wise to have more than the minimum the builder is required to provide. Look at clever ways of incorporating them into your design.

- Conventional tanks or bladders under a deck.
- Narrow tanks along a fence or as a fence replacement. At least one style can have others connected to them as money becomes available or the need arises. Slimline tanks suitable for verandahs or balconies are also available.
- Tanks behind the shed.
- A cylindrical tank in a corner.

Use grey water

There are numerous ways of reusing grey water in the garden. The smart, but expensive, option is to have a purpose-designed grey water system installed at the time the house is built. Some eco-friendly housing estates are incorporating this into new houses and I'm sure the trend will spread. Digging up the backyard to retrofit a grey water system so the water is delivered via trenches throughout the garden is messy, inconvenient and expensive and needs to be done by a professional. Most of us settle for small-scale adaptations.

Grey water dispersal system at Happy Earth. (Photo courtesy Happy Earth)

The valve can be opened or closed as needed. (Photo courtesy Happy Earth)

Grey water pipe surrounds a fruit tree. (Photo courtesy Happy Earth)

Water from the washing machine is piped into a small tank outside the window.

First collect your water

You have several sources of reusable grey water in your home: laundry, bathroom and kitchen.

Laundry

Divert the water from your washing machine into a small tank outside the laundry. From there it can be bucketed onto the garden, or run through dripper or seeper hoses. If there is no room for a tank outside the laundry, in most cases the outlet hose can be directed into buckets, but this does need to be supervised.

After a couple of summers of catching washing machine water in buckets for the garden, we finally invested in a small tank outside the laundry. A pipe connected to the washing machine hose goes out through the laundry window into the tank. I nearly always use washing balls rather than detergent, so don't have to worry about ingredients in the water affecting my soil/plants. A hose connects to the tap at the bottom of the tank.

A hose connects to the tank and can be directed to several different beds/plants.

Here the hose runs from the tank and is connected to dripper hose along a vegie bed.

This can be directed to several different areas. The tank is on the ground, so pressure is low, making it ideal to dribble out onto selected plants. As well, the hose can be connected to a low-pressure dripper hose running along a vegie bed. Liquid fertilisers are easily added to the grey water in the tank.

Bathroom

The practice of catching shower water in buckets is widespread and many homes have multiple buckets in the shower recess. Children's bath water can be bucketed out as well. However, it is possible to install a diverter valve into the plumbing system to direct the water into a tank outside.

Kitchen

Not all kitchen water can be reused. Water with food solids or fats is considered dark grey and is unsuitable for garden use. However, water used to rinse hands, vegetables or washed crockery can be caught in a basin for reuse. Add to this the dregs from the teapot or coffee pot and cooking liquid from vegetables or pasta, so long as there is no salt or oil added. It seems obvious, but do make sure all this water is cold before pouring it onto the garden.

Grey water cautions

Many regulations surround the use of grey water and these differ from state to state; even

The dripper hose is watering tomatoes and peas.

You can see how slowly the water drips out of this hose.

different councils and water authorities might have different requirements. One thing they all seem to have in common is that a licensed plumber must be employed to undertake any changes to the permanent plumbing of a residence. In sewered areas, if water is to be diverted away from the existing system, permission from the water authority is needed.

If you are using grey water, keep the following in mind:

- Contain it within your own property.
- If water contains faecal matter, such as from babies' nappies, do not use it.
- Grey water must be stored for no longer than 24 hours without treatment.
- Use no dark grey water from the kitchen.
- Choose cleaning products carefully. They might contain high levels of nutrients or be alkaline and raise the soil pH, or contain sodium which can be bad for plants and soil.
- Try to alternate grey water with clean water.
- Take care not to use grey water on leafy vegetables or on any others eaten raw. Never sprinkle vegetables with grey water.
- If you have a system with a grey water diverter, turn it off in wet weather.

See these websites for more information about detergent ingredients: www.lanfaxlabs.com.au, www.greenplumbers.com.

Be systematic

To ensure the available water is properly distributed to where it is needed, devise a simple roster system to follow, otherwise it is all too easy to lose track of where you are up to and some plants are bound to miss out.

List the sources of grey water and the plants you want it to go to. A roster I made during a recent drought had the days of the week across the top and the water sources down the side. I wrote in the plants that would be watered from each source each day.

If and when you are allowed to use irrigation systems or hand-held hoses, a similar system can also be useful.

Protect your plants

Strategies as simple as giving your plants some sun and wind protection when needed can reduce their water needs.

Wind

Strong wind can quickly whip the moisture from plants' leaves. When designing a dedicated vegetable garden, consider its location in regard to the strongest prevailing winds where you live. Use windbreaks of fences, trellis or hardy plants to protect your vegie garden or fruit trees.

Rooftops can be especially vulnerable to wind, so ensure your rooftop garden is adequately protected and that the protection itself is firmly located.

Sun

Though most productive plants need about six hours a day of sunlight, in Australian summer conditions this can easily be surpassed and plants can suffer from too much intense sun, which increases their water consumption.

You can use garden umbrellas or erect temporary shadecloth or sails over some spots. I like the umbrellas because they look good and can be easily opened, closed or moved as needed. In windy conditions they can be wound down and put away to avoid accidents.

Plants that prefer shadier conditions, such as berries and currants, can be positioned so they have the benefit of the shade of the house, shed or large trees in the afternoons. Do not plant them in the ground too close to large trees because the tree's roots will rob them of moisture.

Make sure that any shade protection you use is firmly anchored, especially on exposed rooftops. You don't want your shadecloth or umbrella to go sailing away in a strong wind. A friend of mine covered a whole large vegetable garden with shadecloth; the job was professionally done, not a temporary makeshift. One stormy night the whole lot was ripped off and deposited at the other end of the garden. Never underestimate the potential power of natural forces and plan accordingly.

Innovative watering ways

We all need to be smarter about the ways we use water, especially during drought years, and even more so if we want to grow food plants.

Some of the methods already described are water-efficient in themselves and will permanently reduce the amount of water you need to use. These include:

- Mulch, but ensure that water is applied under the mulch during dry times, such as by drippers, seeper hoses or upside down drink bottles (see below).
- Incorporate organic matter into the soil to ensure it acts as a reservoir that absorbs water.
- Aim for an open soil structure that allows water to percolate through to plant roots.
- No-dig beds usually have an open structure and contain large amounts of organic matter.
- Wicking beds utilise water from the bottom, preventing losses from evaporation.
- Hydroponics uses the same water that circulates around the system.
- Aquaponics not only reuses the same water as it circulates around the system, but grows fish in it at the same time. When the water in the tank needs to be changed, it can be used on the garden wherever needed.

Tips, tricks and products to try

Have a wander through a large department store's nursery or irrigation section to see what water-efficient devices you can find. There are many to choose from, but some watering tricks don't need you to spend any money at all.

Pipe method

Insert leftover lengths of drainage pipe to a depth of 25 to 35 cm into the soil around a plant. You can use one pipe or several for each plant. The pipe should be just protruding above the soil and can be disguised with mulch so it is not visible. Pipes can be filled from a hose or bucket. This is a good method for fruit trees, but should preferably be done at planting time so as to avoid root damage.

Juice bottles

Cut the bottoms off old plastic juice bottles, turn the bottles upside down so the necks are a couple of centimetres into the soil. Pour water into the bottles. The necks can be plugged with coconut fibre to minimise blockages.

Leaky buckets

Place old buckets with holes in the bottoms around selected plants. Pour grey water or hose water into the buckets; it will slowly seep out of the holes.

Baled up

A great idea that I recently read about is to protect vegies, or anything else you think needs it, by placing bales of straw of any type or lucerne hay around the bed, or on the side the strongest winds blow from. The wind protection this gives reduces losses of water through evaporation and transpiration. This barrier can also give a good frost protection. In a year or two, depending on climatic conditions, the bales will have broken down enough to be used as partially (or fully) decomposed mulch or as the basis for a no-dig bed, both of which are further water-saving measures.

Self-watering plant guard

This commercial product is a clear plastic sleeve surround that protects new plants from the elements and some pests, but it has a dual role. It is made of a double layer of plastic formed into tubes that hold water. You fill the tubes with water, which slowly leaks out at the bottom to water plants.

Wetpots®

A system of ceramic pots connected by 4 mm pipe to a storage tank is known as the Wetpot® system. A ceramic pot is buried beside each plant. The storage tank is mounted above the pots/plants and gravity-fed water seeps out into the root zone constantly when the soil is dry, not when it is already wet. Plant roots tend to wrap around the pot to access the water. The storage tank is topped up as needed, either by bucket or hose. Worm juice and herb 'teas' can be added to the storage tank for automatic fertilising of plants. There is no water wastage with this system and plants take only the water they need.

There are three sizes of Wetpots® suitable for small pots, large pots or in the ground. The system is fully enclosed so soil and ants cannot get in to cause blockages. Systems are sold with a 30 litre storage tank, either five or 10 pots and a length of pipe. It is quite expensive to set up, but is a simple and efficient method for a small area or for pots.

Eco bags

This product is good to water fruit trees, especially if you are away from home for extended periods. It is a green, UV treated, laminated vinyl bag that is shaped to sit on the ground around the plant's trunk. It holds 25 litres of water, which slowly seeps through the bag to water a plant for up to four weeks. The bag also acts as a mulch and stifles weed growth. Liquid fertiliser can be added to the water as needed. Bags are easily refilled with a hose or watering can.

Wetting agents
There are two main types of wetting agents available: a thick liquid and a granular or crystal form. These products enable water to spread more easily through the soil particles. They could be useful on sandy soil, but are probably not needed on clay soil. The recommended application rate on very sandy soil is 100 g to 300 g of the crystals mixed into the top 20 cm of soil.

Water crystals do not reduce the amount of water plants use, but hold water in the soil for an extended time so that some (though not all) of it is available for plant use. The addition of organic matter such as decayed manure or coir fibre is likely to be more effective at increasing the available soil water content than water crystals, depending on the application rate. All need to be re-applied, the wetting agent more frequently than the organic matter.

When planting new shrubs and trees, those in pots up to 20 cm diameter will benefit from the incorporation of a slurry of water crystals or liquid into the soil of the planting hole. Soak half a teaspoon of water crystals in half a litre of water for a couple of hours, then mix this into the soil being firmed around the roots of the new plant. Do not add dry water crystals to the planting hole.

> **SMART APPROVED WATERMARK**
>
> It can seem impossible to interpret the advertising hype of some products and know if they really do live up to the water conservation claims of their manufacturers. Smart WaterMark is a national accreditation scheme that independently assesses and verifies products that directly save water. Garden devices are well represented, but there are other categories as well. To date over 150 products have been accredited, but more are constantly being added. Have a look at www.smartwatermark.org or contact PO Box A 812, Sydney South 1235, tel: (02) 9290-3322.

Dripper and seeper hoses
There are a few different styles of dripper and seeper hoses available, which are very water-efficient when it is permitted to use them. They are quite good for vegetable gardens when the plants are in straight rows. Be aware though that seeds or newly planted seedlings will need supplementary watering by watering can, hand-held hose or microsprays until their roots are sufficiently established to reach the watering zone. Dripper hose with outlets at set spacings might also prove impractical for seasonal vegetables planted at different spacings. One season's lettuce or buk choy crop, for example, will need outlets

Soil wetting agents are more useful in sandy soil than in clay.

spaced closer together than the following season's tomatoes.

Dripper irrigation system

The dripper hoses mentioned above have holes at set spacings and will probably not be suitable for fruit trees, which are spaced further apart. An efficient system of watering these is to lay down a line of black polypipe and place drippers with an adjustable flow rate at the required intervals. You might want one dripper per plant, or one on each side. The dripper devices can be inserted into the polypipe or onto lengths of flexible spaghetti tubing that is attached to the polypipe. There are kits available that might suit your needs; you can pick up leaflets where irrigation supplies are sold, or talk to the staff about what you need.

Watering pot plants

In a small garden many of the plants might be in pots. There are advantages to potted plants, especially when all the space available is a courtyard, deck, verandah or rooftop, but there is no question that pot plants do dry out faster than plants in the ground. These hints will help you keep pot plants moist.

- Use a good quality potting mix with wetting agent incorporated.
- Incorporate compost or well-rotted manure into the mix.
- Water pots until you see a little water coming out of the drainage holes.
- Move pots to a shady, wind-protected spot at the hottest time of year.
- Group them in a protected spot under shadecloth.
- Water smaller pots by dunking them for 10 to 15 minutes into a bucket of water.
- Mulch pot plants, but do not allow fine mulch to build up around the stem.
- Sink a smaller pot into a larger one of coir fibre or similar.
- Use saucers under the pots in hot weather, but remove them in wet conditions.
- Waterwell pots, which have a built-in large reservoir at the base of the pot, are a good way of ensuring the plant has access to water for an extended period. However, make sure you use a well-aerated potting mixture or roots could become too damp.
- Water pot plants with a solution of wetting agent, or sprinkle granular wetting agent over the top of the mix and water it in. Do not exceed the recommended rate when using a wetting agent and leave at least three months between applications. Wetting agents should last up to five months.
- Use Wetpots®, as described above.

Choose hardy plants

Though, in general, food plants need more water than many others in the garden, there are some that have been found to be more drought-tolerant. I have compiled these suggestions from information shared through *Grass Roots* magazine.

- Dark coloured vegetables such as purple beans and red, purple or brown lettuce do better than green varieties in hot dry conditions.
- Red-skinned potatoes are hardier than light-skinned ones.

- Purple-flowered peas are hardier than white-flowered ones.
- Red-stemmed chard is hardier than white-stemmed silverbeet.
- Purple and black tomatoes might perform better than red or yellow varieties.

Bush tucker

Bush food plants that originate from dry areas will tolerate dry conditions, once established. To be productive they will need more water, but they are likely to survive droughts and return to productivity once water is available.

In the vegie garden

Try these varieties that seed savers have found to grow well in dry times.

- Amaranth
- Beans: 'Snake', 'Zebra', 'Purple King', 'Dragon's Tongue' and 'Black Turtle'
- 'Bob's' cucumber
- 'Champagne' watermelon
- Climbing snow pea, 'Yakuma'
- Cow pea
- Egyptian spinach
- 'Italian' and 'Brown Romaine' lettuce
- 'Lebanese Purple' eggplant
- 'Peruvian Cherry' tomato
- Pigeon pea
- 'Purple Plum' and 'Black Russian' tomatoes
- Red and green orach
- 'Sweet and Striped' cucumber
- Tree onion
- Warrigal greens (a bush food that can substitute for spinach).

Hardy fruits

Several fruits that are recommended as being drought-tolerant are:

- Feijoa
- Citronelle or bush lemon (the tough rootstock many other lemons are grafted onto)
- Natal plum
- Pomegranate
- A number of bush fruits including muntries, appleberry, rock fig, lilly pilly, desert lime, midjin berry and quandong.

Pest control

There is no denying that many pests will find your produce as desirable as you do and they often have very sneaky ways of getting to it first. You definitely don't want to lose your delicious crops to pests; neither do you want to negate one of the big benefits of growing your own food (its chemical-free status) by spraying poisons onto it to kill the pests. Fortunately, there are a number of simple measures that will ensure that the majority of your fabulous fresh food is enjoyed by you and your family.

Soil

Healthy crops begin with healthy soil. Prepare your soil as described in Chapter 4. Make sure the pH is not too far into either extreme so the correct nutrients are available to plants. Add mulch and organic fertilisers to keep up a constant supply of nutrients.

Timing

Some pests are active for certain periods of the year. Observe the cycles of life in your own garden and use this knowledge to your advantage by planting a pest's preferred tucker at a time of year when it is inactive. For example, after losing several brassica crops to caterpillars of cabbage white butterfly in the early days of my gardening experience, I noticed that the butterflies disappeared by about May and did not reappear until about October or November. Consequently, I now delay planting broccoli and cabbages until there are no more butterflies fluttering around. My broccoli matures later than that of most other people, but at least I get to eat it, without grubs in it.

Crop rotation

Plants that are closely related to each other have similar nutrient requirements, so constantly planting the same or related crops in the same patch of soil, or pot, will deplete the soil of those nutrients. In addition, related plants are susceptible, by and large, to the same diseases, some of which are soil-borne. To minimise the possibility of nutrient depletion and the spread of soil-borne diseases from one crop to another, practise crop rotation, as described in Chapter 5.

Pluck and squirt

In a small garden it is relatively easy to pluck pests such as caterpillars and vegetable bugs from your plants as you stroll around the garden, or while you are harvesting the evening meal. Thrips and aphids can be removed by crushing them between gloved fingers, but don't be too thorough; the beneficial insects (ladybirds, hoverfly larvae, lacewing larvae, flower bugs and several species of wasps) will feed on them if given a chance.

Slugs and snails can be searched out and destroyed during an evening or early morning garden check, especially if it has recently rained. You will soon learn where they like to hide and can even provide some hiding places, which then become traps.

It is worth remembering that most pests, just like most humans, like to hang out together. When you find one bug on a plant, look for others nearby.

If you have tank water, and when water restrictions permit the use of hoses, many pests can be dislodged by a strong jet of water from the nozzle.

Birds and beneficial insects

Not all insects are pests; in fact most are either beneficial or have no harmful effects. When you spray pest insects, even with low-impact, organically acceptable sprays, beneficial insects are likely to be killed or repelled at the same time. Leave them alone and they will deal with your pest problem for free. You can attract beneficial insects to your garden by incorporating a variety of

HELPFUL INSECTS

Some of the insects that do a fine job as unpaid pest insect destroyers include bee flies, hover flies, ladybirds, lacewings, flower bugs, wasps and ants. Often, it is the larval stage of the insect that consumes the pests and the adult stage that depends on the pollen and nectar in flowers. Even the thrips and mites that gardeners hate have species which are beneficial in eating their pesky relatives.

Small birds such as this grey fantail will eat numerous insect pests. (Photo courtesy Happy Earth)

Beneficial and benign insects are welcome visitors to your garden.

flowers such as open-daisy-type blooms, borage, bergamot, tea tree, nepeta and numerous others, including those below that attract nectar-feeding birds. Remember that variety of colour, flower shape and position on the plant will attract a variety of helpful insects.

Birds are wonderful to have in the garden, both for the joy of watching their antics and because they will consume vast numbers of insects. Some flowers that will attract honeyeaters include banksias, callistemons, camellias, correas, epacris, ericas, grevilleas, paperbarks, penstemons, proteas, red-hot pokers, small flowering gums, strelizias, succulents of many types, wattles and yuccas. In addition to the nutrient-rich pollen and nectar within the flowers, honeyeaters also eat insects. These same flowers will attract beneficial insects as well.

Ladybirds control aphids, free of charge. (Photo courtesy Happy Earth)

Bees provide a pollination service of inestimable value.

Attract seed-eating birds, which also eat insects, by planting bankias, casuarinas, conifers, crepe myrtles, eucalypts, native grasses, silver birches, tea trees and wattles.

Poultry pest eaters

I have mentioned previously that poultry can be used as pest controllers and weeders. The secret is that you must control where they have access to, otherwise they can cause more damage and mess than they are worth.

In a previous larger garden we had a medium-sized flock of poultry. As well as secure housing for the night, they had a fenced, treed run in a windbreak area, where they did a very good job of pest control and fertiliser application. In addition, we made a wire enclosure that fit neatly into the area of our no-dig vegie beds. Two or three hens could be caught and put into this temporary home during the day. They scratched over the soil and fertilised it ready for the next crop and ate any pests and their larvae. A shadecloth cover over the wire protected the hens from the sun and avian predators, and kept them inside where we wanted them.

Careful planning can result in poultry working for you without causing damage.

Frogs, lizards, spiders

Frogs, lizards and spiders consume vast numbers of insects and can be encouraged to take up residence in your garden. A small pond with surrounding vegetation to shelter in will be a frog haven. In return, the frogs will eat numerous insects, including mosquitoes, and small slugs. Do not relocate frogs from the wild. If you incorporate suitable habitat into the garden, frogs will come.

Rocks, logs and lengths of plumbing pipe under the shrubbery will give the lizards a home. Depending on their size, lizards will eat anything from a variety of insects and their eggs to mice and snails.

The more spider species you have in your garden the better. Hordes of insects become trapped in their webs. One spider can easily

This handsome specimen would be a useful resident in any garden.

rid your garden of 2000 insects during the 18 months of its life.

Companion planting

There is much folklore surrounding the age-old practice of companion planting and what works in one area might not work in another. It is interesting to try various combinations and watch the results. If they do not work, you have lost nothing and still have many alternative pest control methods to try.

- Aromatic herbs such as mints, rosemary and basil are said to repel many pest insects. Planted among your vegies, they at least might confuse the pests.
- Chamomile around the garden will benefit any plants nearby.
- To repel cabbage moths plant sage, rosemary, marjoram, thyme, onion or garlic nearby. If you have the herbs in pots, they can be moved around as needed. Try interplanting onions among the brassicas.
- Plant hollyhocks near bean plants to attract bean flies away from the crop.
- Onions between carrot rows might repel carrot flies.
- The roots of French and African marigolds exude a substance that repels pest nematodes in the soil.
- Pyrethrum daisies planted as a border might repel a range of pest insects.

Physical barriers

There are numerous simple barriers that will protect young plants until they become established. A snail out for dinner will soon devour your newly planted seedlings, but a more established tougher plant is less desirable to the gastropod taste buds and can survive having a leaf or two chewed with little ill effect. Spend a little time protecting seedlings with a barrier and there will be few losses.

A barrier can consist of a thick layer of material a slug or snail cannot crawl over, such as shell grit, human hair, diatomaceous earth or eggshells around each seedling. Make sure there are no gaps left that a slug or snail can crawl through. Copper apparently gives gastropods the equivalent of an electric shock. It is available as a strip or a long-lasting spray to apply around vulnerable plants.

I often use large plastic juice bottles with the bottoms cut off. These are placed around seedlings, especially brassicas, until they begin to outgrow the bottle. They act as mini hothouses and keep off slugs, snails, cabbage moths and butterflies. Empty food cans serve a similar purpose, but will need a material such as onion bags tied on over the opening to prevent pests from entering. Remember not to leave plastic bottle barriers in place during hot weather or your seedlings might cook.

Nets and exclusion bags made from a variety of materials are used to keep birds, fruit flies and possums off the ripening fruit crop. If using a net, the whole tree or selected branches can be wrapped.

A multipurpose product made from UV stable polypropylene is available in sheets that can be cut to length to drape over vegetables and fruits to protect them from a variety of pests. It drapes either directly over the crop or can be attached to wire or polypipe hoops.

Traps

Some pests can be trapped and disposed of in an appropriate manner.

Slugs and snails

There are a variety of traps recommended for slugs and snails.

- Half-fill a small container with a 50:50 mixture of beer and water, or milk and water, or Vegemite or Marmite dissolved in water. Put it in a spot near where slugs and snails have been active. The pests are attracted to the liquid, fall in and drown.
- Place grapefruit or orange skins, potato skins, shredded carrot, carrot or lettuce leaves in a spot frequented by the pests. Cover the lure with damp cardboard or sacking. Check the trap every day and dispose of pests.
- Make a bait from pyrethrum mixed with molasses and enough water to form the mixture into small balls. Place them inside a length of polypipe where children, birds and pets cannot get to them. Check and dispose of bodies every day.
- Purpose-manufactured snail traps are available commercially.

Earwigs

Earwigs are difficult to dispose of because they seek out such tiny spaces to hide in, but when they are present in large numbers they can cause a lot of damage to seedlings. There are a couple of good earwig traps. Before placing traps, clean up such areas as piles of bricks or timber that they love to live under.

- Roll up corrugated cardboard into a tube and fasten it with string or an elastic band. Put the tube in a dark sheltered spot close to where you have noticed earwig activity. Not only do earwigs like to eat cardboard, but the corrugations mimic their preferred habitat. It might take them a few days to discover this delightful abode. Every few days, knock the tube on the ground or into a bucket to dislodge the earwigs. We feed them to the fish in the aquaponics tank. What you do with them is your choice.
- Put some water into a small container and float a tiny amount of olive oil on top of it. The earwigs apparently are attracted to the oil, fall in and drown.

Fruit flies

As well as using barriers to exclude fruit flies, many organic growers use traps. There are commercial traps and baits available, but it is simple to make your own. One commercial bait is made of protein, sugar and a biological insecticide, which is attractive to both male and female flies; another is based on native essential oils and attracts and kills male flies.

- Use a bait such as Vegemite or citronella oil to attract male fruit flies and orange, peach, banana or plum pulp to attract females.
- Mix the bait with water.
- Place it in a bottle, jar or tin in which you have made a small hole for the flies to enter.
- Hang several traps around in your fruit trees.
- Check every few days and remove dead flies and replace lure.

Codling moth

Codling moths are very fond of apples and pears. The larvae burrow into the fruit, leaving

> **MORE FRUIT FLY CONTROLS**
>
> - Encourage beneficial fruit fly predators such as ants, spiders, ground beetles and birds.
> - Good garden hygiene is important. Clean up fallen fruit. If fruit fly maggots are present, soak the fruit in water for a few days or leave it in a black plastic bag in the sun to solarise. Once the maggots are drowned or cooked, the fruit can be put in the compost. Do not put infested untreated fruit in the compost.
> - Use exclusion bags or sheets to cover fruit.

entry holes that are surrounded by dead tissue. The inside of the fruit goes dark and rots. There is a commercial pheromone trap that will attract both male and female moths.

Another type of trap can be made at home by placing bands of corrugated cardboard around the trunks of trees you want to protect. Caterpillars like to lay their eggs in the cardboard. Every few weeks remove the cardboard and destroy any cocoons. It is important not to leave the bands on the trees for too long, especially in wet and humid conditions, as a fungal condition could develop under the wet cardboard.

Coloured sticky traps

Some insects are known to have colour preferences. You can buy coloured sticky traps that will attract a range of insects. Blue attracts thrips and leafminers. Yellow attracts whiteflies, aphids, leafhoppers and moths. It is simple to make your own by smearing Vaseline onto pieces of plastic cut from ice cream containers and placing them around areas where the pests are prevalent.

Organically acceptable commercial products

There is a wide range of organically acceptable sprays, dusts, oils and pellets readily available from nurseries. Have a wander around the shelves next time you get a chance. Before you buy, look for an accreditation label such as Biological Farmers Australia (BFA), National Association for Sustainable Agriculture Australia (NASAA), Australian Certified Organic (ACO), Bio-Dynamic Research Institute (DEMETER), Organic Food Chain (OFC) or Organic Growers of Australia (OGA).

You can buy snail pellets that will not harm birds or pets and break down to add a trace of iron to the soil, sprays for all manner of insects and oils that smother adults and eggs of scales, aphids, mites, white flies, leafminers and mealy bugs. Read the labels and use according to the directions.

Remember that even these products will often have a detrimental effect on beneficial insects

> **MORE CODLING MOTH CONTROLS**
>
> - Clean up fallen fruit and treat as for fruit fly, above.
> - Have flowers around the garden that will attract beneficial insects, especially wasps, which parasitise the caterpillars.
> - Paint trunks with a band of horticultural glue that prevents larvae from crossing it.

and on people with allergies. There has been some publicity about harmful effects on humans from using derris dust and pyrethrum, so take care.

Fungal diseases

Some fruit trees and vegetables are susceptible to a range of fungal diseases. The list seems ominous, but in most cases prevention is easier than cure and the plant, if grown in fertile, well-aerated soil and given adequate, but not too much water, will not be too badly affected.

Prevention of fungal diseases starts with healthy fertile soil. Check the pH. Fungal organisms thrive in acid soil, largely because the other micro-organisms that keep them under control prefer slightly less acidity and are not present in sufficient numbers to prevent fungi from multiplying out of control. Apply lime to raise the pH.

Fruit trees

Peach and other stone fruits might suffer from curly leaf, brown rot, peach rust, freckle, silver leaf or verticillium wilt. Apple and pear trees are prone to powdery mildew, apple scab and pear scab. In fact, most fruit trees can fall prey to fungal diseases, with the problem being more common in humid areas or during humid summers.

Always collect and dispose of fallen diseased fruit and leaves, but not in the compost. If the temperature in your bin does not become high enough to kill disease organisms, they can spread throughout the garden. If areas of a tree are affected by curly leaf, for example, cut them off and dispose of them. Do not allow them to remain on the ground under the tree where spores can cause reinfection.

Mulch under fruit trees performs another valuable function in reducing the likelihood of fungal spores from the soil splashing onto the plant. Lucerne mulch is said to be mildly antifungal.

Use drip or seeper irrigation so that the leaves do not remain damp for extended periods. Alternatively, water by hand or a hose into upside down bottles or leaky buckets, as previously described.

Vegetables

Of the vegetables, those most often seen with fungal diseases such as downy or powdery mildew are zucchinis, cucumbers, squash and pumpkins. Growing cucumbers and squash on a trellis to encourage good aeration might help. However, my experience has been that powdery mildew only develops late in the season when the crop is almost finished, so I have never regarded it as a problem. In more humid regions, if mildew develops early in the season, vigilance in cutting off affected leaves and in preventative spraying will help.

Fungicidal sprays

Several types of commercially prepared antifungal sprays are acceptable in organic gardening, but by and large they are preventatives rather than cures.

- Lime sulphur is used for curly leaf, peach rust, black spot and powdery mildew.

- Bordeaux, homemade or bought, is used for curly leaf, black spot and brown rot.
- White oil is used mainly for sooty mould on citrus trees.
- Australia's first organically certified fungicide, Ecocarb®, controls powdery mildew. It is based on potassium bicarbonate (bicarb soda) and works by making the leaf surface more alkaline. It is possible to make your own bicarb soda spray, see below.
- In addition, there are numerous homemade sprays that are effective preventatives, see below.

Homemade sprays

There are multitudes of homemade sprays you can use to kill or deter pests and fungi. I will give only a few here, while admitting I seldom use any of them because I have more to do than fiddle with cooking up pest control sprays when the other organic practices I follow usually keep my garden healthy.

Be aware that most homemade sprays do not single out the pest you are aiming for, but will affect beneficial insects and maybe frogs and aquatic life as well. Keep all sprays away from children and pets and have equipment kept only for this purpose.

Insect pests

Eucalyptus spray
This is effective for controlling soft-bodied pests such as caterpillars and cockroaches, ants and beetles. Use 10 mL eucalyptus oil to 500 mL water. Add 10 mL detergent as an emulsifier. Shake well before use.

Garlic spray
This is probably the most well-known and widely used general-purpose natural insecticide. Make your own or buy a commercial product.

Soak 90 g chopped garlic in two teaspoons vegetable oil for 48 hours. Dissolve 90 g pure soap in 600 mL warm water. Add to the garlic and oil. Filter and store in a sealed glass or plastic container. Use one part solution to 99 parts water. Increase the strength if necessary.

Molasses spray
Molasses will repel beetles, caterpillars and nematodes. Dilute 20 mL molasses in four litres of hot water. Allow the mixture to cool before spraying.

For nematodes, put the mixture into a watering can and drench the affected soil. This will be harmful to earthworms so use only if necessary.

Oil sprays
These are great for suffocating sap sucking pests and their eggs. Use for scale, thrip, mealy bug, white fly and spider mite. Spray it on deciduous fruit trees after leaf drop and before new buds burst when the temperature is less than 25°C.

Add 125 g grated pure soap to one litre of vegetable oil in an old saucepan. Boil, stirring until the soap has dissolved. Cool. Dilute one cup oil/soap in 20 cups of water. Make up only the amount you intend to use at one time or the remainder will separate and be unusable.

Add half a cup of dishwashing detergent to two cups of sunflower oil. Shake well. Before use dilute two dessertspoons per litre of water.

Pyrethrum spray
Soak 2 tablespoons of pyrethrum flowers in 1 litre of hot water for two hours. Strain and cool before use. Strengthen if necessary. This will kill beneficial predators and could harm bees, so use with caution. Spray at night to minimise the risk of harming beneficial insects.

Chilli spray
This is said to be good to rid the garden of caterpillars and red spider mites. Blend two cups hot chillies with two cups water. Strain and use immediately. Wear gloves and do not allow the mixture to touch sensitive skin or eyes; it burns.

Fungal diseases

Milk spray
Red-legged earth mites dislike the waxy layer left by this milk spray and it is also an effective fungicide to control powdery and downy mildews. Dilute one part milk to nine parts water and spray as required.

Bicarbonate of soda
To control powdery mildew on fruits and vegetables dissolve 1 level teaspoon of bicarbonate of soda in 2 litres of water.

Seaweed spray
Use seaweed to control curly leaf, black spot, brown rot, canker, silver leaf and powdery mildew. It is a preventative, not a cure. Use every few weeks all around the garden; it is a wonderful plant tonic too. Use a commercial spray or make your own where you have legal access to seaweed. Wash the salt from a bucket of seaweed. Cover it with water and soak for two to three weeks. Strain and dilute until it is the colour of weak tea.

Compost spray
A spray made from well-decomposed compost is claimed to control a range of fungal diseases, including botrytis (grey mould), potato blight, apple scab and phytophthora (root rot). Soak some well-rotted compost, about six months old, in a

---

ACTION PLAN

- Easy weed control methods:
  - no-dig beds
  - solarising
  - sheet mulching
- Install tanks
- Use grey water
- Protect plants
- Try innovative watering ideas
- Safe pest control measures:
  - good soil
  - timing
  - crop rotation
  - pluck and squirt
  - incorporate biodiversity
  - companion planting
  - barriers
  - traps
  - organic commercial products
  - homemade sprays.

drum covered by three to nine times its volume in water. Stir a couple of times during the soaking period, which should be at least a week. After three weeks of soaking, the mixture should be strong enough to control botrytis. Strain liquid off and use undiluted. The sludge can be used on the garden.

Compost spray works by preventing fungal spores from settling and colonising the plant. Spray weekly during humid weather and ensure all surfaces are covered. Repeat spraying after it rains.

Vegetable oil spray
A spray made from vegetable oil such as sunflower, olive, canola, peanut, soybean, grapeseed or safflower oil will control powdery mildew and sooty mould. To a litre of water add 10 g of oil and three drops of liquid detergent. Use immediately. See also the oil sprays above.

PART TWO

ALL ABOUT THE PLANTS

I am not going to attempt to describe every possible food plant you might want to grow, nor even every plant mentioned so far in this book; there are simply too many choices. Those described in this section have been chosen for a variety of reasons, including suitability for small spaces, multiple uses, productivity and great taste, though not everyone's taste buds will necessarily agree with mine.

For example, zucchini, though very productive, has not been included because it does take up a lot of space for an extended period, is not generally a great favourite and does not keep or preserve well. However, if your family loves it, by all means include it in your garden. Eggplant is another vegetable not included here because it is not highly productive, takes a long time to mature and is usually not well liked.

If your space is very limited, your choices will be based on criteria relevant to your situation, such as what your family likes to eat and how much sun or shade your area receives. If your favourite cuisine is Thai, you might like to grow some Asian greens, lemon grass, coriander, ginger and galangal. If Mediterranean cuisine is your family's preference, tomatoes, capsicums, eggplants, garlic, parsley and basil will suit you better.

The choices are numerous; have fun with them.

VEGETABLES

Grow your vegetables in a dedicated plot, in pots or scattered throughout the garden. It might take a little trial and error before you discover what grows best in your particular climate and the microclimates within your garden. The following advice will give you some general guidelines as a starting point.

It is possible to extend the growing season or to grow vegetables, and other foods, that would not normally thrive in your location by creating suitable microclimates. However, these methods require time and attention and results might not be as successful as they would be in the plant's preferred climate and conditions. My advice in general is to try these methods if you have the time and interest, but otherwise stick to plants known to be suited to your area.

Where I have made suggestions about cool, warm and hot climates, they are based on the recommendations of the Digger's Club (also known as Digger's Seeds), one of Australia's major suppliers of open-pollinated seeds.

Cool: Tasmania, Canberra, Ballarat, Orange.

Warm: Melbourne, Adelaide, Sydney, inland areas.

Hot: Perth, Brisbane, Darwin.

Top 10 for nutrients

Of the commonly eaten vegetables, the 10 most nutritious are broccoli, spinach, Brussels sprouts, lima bean, peas, asparagus, artichoke, cauliflower, sweet potato and carrot. You might not grow all of them in your garden, and they might not all be suited to growing in a small garden, but you can certainly include a number of them in your plant choices.

Asian greens

A number of vegetables fall into the broad category of Asian greens, including buk choy, baby buk choy, pak choy, mizuna, choy sum, tatsoi, Chinese mustard and Chinese cabbage. There is confusion over the naming of many plants in this category because some are very similar physically and some are called by numerous names, both in English and in several Asian languages.

Buk choy (or bok choy), for example, means 'white vegetable' in Cantonese, but in Australia it refers to the white-stemmed variety of *Brassica rapa* var. *chinensis*. Baby buk choy is a dwarf variety of the same subspecies. The green-stemmed variety is called pak choy. To go into detail about the profusion of names would only lead to bewilderment.

Buk choy ready to be eaten.

The two great advantages of this category of greens are that they are fast growing and generally quite small. This means they can be grown between other, larger, slower maturing plants to produce a quick crop before the larger plant has spread too much. It also makes them very suited to growing in pots.

Pak choy and buk choy

Sow
Grow from seedlings or from seed planted directly in the ground, September to April in a cool climate, any time in a hot or warm climate. Minimum soil temperature needed for germination: 10°C.

Soil
Grow in fertile soil with plenty of organic matter. After sowing the seeds, water them with a teaspoon of Epsom salts dissolved in four litres of water.

Use
The stems and the leaves have distinctive flavours. Use the leaves raw in salads or throw them into a stir-fry for the last minute of cooking. The stems take a little longer to cook, so if the leaves and stems are being used in the same dish, add the chopped stems first. Alternatively, serve steamed or lightly boiled.

Nutrition
A good source of folate, iron, calcium and vitamin C. The leaves contain beta-carotene and glucosinolates, said to reduce the risk of cancers and heart disease.

Harvest and store
Ready for harvest: about six weeks.

Cut individual leaves to chop into a salad or the whole mature plant when the head is still quite tight. If flower heads begin to develop, the plant can still be eaten, but is likely to be tougher. Best eaten fresh, but will keep in a plastic bag, refrigerated to less than 5°C for about a week.

Save seeds
To let plants flower and seed so seeds can be saved means you miss out on eating them.

Buk choy on the left side of the aquaponics bed.

However, they can sometimes go to seed quickly (known as bolting) if the weather becomes hot suddenly. Paradoxically, the seeds take a while to mature and dry. If you are willing to leave them long enough, collect seeds from these plants, or shake them around the garden where you would like more plants to grow. Alternatively, working on the theory that seeds from bolters are more likely to grow into plants that bolt, if you really want to save seeds, you will have to sacrifice the best plant or plants. Asian greens cross-pollinate very readily. However, they are such quick growers that you can leave one variety to flower and seed while growing and harvesting another.

Others to try

Grow and use these in a similar way to pak choy and buk choy.

Mizuna greens and Chinese mustard

Mizuna greens (*Brassica rapa* var. *nipposinica*) and Chinese mustard (*Brassica juncea*) are similar in flavour and use. The leaves are used in salads or stir-fries. Young leaves have a mildly mustardy taste, older leaves become stronger in flavour.

Choy sum or flowering white cabbage

Brassica rapa var. *parachinensis*

Similar in appearance to buk choy and pak choy, but with more slender stems, it is the developing tender, sweet flower shoot that is most valued with this plant. The whole young plant can be used in stir-fries or lightly steamed, or the young leaves and flower shoots can be eaten raw in salads.

Bush beans and lettuce in a tank bed.

Beans

Phaseolus spp.

There is a place for beans, commonly referred to as 'French' or 'snap' beans, in every small garden. Bush bean (*Phaseolus vulgaris*) varieties take up little space, are quite useful to grow in front of or between larger plants and are a good choice for pots. Climbing varieties (also *Phaseolus vulgaris*) take up little horizontal space, but do need a reasonably strong supporting frame or trellis. Climbing beans are very much more productive than

'Lazy Housewife' climbing bean.

'Violet Queen' bush bean.

are bush varieties. Runner beans (*Phaseolus coccineus*) are climbing beans that live for a number of years, often said to be seven, but it is variable. They die down to a root mass over winter and reshoot in the spring. Runner beans could produce for a month or more longer than other varieties.

All types of beans fix nitrogen in nodules that grow on their roots, so long as the right bacterium is in the soil. The nitrogen becomes available for other plants to take up when the beans die, though small amounts are released while the bean is growing. In a crop rotation, plant them either after a nitrogen-hungry crop, such as brassicas, to replace soil nitrogen, or before the brassicas so the nitrogen is available for the following crop.

When the bean crop has been harvested, either put the plants into the compost or mow over them and use the chopped residue as mulch.

Sow
Grow from seed planted directly in the ground, generally in spring to summer, after the likelihood of frost has passed.

Bush beans: October to January in a cool climate, September to February in a warm climate and March to September in a hot climate.

Climbing and runner beans: October to December in a cool climate, September to January in a warm climate and March to September in a hot climate.

Minimum soil temperature needed for germination: 15°C.

Soil
Beans will tolerate moderately acid soil, but spread lime a few weeks before sowing on very acid soil. They will grow well in most soils, except those that are very sandy. Once plants are growing well use mulch to prevent the shallow roots of bush beans from drying out.

Use
Eat young beans raw or cooked. The whole pod can be eaten, but if left too long they can become tough. Some varieties are suitable to either shell and eat the beans only or to leave longer on the plant and harvest to dry the beans for storage. These include 'Flageolet', 'Red Kidney' and 'Borlotti'.

Very young broad beans (see below) can be eaten pod and all, but usually the seeds are removed from the pods before being cooked.

Nutrition
Dried beans have long been used as a protein source, especially when combined with corn. Beans are high in carbohydrates and contain potassium and iron and vitamins A, B1 and B2.

Harvest and store

Runner beans are quick to produce the first crop, about six weeks, and produce over a lengthy period, as much as four months. Other climbing beans and bush beans will start to produce in about nine weeks and give you a harvest for over three months.

Cut beans from the plant rather than pulling them, especially with bush beans; they are quite brittle and it is easy to pull off more than you want and damage the plant. Bush beans are shallow-rooted and an enthusiastic pull might uproot the whole plant.

Beans will keep in a plastic bag or airtight container in the fridge for a week or more. Broad beans will keep for longer if left in the shells. Dried beans will store in the pantry in an airtight container for as much as a year. Any excess crop is easily frozen or incorporated into pickles.

Save seeds

Beans are one of the easiest plants to save seeds from. Let a few pods mature before harvesting them, then shell and dry the seeds. Cross-pollination can occur, but can be minimised by separating different varieties (a climbing and a dwarf for example) in different areas of the garden. Alternatively, stagger the crops so you have different varieties flowering at different times.

Broad beans
Vicia faba

Grow broad beans in the cooler months. They will grow over winter and start producing in

Broad beans harvested and ready to cook.

early to mid spring. They grow tall and will probably need staking in windy areas. Grow them at the back of a rectangular bed or in the middle of a circular one.

Plant seeds directly in the ground. In cool climates sow from March to August and in warm and hot climates from April to July.

Minimum soil temperature needed for germination: 10°C.

BROAD BEAN CAUTION

Some people, especially those of Mediterranean origin, can suffer from a disease called favism that is caused by consumption of broad beans or inhalation of their pollen. Symptoms might appear immediately after or within days of consumption and include breathlessness, nausea, fatigue, stomach pain, back pain, fever and chills. Recovery is usually spontaneous and occurs within one or two days. Favism can be fatal for young children.

Stake or otherwise support broad beans and grow them behind a smaller crop.

Beetroot
Beta vulgaris

For those who like beetroot there is a choice of colours, including golden and concentrically red and white striped. They take up little space and there are mini varieties available. Grow them as an edging in front of other vegetables or in the flower garden. They are very suited to growing in pots.

Sow
Sow seeds directly into the ground or grow from seedlings. In cool climates sow from September to February, in warm climates from July to March and in hot climates from April to July.

Baby beetroot growing with capsicum.

Minimum soil temperature needed for germination: 12°C.

Soil
Beetroot does not like too much fertiliser, so grow plants where a previous crop has been fertilised. A light well-drained soil is preferred and very acid soil should have lime spread a few weeks before planting the crop.

Use
The beetroot root can be cooked or grated and eaten raw in salads. The leaves are edible and some varieties are grown predominantly for the tasty purple salad leaves, which look decorative in the garden as well. Eat young leaves raw and cook older ones as you would silverbeet.

Nutrition
The root part is a source of potassium, phosphorus, magnesium, sodium, iron, calcium, vitamins A, C and B3, folic acid and biotin. The leaves contain vitamins A and C, iron, calcium, potassium, folate and beta-carotene.

Harvest and store
Cut leaves to use in salads or stir-fries as required. The roots can be pulled for use from about eight weeks to 20 weeks. Younger roots are good grated and eaten raw. Older roots need to be cooked or pickled. After pulling the beets up, remove the leaves by breaking them off at least 3 cm from the root to prevent bleeding during cooking. Long, slow cooking is usually recommended. Scrub well and cook beets whole, either by boiling

or baking. When cooked, rub the skin off and use the flesh as desired. It is good chopped and used in salads.

The roots will store in a plastic bag or airtight container in the refrigerator for several weeks. Pickled beets can be stored indefinitely in the pantry.

Save seeds

Beetroot needs to be left to flower and seed, which can take quite a long time before seeds are ready to collect. This vegetable is not really suitable for seed saving in a small garden when you want a quick turnaround of crops. If you do want to save the seeds, let two or three plants of the one variety flower and set seeds.

Broccoli

Brassica oleracea

Reputed to be one of the best vegetables for preventing cancers, diabetes, osteoporosis, high blood pressure and heart disease, broccoli is worth finding space for.

Sow

Buy seedlings or grow from seed indoors and transplant into the garden.

Sow at any time of year in cool climates, from June to March in warm climates and from February to June in hot climates. I like to wait until the weather is too cold for the cabbage moths and butterflies to be flitting around, May to June in my area, before planting out seedlings. That way I do not have to worry about controlling these pests.

This healthy broccoli was grown in an aquaponics bed.

Minimum soil temperature needed for germination: 10°C.

Soil

Broccoli is a heavy feeder, so fertilise the soil well before planting and during growth. Slightly acid soil is not a problem, but very acidic soil should be limed before planting.

Use

Broccoli is usually lightly boiled and served as a side dish, though florets are a crunchy addition to salads and lightly cooked in stir-fries. The stems contain useful amounts of nutrients and can be stir-fried or grated and eaten raw. A tasty combination salad is grated broccoli stem, beetroot and carrot.

Nutrition

Broccoli is very rich in vitamins C, K and A. In fact, one cup of steamed broccoli provides about twice the daily requirement of these vitamins. It is a good source of vitamins B1, B2, B3, B5 and E, folate, manganese, potassium, phosphorus, magnesium, protein, omega 3 fatty acids, iron, zinc and calcium.

The phytonutrients sulforaphane and indoles have anti-cancer effects, especially for lung, colon, breast and ovarian cancers. Eaten in conjunction with tomatoes, broccoli is even more beneficial (see tomato listing).

Harvest and store

The first heads are ready to harvest in about 12 to 16 weeks. Cut them quite low down with a slanting cut. The plants will continue to produce side shoots indefinitely, years in some cases, if you can keep the caterpillars off them, but they will become progressively smaller. The side shoots form quite quickly and you could be cutting them every two weeks. If you leave them, they will flower and seed.

Broccoli is best eaten fresh from the garden, but will keep wrapped in plastic in the fridge for a week or two.

Save seeds

It takes some time for flowers to form and seeds to mature, so your space will be taken up by an overgrown broccoli plant for months. It will also be attracting unwanted pests. This is another one I think not suitable for seed saving in a small garden. If you do decide to save the seeds, do not allow other brassicas to flower at the same time as cross-pollination could occur.

Capsicums, sweet

Capsicum annuum

Different capsicum varieties growing in an EarthBox®. (Photo courtesy EarthBox Australia)

Capsicum is a warm climate vegetable and needs a long period of heat for the green fruit to turn red, or yellow, or orange, when its flavour is at its best. It is versatile, nutritious, decorative and suited to growing in pots. In cooler areas, grow it in a pot so it can be moved to a warm microclimate, such as against a north-facing brick wall, where it is more likely to ripen properly than it will in the open garden.

As well as the sweet capsicums the genus contains chillies or hot peppers, for those who enjoy a more fiery taste.

Sow

Buy seedlings or sow indoors and transplant seedlings to the garden. In cool climates sow from September to November, in warm climates from August to December and in hot climates from April to September.

Minimum soil temperature needed for germination: 18°C.

Soil

Capsicums need fertile, deep, well-drained soil, so fertilise before planting and again once fruit have set.

Use

Eat capsicums raw in salads or cooked in stir-fries, soups and casseroles. Many cuisines, from Asian to Italian, incorporate the colours and flavours of this versatile vegie. For those with more tender taste buds, use the hot chillies in moderation; they are often dried and used as a flavouring.

Nutrition

Capsicums are rich in vitamins C and A and also contain vitamins B1, B2 and D, zinc, rutin, beta-carotene, iron, calcium, potassium, magnesium, phosphorus, sulphur, sodium and selenium. No wonder they have a reputation as a health food and are one of the heart-smart, cancer-preventing foods. Fully ripe coloured capsicums contain far more nutrients than do the green unripe fruits.

Harvest and store

Capsicums can be harvested and eaten when green and of a good size, but are much better left until they are fully coloured. Cut rather than pull them off the plant as stems are brittle and easily damaged.
They will keep for a week or two wrapped in plastic in the refrigerator. Chillies are easily dried by threading them onto a string and leaving in an airy place. Once dry, they need to be stored in an airtight container away from light.

Save seeds

Cut a fully ripe capsicum in quarters lengthways and brush the seeds out with the back of a knife. Keep in an airy spot until very dry before storing. Cross-pollination is common (even between capsicums and hot

Carrots in a straw bale bed.

chillies, which belong to the same species) if different varieties are grown close together, so stick with one variety in a small garden if saving seeds is your aim, or grow different varieties in separate areas of the garden.

Carrot

Daucus carota

Carrots are very nutritious, take up little space and keep well. Grow them after a

Carrots in an aquaponics bed with vermiculite medium.

fertilised crop and do not add any fertiliser because too much will cause them to grow misshapen; they are still edible, but awkward to peel and store. There are purple, white, red and yellow varieties available and round shapes as well as the traditional long tapered shape. Use them as a border in front of taller crops or in the flower garden. They are suitable to grow in pots.

Sow
Grow seed directly in the ground. Mix it with coarse sand and shake out of a container with appropriate-sized holes punched in the lid to minimise the need for thinning of the crop. Otherwise, sprinkle thinly by hand along the prepared row.

In cool climates sow seeds from September to February, in warm climates from July to March and in hot climates from February to November.

Minimum soil temperature needed for germination: 12°C.

Soil
Carrots do not need much fertiliser, so grow them where a previous crop has been fertilised. They are best grown in light, finely textured, well-drained soil.

The soil must be kept damp until seeds have germinated. If you are away from home and unable to check this during the day, cover the rows of seeds with sacks, shadecloth or planks of wood and check each evening to ensure the soil is still moist. The shadecloth or other cover can be left until seedlings are about 2 or 3 cm tall.

Remove it at night so they are not exposed to the sun straight away. It is a good idea, if the weather is hot, to rig up a length of shadecloth over, but not sitting on, the seedlings until they have established and are growing well.

Carrots require a bit of fiddling to nurse them through germination, but are very hardy after this stage.

Use
Eat them raw as sticks or grated, add them to salads or cook them in stir-fries, stews, soups or roasts.

Nutrition
Carrots are rich in vitamin A and beta-carotene and contain useful amounts of vitamins B3, C and E, along with potassium, calcium, iron and zinc. Recent research has shown that cooking reduces the vitamin C content, but makes the beta-carotene and antioxidants more readily available, so enjoy them both cooked and raw for maximum benefit.

Harvest and store
Carrots can be ready to harvest in eight to 18 weeks, but I have always found them to take longer than this. The rows need to be thinned to allow the carrots to grow without crowding; when they reach a usable size the thinnings can be eaten. Carrots will keep fairly well in the ground as long as frosts are not too severe, or can be buried in clean sand in a polystyrene box and kept in a dark place. They will keep for weeks in a plastic bag in the refrigerator.

Save seeds

This is another plant that needs to be left in place for a long time to flower and seed. The seedy plant will grow over a metre tall and spread to be straggly and surprisingly wide, so seed saving is not recommended for a small garden. On the plus side, the flowers attract numerous beneficial insects. Different varieties of carrots cross-pollinate freely, so it pays to stick to one variety in a small garden if you want to save the seeds.

Chinese water chestnut
Eloecharis dulcis

This unusual vegetable is worth a try for anyone who has a shallow garden pond, old bathtub or child's wading pool that could be put to a productive use. Water chestnuts are rush-like swamp or edge-of-pond plants and do have specific growing requirements. However, I am currently trying some in pots with large saucers kept full of water and so far they are growing well. We also have some doing well in the aquaponics system.

Sow

Water chestnuts grow from corms, planted about 5 cm deep with the growing tip pointing upward. The sowing rate for maximum productivity is two corms per square metre, but I am sacrificing productivity for convenience, just to see how it goes in my area, and have four corms per 45 cm pot. Under ideal conditions, a single corm can multiply to over 50.

Plant in early spring, but after the frosts are over in your area. A minimum soil temperature of between 20°C and 25°C for the whole growing season is recommended.

These plants need lots of water. Let them grow to about 10 cm tall and then flood them to a depth of between seven and 10 cm. This level should be maintained for the remainder of the growing season of at least seven months without frost. You could plant them in pots until they reach 10 cm high and then plunge the pots into the water source.

Soil

A rich sandy loam is the preferred soil, with a pH of 6.5 to 7.2. Lime the soil before planting if it is acidic. They will grow in slightly alkaline conditions and even in brackish water. Use plenty of compost and well-decomposed animal manure, never fresh, which would lead to lush leaf growth and poor corm formation.

Chinese water chestnuts growing in a pot with a generous saucer for watering.

Use

The corms need to be peeled and are then used in stir-fries or soups, or can be eaten raw. The raw corms have a sweet flavour reminiscent of coconut and are quite crunchy. The texture remains after cooking, but the sweetness is less noticeable.

Nutrition

Water chestnuts are about 19% carbohydrate and a good source of B vitamins. Raw corms contain the natural antibiotic puchine.

Harvest and store

In late autumn the leaves will turn golden-brown. When this happens, drain the water off, or take pots out of the water, to harden and sweeten the corms. Leave them for three to four weeks before harvesting. The skins should be a rich chestnut colour. They will keep in the fridge for several weeks, or you can freeze them.

Save corms

Save some large corms to replant in spring.

Cucumber

Cucumis sativus

There are both bush and vine types of cucumber and the fruits range from tiny to enormous, up to a metre long for some varieties. Small bush varieties will take up less space than a sprawling vine and are very suited to growing in pots; however, a vine can be trained to grow on a tepee or trellis and take up little horizontal space. In addition,

Two varieties of cucumbers.

vines along the ground can be grown as an understorey for other, taller crops such as corn.

Sow

Buy seedlings or grow seed directly in the ground, or start off indoors and transplant to get an earlier crop. Do not plant outside until the danger of frosts is over. Pinching out the growing tips will encourage more flower and fruit production.

In cool climates plant from October to December, in warm climates from September to January and in hot climates from July to October.

Minimum soil temperature needed for germination: 15°C.

Soil

Cucumbers prefer well-drained, moderately fertile soil with a pH of 6 to 7.5. They have a high water need so benefit from soil with added organic matter. Mulch will help conserve water in the soil and also prevent fruit of vine-type plants from being in contact with the soil, which can result in the fruit rotting.

Cucumbers and other cucurbits are often grown in a mound. The mound is built up with compost and organic matter, similar to a no-dig bed, and soil is raked over it. Seeds are planted into holes in the mound. The warmth of the decomposing organic matter speeds seed germination and the nutrients encourage quick growth.

Use
Cucumbers are usually eaten raw in salads. Immature fruits can be pickled. The young leaves can be used in salads.

Nutrition
Cucumbers are a good source of vitamin C and contain useful amounts of molybdenum, vitamin A, potassium, manganese, folate and magnesium. The skins are edible and contain silica, potassium and magnesium.

Harvest and store
For pickling, harvest fruits when they are about 10 cm long. There are varieties especially recommended for pickling, including 'Perfection Pickling', 'Chicago Pickling' and 'Mineu'. Dual-purpose salad and pickling varieties include 'Lebanese Mini Muncher', 'Japanese Climbing' and 'Midget'. Cut fruit from the plant rather than pulling as cucumbers are shallow-rooted and it is easy to pull the whole plant out.

Fruit can be ready to harvest for salads in about eight weeks. Harvesting the fruit as soon as it is ready will encourage more flowering and fruit production over an extended period. If the plant's energy goes into growing huge fruits, there will be fewer of them.

Cucumbers will keep in the refrigerator in a plastic bag for at least a week.

Save seeds
Cross-pollination of different varieties is common, so grow only one variety in a small garden if you want to save seeds. Leave fruits on the vine to fully mature. Cut the fruit open and scoop out pulp and seeds. Wash the pulp away from the seeds and let them dry well on absorbent paper before storing.

Lettuce
Lactuca sativa

The variety of lettuces and other salad greens available is large. Lettuce can be broadly divided into hearting, nonhearting, butterhead and 'Cos'-type varieties.

Hearting varieties such as 'Great Lakes' and 'Iceberg' are satisfyingly crunchy in a salad, but have less flavour than most nonhearting ones. They are usually slower to mature than other types. The great benefit of nonhearting

Nonhearting 'Australian Yellow' lettuce ready to eat.

Lettuce growing in a straw bale bed.

or loose-leaf varieties such as 'Australian Yellow', 'Flame', 'Oakleaf' and 'Lollo Russo' is that you can cut a few leaves whenever you need them and the plant will keep on producing for an extended period. With hearting varieties, you only harvest each plant once. As well, all the lettuces mature at the same time and do not keep well. Thus, if you have planted a punnet of 'Icebergs', they will all be ready to pick within a week of each other and probably will go slimy in the fridge before you can eat them.

Butterhead varieties include 'Red' and 'Green Mignonette', 'Sangria' and 'Buttercrunch'. They form loose heads of smooth leaves. 'Cos' (also known as 'Romaine') types have a medium-tight heart with stiff upright leaves. Varieties include 'Cos', 'Brown Romaine' and 'Verdi'.

Lettuce are quick-maturing and can be planted between other slower maturing crops. They are ideal to plant in front of taller crops and are exceptionally well suited to growing in pots.

Sow

Buy seedlings, sow seed directly in the ground, or sow indoors and transplant seedlings into the garden or pots outside. Mix seeds with some coarse sand, as for carrots, to obtain better spacing. Germination is fairly quick. Soil must be kept damp until seeds germinate. Thin seedlings to about 30 cm apart for hearting varieties. Nonhearting varieties can be much closer.

In cool and warm climates sow at any time, in hot climates sow from March to August. However, most lettuces do not thrive in extremes of climate, so avoid planting in very cold weather, when seed might rot in the ground, or in very hot weather when plants might bolt to seed. One advantage of growing lettuce in pots is that they can be moved into dappled shade or sunlight, as needed. 'Cos' types are more heat- and cold-tolerant than other varieties. Red-leaved varieties are more heat-tolerant than are those with green leaves.

Minimum soil temperature needed for germination: 12°C.

Soil

Lettuce has a high nitrogen requirement, so prepare the soil with compost and rotted manure, not fresh. Soil should be well drained and not too acidic; a pH of 6.5 to 7.5 is preferred. Liquid fertilisers applied every two or three weeks will keep the crop growing well. However, I prepare the soil well, as described, and usually only fertilise with a weak liquid mixture of fish fertiliser and seaweed once or twice during the crop's growth. Lettuce is shallow rooted and has a high water requirement, so apply mulch to keep the soil damp. If plants are stressed by the soil becoming too dry, they are likely to taste bitter and bolt to seed.

Use

Eat fresh in salads. Where space is very tight, grow a mixture (both mixed seeds and punnets of mixed varieties are available) and cut the leaves as you need them for tasty and attractive mixed salads. Combine lettuce with homegrown sprouts and sprinkle grated carrot or beetroot over the top for a simple and nutritious salad.

Nutrition

Lettuce contains vitamins A, C and E as well as potassium, iron and calcium. Red-leafed varieties contain about three times the antioxidants of green varieties.

Harvest and store

Hearting varieties can be ready to harvest in eight to 10 weeks; loose-leaf types can be cut from about five weeks. Always cut leaves, do not pull the plant or it will come out of the ground. Lettuce will keep in the refrigerator, wrapped in plastic or in an airtight container, for at least a week.

Save seeds

Plants must be left to flower and seed. If you save seed from plants that have bolted, the progeny are likely to inherit this characteristic. Lettuce varieties will readily cross-pollinate so grow only one variety in a small garden if you want to save seeds. They are quick to mature, so it is possible to have one variety in flower and seeding while you are growing and harvesting another.

Others to try

There are more greens (and reds, and burgundies) than simply lettuce to make tasty, eye-pleasing salads from.

Mixtures

Mixtures are available in both seed and seedling form. The seedlings in punnets from nurseries are usually made up of a variety of lettuces. Seed mixtures (often known as mesclun) might include rocket, endive and chervil as well as lettuces.

Rocket
Eruca sativa

Also known as arugula or roquette, rocket can be grown alone or as part of a mixture. Its strong peppery flavour might not be to everyone's taste, but mixed with other leaves rocket adds zing to a salad. It freely self-seeds so if you like it, leave it to go to seed and shake the dry pods around where you want the plants to grow.

Watercress
Nasturtium officinalis

Watercress can be grown in soil or water. Its leaves are high in antioxidants and have a mild mustardy flavour.

Radicchio
Cichorium intybus

The thick strongly flavoured leaves of radicchio are wine-red with cream ribs, making it a very decorative addition to salads. Use cautiously; it is quite bitter and probably an acquired taste. The hearting variety used as a salad vegetable has been developed from chicory.

Onions
Allium cepa

Onions are so commonly used in all kinds of cuisines that it is worth finding space for some. Many varieties store quite well, so a single harvest for the year can keep a family in onions for months. The traditional bulb-type onions do take some time to mature, so it could suit space-strapped gardeners to grow alternatives such as spring onions or chives.

Sow
Seed can be sown into a fine seedbed and later thinned to a spacing of about 10 cm. However, as onions take so long to mature and the germination and growth to seedling stage makes this even longer, I prefer to buy seedlings in punnets. Separate seedlings and lay them semi-upright in a prepared shallow furrow so each plant is supported by the soil at the back of the furrow. Gently push the soil from the front of the furrow to cover the roots. Within a week the onion seedlings should be standing upright.

There are early, mid and late season onion varieties, referring to when they are planted. Early varieties include 'Gladallan', 'Lockyer Early White' and 'Barletta'; some mid season varieties are 'Odourless' and 'Creamgold'; and late varieties are 'New Australia Brown', 'Brown Spanish', 'Pukekohe', 'Red' and 'Long Red Florence'.

Early varieties: in cool and warm climates plant from March to June and in hot climates from February to May.

Mid varieties: in cool and warm climates plant during winter. These are not suited to growing in hot or very cold climates.

Late varieties: in cool and warm climates plant from July to October. In general, these are not suited to the tropics.

To simplify matters, buy seedlings as they appear in the nurseries and they should be varieties suited to grow at that time of year.

Minimum soil temperature needed for germination: 10°C.

Soil
Onions prefer moderately rich (but not overfertilised), friable soil and good drainage. Too much nitrogenous fertiliser will

Red onions just harvested.

encourage leaf growth rather than bulb. Manure spread too close to seedlings will encourage onion maggots. Onions prefer a fertiliser with potassium, so blood and bone with potash is a good choice. Alternatively, spread wood ash and rake it in a couple of weeks before planting. The preferred pH is 6 to 7. Sprinkle acidic soil with lime or dolomite before planting.

Use

Depending on the variety, onions can be eaten raw in salads or cooked in a wide range of dishes. Some varieties are suited to pickling; these include 'Barletta' (harvested early) and 'Borettana Yellow'. 'Barletta' (harvested when mature) and 'Long Red Florence' are good salad onions.

Nutrition

Onions contain vitamins B6, B1, K and C, folic acid and sulphur. They are reputed to lower blood pressure, cholesterol and blood sugar.

Harvest and store

Stop watering when some of the onion tops begin to turn yellow. Once a few of the tops begin to dry and fall over, knock over the rest of them and wait about two weeks before pulling them out of the ground. If they do not come out easily, leave them a while longer. They will store better if you do this. After pulling them out of the ground, leave them on a well-ventilated dry surface, not in bright sunshine, for two weeks for the skins to harden. Do not allow them to get wet during this time.

To store, rub loose dirt and skins off and cut the tops off a few centimetres from the bulb. Store the onions in nets or cut-off pantyhose legs and hang them in a cool, dry, well-ventilated place; the rafters of a shed or garage are suitable, or maybe you have a large airy pantry.

Alternatively, leave the tops on and plait or tie them together in bunches to hang. They look decorative in the kitchen, and are ready to hand, but will not keep as well as those stored in dry, cool conditions if your kitchen tends to become steamy.

Bulbs with a thin neck and a flattened root end are said to keep the longest, so eat those with thick necks and rounded bulb bottoms first.

Some varieties store better than others with 'New Australian Brown' and 'Creamgold' having reputations as being the best keepers. 'Brown Spanish' and 'Pukekohe' will also store well. In general, the late varieties store better than the early ones.

Save seeds

Onions take a long time to form a flower head and set seeds, and the seeds have a limited viability, making them one of the less suitable vegetables for seed saving in a small garden. If you do leave a few to seed, make sure they are of the one variety because different varieties will cross-pollinate. Carefully cut off the seed heads when you can see they are full of black seeds. Place them in a paper bag or open container to dry for a week or two. Shake the seeds out of the heads into an airtight container. Use within a year.

Others to try

Tree onions
Allium cepa var. *proliferum*

Tree onions form clusters of thickened leaf bases, rather than true bulbs, but also produce clusters of small bulbs on top of the leaves. Both leaf bases and onion clusters can be eaten or used for propagation purposes. Clumps are easily divided. If left alone, the bulb clusters at the top will often fall to the ground and take root to form new plants. The small bulbs sometimes begin to sprout new leaves while still attached to the plant. Tree onions are perennials and once you have a few clumps established in the garden you are likely to have them forever.

Spring onions
Allium cepa var. *aggregatum*

Spring onions are easy and quick to grow and perform well in pots. The common type of spring onion has no true bulb, but a thickened white stem at the base, darkening to green at the top. Both sections are eaten, often raw in salads, but the outside green leaves can be fibrous. There is a variety with a swollen red bulb and emerald green leaves, called simply 'Red', which is high in antioxidants.

Other varieties of *Allium cepa* var. *aggregatum* include potato onions and French shallots. These produce clusters of small bulbs at the base of each plant, rather than a single bulb.

Bunching/Welsh onions
Allium fistolosum

Also known as Japanese bunching onion or Japanese leek, this species has thick hollow leaves and forms a swollen leaf base instead of a bulb. It is the base of the leaf that is most often eaten, though the leaves can be snipped and used in salads. Bunching onions generally grow as a perennial and clumps can be separated to form more plants. They grow more quickly than bulbing onions and are more suited to warm climates. They grow well in pots.

Peas
Pisum sativum

Peas are one of the legumes that return nitrogen to the soil, provided the bacterium needed for nodules to form on the roots is in the soil. They grow best during the cooler seasons so can follow a heavy feeding crop such as tomato or corn and be grown on a trellis behind a brassica crop, or on a wire frame between brassicas.

Varieties include the traditional green pod peas, purple or golden podded types (which

Peas growing on wire frames behind broccoli.

Peas in an aquaponics bed.

still have green peas inside) and dwarf varieties that do not need support. With snow peas and sugar snap peas the whole pod is eaten before the seeds inside develop fully. These are sometimes known as 'mangetouts' (eat all).

Sow

Seedlings can be bought, but peas are easy to sow directly in the ground. If growing in rows, scrape a furrow in the soil about 5 cm deep, drop the peas in at spacings of 8 cm to 10 cm and rake or push the soil from the side of the furrow over them. I find that they can be grown closer together and will help support each other. Alternatively, use a wire frame to support them and poke holes into the soil around the frame to plant the seeds in. Six to eight seeds can be planted into a 20 cm to 30 cm diameter pot. Dwarf varieties will need no support, climbing types will need a frame in the pot to twine around. If growing during wet conditions, do not water peas until after they germinate because the seeds can easily rot in the ground.

In cool climates sow from January to October, in warm climates from February to August and in hot climates from March to July. However, they are susceptible to frosts, especially when young, so time your planting to avoid frosts in your area. I find, in northern Victoria, mid spring planting avoids frosts and the crop matures before the worst heat of summer. Alternatively, I might plant peas in autumn, after the summer heat, so plants are big enough to survive winter's frosts and crop from mid to late spring. It is important to know your area's usual weather conditions and plant accordingly.

Minimum soil temperature needed for germination: 10°C.

Soil

Peas do not need a lot of fertiliser, especially not high-nitrogen fertiliser. If the previous crop has been well fertilised, the peas will probably have enough nutrients. They prefer neutral to slightly alkaline soil with a pH from 6.5 to 7.5. If your soil is acid, apply lime or dolomite a week or two before planting and water it in well.

If the soil is poor and fertiliser is needed, prepare the furrow twice as deep (about 10 cm) and spread your chosen fertiliser along the bottom, cover it with 5 cm of soil and put the peas on top, then cover them with another 5 cm of soil. In very cold and damp soil, seed can be sown more shallowly, about 3 cm deep.

Use

Eat peas lightly cooked or raw, in salads and stir-fries or as a side dish. Snow peas and sugar snap peas are very easy to overcook, a quick blanch or stir-fry is all that is needed.

Nutrition

Peas are high in vitamin K, manganese and vitamin C and contain useful amounts of vitamins B1, B2, B3 and B6, as well as protein, magnesium, copper, iron, zinc and potassium. They also contain purines, which break down to form uric acid, so people who suffer from gout or kidney disease should limit their consumption.

Harvest and store

Most peas will be ready to harvest in about 10 weeks and the bulk of the crop will be produced over only a few weeks. Stagger planting and sow only a few seeds at a time to extend the harvest. Pick traditional pod peas when the pods are full but still young; older peas become quite starchy. Snow peas and sugar snap peas should be harvested when the peas are just visible inside the pods. Harvest every day or two so peas do not become too big and stringy.

Store peas in the refrigerator in a sealed container for up to a week. Pod peas are easy to blanch and freeze. Snow peas and sugar snap peas do not freeze well and are best eaten fresh, straight from the garden.

Save seeds

Peas are easy to save for seeds. Leave a few peas on each plant to develop fully and save for the next season's crop. Dry seeds in an airy place before storing in an airtight container. Try not to plant different varieties close enough that they can twine together because you will not know which seeds you are saving.

Potato

Solanum tuberosum

Potatoes are cheap to buy so you might not see any reason to grow them at home. However, they are fun to grow in that there are numerous space-efficient methods to try. You might not be able to grow anything like the quantity your family needs, but you can specialise in one or two less common varieties that you particularly enjoy eating and have difficulty buying.

Sow

To begin your potato adventure, buy certified seed potatoes of the variety you prefer.

Potatoes growing in a pot.

Temporary shade cover for potatoes in hot weather.

Potatoes are grown from other potatoes that have begun to sprout or form eyes, not from seed. I like to grow 'Kipflers', which are banana- or sausage-shaped and excellent in salads. These are seldom available in supermarkets, so it feels like a real luxury when I harvest and cook my small crop.

Potatoes are frost-tender and do not like very hot weather; a mild climate is best, but you can easily provide shade in the summer to prevent plants from bolting to seed. In cool climates sow sprouted tubers from August to September, in warm climates from July to December and in hot climates from February to September.

Minimum soil temperature needed for planting: 12°C.

Before planting, leave the tubers, which should already have formed tiny buds or 'eyes', outdoors for a week or two to encourage the formation of strong shoots. Some research has found that if the seed potatoes are left until the shoots are quite long, 12 cm to 30 cm, and the shoots are laid horizontally in the planting trench/hole, productivity is significantly increased.

Large seed potatoes can be cut into smaller segments, as long as there is at least one eye on each part. Allow the cut surfaces to dry before planting.

A plethora of choices

You can grow your potatoes the conventional way in trenches, planted 10 to 15 cm deep with about 25 cm between plants. Lightly cover the tubers and, as they grow, keep mounding soil, compost and/or mulch on top of them until they are growing in hills. Remember, new tubers form above the seed tuber, not below, and if they are exposed to sunlight they will turn green and be poisonous so cannot be eaten.

A good method for small spaces is to grow potatoes in pots, polystyrene boxes, old bathtubs or tubes formed from wire mesh. One-third fill the container with a mixture of good soil and compost or vermicompost. Place sprouted tubers on top of the soil mixture, sprouts up, and gently cover them with soil, trying not to damage the sprouts in the process. As leaves appear, cover them with more soil, mulch or compost until the container is full.

Similarly, grow potatoes in a no-dig bed, perhaps to make use of a weedy patch or part of a lawn area. Cover the soil with thick cardboard or layers of newspaper. Cover this base with straw and wet it thoroughly. Put your soil/compost mixture on top and follow instructions as for growing in a container. A surround of straw bales will insulate the crop from weather extremes, retain moisture and partially decompose while the potatoes are growing so it can be used in a new no-dig bed.

To grow potatoes in an existing no-dig bed, scoop a large hole for each tuber, add topsoil or compost to the hole if needed (this will depend on the stage of decomposition of the bed), drop in the tuber, cover it with material from the bed and push more over the leaves as they grow. If the bed is largely undecomposed, alternate bedding material and compost or vermicompost.

Regular fertilising with seaweed, fish emulsion, Bokashi liquid or compost tea, especially for pot-grown potatoes, will be beneficial.

Soil

Potatoes prefer well-drained, well-aerated, slightly acidic, fertile soil which has plenty of potassium. Sources of potassium include blood and bone with potash, ash from a wood fire, seaweed fertiliser or a mulch of oak leaves. Too much nitrogen will result in luxuriant leaf growth and few tubers. Grow them in a sunny spot, but provide some sun protection if you are growing them in the middle of summer.

Use

Potatoes are the world's most widely grown non-grain food and are used in numerous ways. Different varieties are often recommended for different uses.

'Bintje': boil, fry, salads.

'Coliban' (the one most often found in supermarkets): bake, mash, steam.

'Desiree': boil, bake, gnocchi.

'Dutch Cream': boil, bake.

'Kennebec': boil, bake, fry, mash.

'King Edward': mash, bake, fry.

'Kipfler': steam, boil, salads.

'Nicola': mash, bake, boil, salads.

'Pink Fir Apple': boil, salads.

'Pontiac': bake, boil, grate.

'Sebago': boil, bake, mash, fry.

Nutrition

Potatoes are high in carbohydrate and vitamin C and a good source of potassium, iron and vitamin B.

Harvest and store

After potatoes have flowered, you can dig into the hills or no-dig bed and extract a few 'new' or thin-skinned potatoes for immediate use. These are great to use in salads, but will not store well. Wait until the leaves have nearly all died off, cut off the top growth (haulms) and leave the potatoes in the ground, unwatered, for at least a week before digging up the main crop. The skins should be quite hard. Leave the dug potatoes to dry for a few hours, brush excess dirt off and store in a cool, dry, dark place. Unblemished potatoes will store for months. Use any damaged potatoes first. Scattering dried lavender, sage and rosemary among your stored spuds is said to suppress sprouting and inhibit bacteria formation.

The easiest way to harvest potatoes grown in containers is to put a sheet of heavy duty plastic on the ground at the base of the pot and tip the contents onto it.

Save tubers

To avoid diseases, it is best to begin with purchased certified tubers. Once you have healthy stock growing, you can save some of your own tubers. There are nearly always some near the surface of the soil that have turned green. Store these in a cool dry place to use as seed for the next season's crop. Any stored potatoes that begin to form shoots can also be used as seed. As long as you practise crop rotation and avoid diseases, this system should work well. If you have an unhealthy crop, begin again in a new area with new certified seed. Many people prefer to start fresh each year, and in some potato-growing areas, this might be a legal requirement.

Pumpkin
Cucurbita maxima

Turn your back and a pumpkin vine planted in a moment of weakness, or optimism, will have sprawled all over your garden. You might think this vegie is not a good choice for a small area, and you could be right. However, if you do have a space going to waste, pumpkins will cover it very quickly and produce enough fruits to feed a family for months. As well, there are varieties that produce small fruits and these can be trained to grow on a trellis to take up little ground space.

Sow

Buy seedlings or sow seeds directly into the ground once frosts have finished in your area. Pumpkins need a long growing season for fruits to mature and, in frost-prone locations, they need to be harvested before the first winter frosts. In cool and warm climates plant from after the frosts until December, in hot climates plant from July to October. Pumpkins are prone to developing powdery mildew on the leaves so very humid areas might not suit this vegie.

Minimum soil temperature needed for germination: 15°C.

A variety said to be resistant to powdery mildew and worth trying in humid climates is 'Bohemia'. For space efficiency, the varieties 'Delicata Mini Sweet Bush' and 'Golden Nugget' are bushier than most others and 'Potimarron' and 'Green Chestnut' have small fruits and are suitable to grow on a trellis.

Soil

Pumpkins will grow in almost any soil, as long as the drainage is good, but will thrive in fertile soil rich in organic matter. Though the preferred pH is 6.5 to 7, pumpkins will still grow in soil with a pH as low as 5.5. The best results I have had with pumpkins were those

Part of one season's generous pumpkin harvest (yellow zucchinis on top).

planted in a new no-dig bed. See Chapter 3 for details.

Though pumpkins can be grown in any sort of bed, the following simple method seems to suit them. Build up a mound of good soil about a metre square enriched with compost, decayed manure and any other organic goodies you have available. Plant four seeds or seedlings per mound, one on each side. A moat around the mound and a saucer-shaped depression in the centre will help with watering and mulch will conserve soil moisture. Be careful what you plant them near because they will spread. If you can, spread thick cardboard covered with straw over the surrounding area so the fruits will have a clean surface to rest on. Alternatively, as the fruits form, place cardboard and straw under each one.

Pollination

Pumpkins and other cucurbits (zucchinis, cucumber, squash) produce male and female flowers. For fruit to form it is necessary for pollen to be transferred from the stamen of the male flower to the stigma of the female. Usually bees do this job for us. It is easy to recognise male and female flowers. The male has a long slender stalk and the female has a shorter, slightly thicker stalk with a small round bulge at the bottom of the flower, which is the part that grows into the fruit if fertilisation occurs. Inside, the female flower has a short, thick stigma and the male has a longer, thinner stamen. There are always many more male flowers than females.

The pollination rate can sometimes be poor if bees and other pollinators are in short supply

Bees in a male pumpkin flower.

or in very hot weather. Sometimes it seems that very few female flowers are produced. Snipping off the growing tips of the vines often stimulates production of more female flowers. It might be necessary to try hand-pollination, which is best done early in the morning when flowers have just opened and pollen is plentiful. Simply break off the petals of a male flower and paint the pollen from the stamen onto the stigma of a female flower.

Now plant some more native plants and other vigorous flowers elsewhere in the garden to attract pollinators.

Female pumpkin flower.

Male pumpkin flower.

Use

The culinary uses of pumpkin are varied. The fruit can be cooked with or without the skin. Serve it boiled, mashed, roasted or barbecued. Pumpkin soup made from your stored supply is a great winter warmer. Use mashed pumpkin in scones, bread or cake. Make a pumpkin pie, either sweet or savoury. Try roasted pumpkin and feta risotto. If you are really keen, you can stuff, batter and deep-fry the flowers. The seeds can be dried in a slow oven as a nutritious snack food.

Nutrition

Pumpkins are a very good source of vitamin A and also contain useful amounts of vitamin C, vitamin B5 (pantothenic acid) and folate.

Harvest and store

Fruits are best harvested when the vine dies off, but can be cut before this for immediate use, as long as the stalk is dry and hard. To maximise storage life, cut the stalks at least 5 cm from the fruit. If any stalks break off at the fruit join, use them quickly as this broken area allows decomposition organisms to enter the fruit and it will not keep.

After harvesting the fruit, leave it in the sun for a few days to dry and toughen the skin. If there is a possibility of frost, move your harvest to a sheltered area. Store in a cool, dry, dark place, preferably with plenty of air circulation and try not to have them touching. Any blemished fruit should be eaten first. The pumpkins closest to the central root are the oldest and will store the longest, provided they are unblemished and have been cut with long stalks attached.

Save seeds

Pumpkin seeds are very easy to save by simply scooping them out of a pumpkin of the desired size and taste, washing the pulp off and letting them dry. However, there is a little more to this story. Pumpkin flowers are very promiscuous and will readily pollinate with other varieties of pumpkin as well as other members of the cucurbit family. This means that if the bees that pollinated your pumpkin had already visited one of a different variety, or even a squash or zucchini, the resulting fruits could be of inferior quality.

To prevent this from happening, either grow no other cucurbits in your garden (but you cannot control what other nearby gardeners plant), or hand-pollinate selected flowers, as described above. Once you have done this, tie a paper bag over the female flower until the pumpkin begins to form, then you can safely remove the bag. You will need to mark fruits resulting from this pollination to make sure you save seeds from the correct ones.

Round radish.

Radish

Raphanus sativus

Radishes are very quick growing and suitable to grow in spaces between other crops or as a low-growing border. They grow well in pots and, because of their size, small pots will do.

'French Breakfast' radish.

Radishes growing in vermiculite in an aquaponics bed.

As well as the traditional round red kind, there are white radishes, egg-shaped and carrot-shaped varieties, even a variety called 'French Breakfast' that is red at the top, fading to white at the bottom.

Sow

Radishes are easy to sow from seed directly in the ground. In warm weather seeds can germinate within days, making this a good crop for impatient gardeners. Seed should be sown about 2 cm deep and needs to be thinned after germination so plants are about 4 cm to 5 cm apart. Thin daikon varieties to 10 cm apart.

Sow at any time of year, but development will be faster in warm weather.

Minimum soil temperature needed for germination: 10°C.

Soil

Most soils are suitable, with daikon varieties needing deeper, more friable soil because of their longer roots. Neutral to slightly acid soil is preferred with a pH of 6 to 7. Keep moist during hot weather for rapid even growth. Intermittent watering might cause roots to split. Radishes have modest fertiliser needs and will do well without extra fertilising where a previous crop has been well fed.

Use
Most radishes are eaten raw in salads, but daikon or Oriental varieties grow larger and are eaten cooked in stews and stir-fries. Young leaves of all varieties are edible.

Nutrition
Radishes are a good source of vitamin C; surprisingly, the leaves contain six times the amount found in the roots. They also contain calcium, molybdenum and folic acid. Daikons are especially high in potassium and copper.

Harvest and store
Harvest salad varieties in five or six weeks. If you like them tiny and tender, begin harvesting in about three weeks. Daikon varieties take longer. Radishes will keep in a plastic bag or an airtight container in the refrigerator for at least a week. Daikon varieties might keep up to three weeks.

Save seeds
To save the seeds radishes need to be left in place to flower and form seed pods. Different varieties flowering at the same time can readily cross-pollinate, so only grow one variety in a small garden or organise plantings so that one variety is flowering while another is coming to maturity and being harvested.

Swiss chard in a straw bale bed.

Silverbeet
Beta vulgaris

Silverbeet can be grown year round and produces over an extended period for a valuable supply of greens. Interestingly, it is the same species as beetroot, but without the edible root bulb. Observant readers will have noticed that the two plants have the same botanical name. Several different varieties are available, with the coloured-leaf type making a very decorative effect in the vegie garden.

Silverbeet and Swiss chard in an aquaponics bed.

Varieties with coloured leaves and stems are usually referred to in Australia as Swiss chard or rainbow chard.

It is a biennial, growing over two years and usually flowering and seeding in the second year. However, frosty weather in winter will often precipitate flower and seed formation in spring. If you live in a frosty area, sowing in spring or autumn will extend the productive life of your silverbeet.

Sow

Silverbeet can be sown at most times of the year except during the coldest months. It is quite easy to grow from seed sown directly in the ground, but can be bought as seedlings in punnets. Seeds are large enough to handle individually, so can be dropped into a shallow furrow about 10 cm apart. Rake or push soil over the seeds and firm down. Keep the soil damp until seed germinates. A light sprinkle of mulch will help conserve soil moisture.

In cool climates sow from August to February, in warm climates from July to March and in hot climates from April to July.

Minimum soil temperature needed for germination: 12°C.

Soil

Silverbeet is a heavy feeder so the soil needs to be well prepared with compost and decayed manure. If growing from seed, rake over the soil to break up any lumps. Silverbeet does not like acid soil and the preferred pH is 6.5 to 7. If your soil is acidic, sprinkle lime or dolomite a week or two before planting and water it in well. For continuous growth keep plants well-watered and use a liquid fertiliser such as fish emulsion every few weeks. Once plants are established, mulch will help keep moisture in the soil. Water stress can cause plants to bolt to seed.

Use

Stems and leaves are eaten lightly boiled or steamed, either as a side dish or in stir-fries. If using both sections together, partially cook the stems first and throw the chopped leaves in after a couple of minutes. Young leaves can be eaten raw in salads.

Nutrition

Silverbeet/chard is a powerhouse of nutrients, containing large amounts of vitamins K, A, C and E and smaller but still useful amounts of vitamins B1, B2, B3, B5 and B6. In addition, it contains magnesium, manganese, potassium, iron, copper, calcium, zinc, folate and biotin.

Harvest and store

Cut leaves as required. Smaller leaves are tenderer than large ones. Once cut, leaves can be wrapped in plastic and stored in the refrigerator for up to a week, but if you have it growing in the garden you only need to cut as much as you intend to use at one time.

Save seeds

This is another plant that needs to be left in situ to flower and seed. It can take a long time and require a large area. I think it is one of the plants less suitable for seed saving in a small garden. If you do want to save seeds, plants need to be kept separate from beetroot and other silverbeet or chard varieties, or ensure they are flowering at different times.

Others to try

Spinach

Spinacea oleracea

Spinach and silverbeet are often thought to be different names for the same plant. In fact, spinach, properly known as English spinach, is a different genus and species. The leaves are smaller and less crinkly than those of silverbeet. It is more suited to cool climates, is an annual rather than a biennial and leaves are ready to harvest quite quickly. Soil and water needs are similar to silverbeet. Its nutritional properties are similar to those of silverbeet, but the nutrient content is even higher.

In cool climates plant it from February to August, in warm climates from February to June and in hot climates from April to June.

Minimum soil temperature needed for germination is 10°C.

Ceylon spinach

Basella rubra

Anyone living in the tropics or subtropics might find that Ceylon or Malabar spinach is more suited to their climate than are either silverbeet or English spinach. It is a perennial climbing vine growing to about two metres high with thick dark green leaves that can be harvested at any time. It needs fertile soil and plenty of water, is heat-tolerant and frost sensitive, especially when young.

Ceylon spinach is used in similar ways to silverbeet and English spinach. It is high in vitamins A and C, calcium and iron.

Tomato

Lycopersicum esculentum

The thought of eating fresh homegrown tomatoes is probably the incentive that convinces many people to become vegetable growers. Once you have tried homegrown, you will realise how lacking in taste and texture most commercially available tomatoes are. More than anything else, it seems, tomatoes are grown for consistent size, uniformity of ripening and toughness to withstand transportation without damage. Taste appears to have been forgotten. Your

Tomatoes growing in an EarthBox®. (Photo courtesy EarthBox Australia)

Tomatoes growing in an aquaponics bed.

homegrown tomatoes might have a few blemishes, they might be of different sizes and shapes and ripen inconsistently, but the taste will astonish you.

There are so many varieties to choose from, not all of them red. You can choose yellow, purple, black, orange, green stripes and orange stripes. Shapes and sizes are equally varied.

Tomatoes are classified in a couple of different ways. The first is whether they are early, mid or late season (how soon after planting they begin to produce fruit). The second is by size and growth habit, whether they are dwarf, determinate or indeterminate. Dwarf plants grow into a small bush that does not need staking. Determinate plants stop growing once a certain number of nodes has been reached, so plant height is more or less predetermined. Indeterminate plants tend to grow taller and have more of a sprawling growth habit, their height not being limited by the number of nodes produced.

None of this needs to concern the home-grower unduly. Just choose a variety or two that appeals to you. For growing in pots, dwarf varieties might be preferred; however, it is quite easy to place a wire frame over the pot to contain the tomato so it does not fall over. Any tomatoes other than dwarfs will benefit from staking of some sort. I prefer to use wire frames/cages with the tomatoes growing inside. It is very common for tomatoes tied to stakes to fall over with the weight of fruit and/or in strong winds and break where they are tied. The cages look neater in the garden as well.

Early season varieties: many of the smaller tomato fruits fall into this category, including 'Brown Berry', 'Galapagos', 'Red Fig', 'Beam's Yellow Pear' and 'Green Grape'. Medium-sized fruits include 'Ida Gold', 'Tommy Toe', 'Tigerella', 'Black Zebra' and 'Purple Russian'. Two good early varieties that are also dwarfs, therefore very suitable for pot growing, are 'Siberian' (which is also cold-tolerant) and 'Principe Borghese' (good for drying).

Mid season varieties: 'Green Zebra', 'Black Russian', 'Black Krim', 'Hungarian Heart' and 'Grosse Lisse'.

Late season varieties: 'Mortgage Lifter' and 'Brandywine'.

Sow

Buy seedlings in punnets or grow your own from seeds germinated indoors. Advanced tomato plants are widely available in individual pots, many of these are grafted and claimed to produce more prolifically than ungrafted plants. A test some years ago by Digger's Seeds compared unpruned seedlings of 'Grosse Lisse' (Australia's most popular tomato) with grafted plants. The surprising finding was that the unpruned seedlings produced almost double the weight of fruit of the grafted plants.

Another surprise was that unpruned plants of 'Grosse Lisse' and 'Tigerella' far out-yielded pruned plants, which puts paid to the common myth that you need to pinch out lateral growths (those that form in the 'V' where the side branch meets the main stem) to increase productivity.

Open-pollinated, or heirloom, varieties have been found to out-yield some common popular hybrids.

In cool climates sow from September to December, in warm climates from August to December and in hot climates from March to June. Tomatoes are sun lovers and frost-sensitive, so you need to wait until all danger of frost in your area has passed before planting them in the open garden. If you have a frost-protected spot such as a north-facing brick wall, it is possible to start them in pots near the wall and move them into a more open position later, or transplant from the pot into the ground. In areas with short summers, it is wise to avoid late season varieties that might not have time to ripen.

Minimum soil temperature needed for germination: 15°C.

When plants are ready to go into the open garden, choose a spot in full sun and with enough wind to ensure pollination of flowers. Tomato flowers depend largely on wind for pollination, so if the area is too well protected, flowering and fruit set will be limited. However, if it is too windy, plants are prone to breaking, especially once they are laden with fruit. Flavour intensity can be reduced in cool weather or if tomatoes are planted in the shade, but in very hot areas, some shade during the afternoon will reduce plant stress and water consumption. Tomatoes must be kept well watered. Inconsistent watering (along with low soil pH) is a contributor to a condition known as blossom end rot. Mulch well to conserve soil moisture.

Soil

Tomatoes need deep, fertile, well-drained soil. Prepare the soil well several weeks before planting by digging in decomposed manure, compost or worm castings, or a mixture of all three. Pelletised manure is a good alternative if other products are not available. If your soil is already fertile, leave the manure application until after the first flowers form, otherwise the plants could produce lush leaf growth at the expense of flowers.

Tomatoes do not like acid soil, which can contribute to 'blossom end rot' where the bottom part of the fruit rots. Test the pH and lime the soil before planting if the pH is lower than 5.5.

Tomatoes can be planted deeply in the soil. Break off the lower leaves and plant so the soil comes to above where they were. This encourages roots to form from the former leaf nodes and the plant will be more stable in the ground. Some people plant with only the top leaves above the soil, but if conditions are cool and damp, the stems could rot before roots form.

Use

The small-fruit varieties are most often used in salads. However, any tomatoes can be eaten raw or cooked in a variety of ways. When fruit is prolific use it for juice, or freeze, dry or bottle it.

Nutrition

Tomatoes are very rich in vitamins A and K and contain many other beneficial nutrients, including vitamins B1, B2, B3, B5, B6 and E as well as molybdenum, potassium, manganese, chromium, folate, copper, magnesium, phosphorus, iron and protein.

They also contain the phytonutrient lycopene, which has antioxidant, cancer-reducing properties and is beneficial in reducing the incidence of heart disease. Research has found that tomato and broccoli eaten together are even more beneficial. The lycopene is more concentrated in tomatoes that have been cooked to a paste or sauce, but broccoli's beneficial effects are reduced if it is overcooked and it is best eaten lightly steamed.

Harvest and store

Early season tomatoes might be ready to harvest in about eight to 10 weeks, mid season in 10 to 12 weeks and late season in 12 to 14 weeks, depending on conditions in your area. Production will be quicker in warmer weather than it will be if you try to plant out too early when night temperatures fall too low.

Tomatoes taste better if left to fully ripen on the plant; however, often it is necessary to harvest them unripe to beat pests and predators, including birds and possums. As long as a tinge of colour is showing, the fruits will ripen inside at room temperature before being stored in the refrigerator.

There are numerous ways of preserving the harvest if you have plenty. I think the easiest and most versatile is to pulp a quantity, bring it to the boil and cook for a few minutes, or long enough to reduce the liquid and concentrate the flavour, then cool and freeze in meal-sized amounts. The frozen pulp can be used in soups, pasta sauces, and to flavour just about any winter meal.

Save seeds

Choose a few of the best fruits and allow them to fully ripen on the plant. Perhaps tie a net or bag over them if you think it is possible they will be mistakenly harvested by others or devoured by pests. Squeeze the pulp into a sieve and wash the flesh from the seeds. Leave them to dry on absorbent paper before storing in an airtight container. If you grow more than one variety, either stagger planting so they are flowering at different times or have them in different areas of the garden. Tomatoes are largely self-pollinating so the chance of cross-pollination is slight.

FRUITS

The number of fruits that can be grown in small gardens has increased dramatically with the widespread availability of plants grafted onto dwarfing rootstock and those specifically bred to be small. Even mangos, mulberries, pears and avocados, which usually mature to be large trees, can now be bought as dwarf plants. This means they are very suited to growing in pots or in many small spots around the garden. There is no longer any excuse that you 'don't have room' to grow fruit. If you have a garden of any size, or a balcony, verandah or rooftop, you can grow fruit.

The fruits I have chosen to describe offer a wide variety of choices to suit most locations in the garden, sun or shade, and most climates. If you are very short on space, try growing trees espalier-style on a lattice, or choose plants that have a naturally climbing habit and grow them against a fence or on a specially constructed arbour.

Fruits that are generally considered to be suited to tropical or subtropical areas will grow in temperate locations if a suitable frost-free microclimate is available, but they might never produce as well as they would in their preferred habitat. People with large gardens might have space to experiment with plants outside their climate zone; those with small gardens will find that choosing plants suited to their climate ensures greater productivity, and usually less maintenance.

Maximise your space efficiency by growing smaller bushes that prefer dappled shade in pots under the canopy of larger trees and encouraging climbing plants to take up vertical space. Plant fruits that require more care and frequent harvesting, such as strawberries, closer to the house.

If you have space for a designated 'orchard', try growing green manure crops under the trees and mowing the crop to both mulch and fertilise the fruit trees. Poultry pecking around the ground in the orchard will help control pests and fertilise the trees. Do make sure they cannot scratch around the base of the trees and cause root damage, or even scratch out young plants.

Acerola

Malpighia glabra

Also commonly called Barbados cherry, the acerola is a plant for tropical and subtropical areas. Young plants are frost-tender, but when mature they tolerate colder temperatures. Make sure newly planted acerolas have frost and wind protection. Mulch well to conserve soil moisture and fertilise with decomposed manure spread under the mulch in early spring and summer. Keep well watered during dry times, especially during flowering and fruiting.

The plant grows from three to four metres high and is a bushy decorative shrub with glossy dark green leaves. Prune acerolas in autumn, after the harvest, by thinning the top growth to keep the plant bushy and compact.

The fruit is bright red and cherry-like with a thin skin. The flavour can vary in tartness depending on variety and stage of ripeness. When ripe it is said to have a good balance of acid and sweetness and be similar to an apple in taste. Fruits are very high in vitamin C, containing as much as 50 times that of an orange; however, the vitamin C content is said to be highest in the tart, unripe fruit. The fruit is eaten raw or can be made into jam or jelly.

Plants usually begin to bear fruit over an extended period from spring to autumn in the second year. Harvest when deep red and eat within a day or two; this fruit does not store well. Unripe fruit will keep in the fridge for up to a week or the juice can be frozen.

Varieties to look for that produce sweet fruit are 'California Honey', 'Florida Sweet' and 'B17'.

Apple
Malus domestica

Though apples are not usually expensive to buy, you can't beat the flavour of a homegrown crunchy apple. Many varieties are available as dwarfs, including the favourites 'Granny Smith', 'Gravenstein' and 'Snow'. As well, there is the specially bred 'Ballerina'

A variety of apples ready to eat.

apple with its columnar growth habit that makes it ideal to grow along a path, as a hedge or in a narrow bed. Dwarf apples are suited to growing in pots or small spaces and lend themselves very well to espaliering against a wall.

Apple trees can withstand severe frosts; indeed, for the flower buds to form and mature properly most varieties need from 1000 to 2000 hours per year of temperatures below 10°C. If you live in warmer climes and love apples, don't despair, there are a few cultivars with a lower chilling requirement. Some that could suit include 'Tropic Sweet', 'Anna', 'Dorsett Golden' and 'Granny Smith'.

Another fact that needs to be kept in mind when buying apple trees is that most varieties will be more productive if they have cross-pollinated with another. This need not cause too much concern as there are plenty of apple trees around in most locations, making it highly likely that the bees pollinating your apple blossoms have already visited others nearby. Pollen from 'Jonathon' blossoms will

Apple tree with hoops in place to be netted.

pollinate nearly any other variety. 'Gravenstein' and 'Mutsu' varieties do not self-pollinate, so you will need to ensure that there is a different variety nearby before buying either of these.

Apple trees are usually bought open-rooted in the winter when they are deciduous. It is best to have your hole or pot prepared so they can be planted as soon as you get them home. However, if you are not able to plant them straight away, keep them in damp sawdust, or loosely cover the roots with soil in a corner of the garden and keep the spot moist until planting.

Make sure new trees are well mulched and the soil is kept moist. It is important that trees have adequate water when fruit is forming in spring and in early summer (or autumn for late maturing varieties) when next season's buds are developing. A sunny position with afternoon shade in hot areas is preferred. Apples do better in areas with mild summers, so if summers get hot where you are, provide adequate shade by means of an umbrella, shadecloth or leafy nearby tree.

Fertilise with blood and bone with potash, plus any combination of decomposed manure, compost or worm castings in spring and autumn. Pelletised manures are also suitable. Apples need potash, so if you can't get blood and bone with potash it will have to be supplied separately and mixed with the chosen fertiliser. Anyone with an open fire can spread some ash around the root zone under the mulch.

Prune after fruiting and again in winter when the tree is without leaves to clean it up and train it to the shape you want. Remove dead or diseased branches, any growing inward or rubbing against each other and any that are growing in a direction you don't want. Remove old or weak shoots. Apples mainly fruit on spurs that grow off old wood. Old spurs can be thinned out. Cutting back the previous season's growth by about two-thirds will encourage the formation of healthy new fruiting spurs. Cut back to just above a bud that is pointing in the desired direction of growth. Make all pruning cuts diagonal and close to the branch.

While the tree is in leaf it can be lightly pruned to tidy up the shape and remove any dead or damaged areas. Pinch out the leafy growing tips of vigorous lateral branches to encourage a compact shape. A lateral growth is one that forms in the 'V' between a leaf stem and the main branch.

Apricot

Prunus armeniaca

The flavour of homegrown, sun-ripened apricots leaves the commercial version for dead, which is all the reason you need to

Ahh, the flavour of sun-warmed apricots.

grow your own. Grow apricots in full sun and with plenty of airflow around the tree. They are available on dwarfing rootstock or as part of a multi-grafted fruit salad tree. The flowers are self-fertile, so no other tree is needed for pollination.

Apricots have a chilling requirement of about 800 hours and there are no low-chill varieties, so if your area is warmer than this in winter, apricots are not for you. Though the trees are frost-hardy when dormant, flower buds can be damaged by frosts in spring. Choose mid to late fruiting varieties such as 'Goldrich', 'Trevatt', 'Tilton', 'Moorpark' and 'Morocco' if spring frosts are a concern.

If summer temperatures exceed 40°C fruit can be damaged, so provide some shade in extreme heat. If your summers are usually very hot, choose apricot varieties that fruit early, say in late spring or early summer, to avoid fruit ripening in the hottest weather. Some early fruiting varieties are 'Glengarry', 'Caselin' and 'Divinity'.

As with other deciduous trees, plant them in winter when the tree is dormant. Keep the soil moist, especially during flowering and fruiting. Keep watering the tree after harvest to encourage the formation of next season's flower buds.

Apricot trees are best fertilised after fruit is harvested. Use decomposed manures, compost and worm castings. Apricots do not need a high-nitrogen fertiliser so minimise use of blood and bone, pelletised manures and poultry manure.

Apricots form flower buds on one-year-old branches, or, as the tree matures, on spurs growing off older wood. This has repercussions for pruning. If too much of the previous season's growth is removed, there will be little fruit. Leave some one-year-old and some two-year-old shoots. Prune in summer after fruiting and again in autumn or winter, after the leaves fall. Remove dead, diseased, damaged, crowded, crossing or inward growing branches. Vigorous lateral growth can be cut back.

Babaco

Carica pentagona

The babaco is a quick-growing shrub reaching only about 2.5 metres high. Its growth habit is similar to that of the related pawpaw, forming a long thin trunk with a canopy of fleshy leaves at the top. This makes it ideal for narrow areas or corners. It is very productive and the fruit can be eaten unripe (cooked as if it were a vegetable) as well as ripe as a refreshing aromatic raw fruit. The ripe fruit is said to taste like a combination of pineapple, pawpaw and strawberry.

Babaco fruits grow big. (Photo courtesy Happy Earth)

Happy babaco grower Alison Mellor. (Photo courtesy Happy Earth)

Babaco can grow in cooler areas than pawpaw and a subtropical frost-free climate is ideal. Hot, dry summer conditions can cause fruit to become sunburnt or to fall from the tree before it is mature. Deep, well-drained soil with generous amounts of organic matter worked in is necessary. Plants are shallow-rooted so make sure to put them in a wind-protected spot or erect a windbreak.

The ideal planting time is spring. For quick growth and high productivity a spot in full sun is best. Mulch well and spread poultry manure and other organic fertilisers under the mulch, but not against the trunk. Keep well watered during spring and summer, but be aware that boggy soil can cause root rot.

Expect to have ripe fruit to harvest about a year after planting. Ripe fruit eaten straight from the tree will have the most flavour. However, if you have a good harvest and cannot eat it all immediately, pick it when about a third of the fruit is yellow and it will keep for as much as a month, even longer in the refrigerator.

After all fruit is harvested cut the stem back to about 25 cm from the ground and let two shoots grow to produce next season's bounty.

Banana

Musa sapientrum

Bananas are an important commercial crop in tropical and subtropical locations and, to control the possible spread of diseases, there are restrictions on backyard growing in some

Bananas are a popular crop in tropical areas.

states. There are quarantine areas, a permit (free) is needed to plant them in residential areas, residential growers can have no more than 10 plants and the varieties you can plant are limited. For more detailed information about these matters and to see whether or not these restrictions apply in your area contact your nearest Department of Primary Industries office. (For Queensland, the state most likely to be affected, ph: 13-25-23 or visit: www.dpi.qld.gov.au.)

In spite of the above, bananas are a very popular home fruit tree in tropical areas. They take up little space, the fruit is delicious and very nutritious and, given the right climate and soil, they are easy to grow. They prefer a hot, wet tropical climate, with wind protection and definitely no frosts. Cold damage can occur if the temperature drops below 5°C.

Deep, well-drained and very fertile soil is needed with plenty of organic matter worked in. The preferred pH is from 5.5 to 6.5, so if your soil is more acid than this, add some lime or dolomite. Bananas need a lot of water and fertiliser. Keep the soil damp by mulching, and a couple of months after planting begin to regularly spread organic fertiliser under the mulch (poultry manure is often recommended).

Buy your first plant from a certified nursery to avoid spreading diseases. After this, propagate from suckers produced by mature plants. You can either remove suckers from the plant, to move your banana into a new area, or let one or two strong suckers develop from each mature plant and remove the old plant by cutting it to ground level once fruit has been harvested. If you leave mature plants they will keep spreading and be unproductive; each stem fruits only once. Plant a new sucker about 40 cm deep and do not water it for the first two weeks unless the weather is dry. Suckers are prone to rot if the soil becomes waterlogged.

In ideal conditions flowers form after six or eight months and the fruit is ready to harvest up to five months later. To protect fruit from pests such as fruit fly and encourage faster development you can tie a green plastic bag over each bunch of fruit a few weeks after fruit formation. Alternatively, wrap a wire netting cage around each bunch, leaving plenty of space for growth, and cover it with bird or fishing net. Cut the bunch from the tree about 30 cm above the first hand of bananas when the top fruits begin to yellow. It can then be hung in a cool spot to finish ripening. Remove fruit from the bunch as it changes colour. A well-fertilised and watered plant can produce a hand of bananas with 13 dozen or more fruit on it.

Regular consumption of bananas might reduce your risk of kidney cancer. A 13-year

Swedish study of 61 000 women aged from 40 to 76 found that eating five bananas a week reduced the incidence of kidney cancer by half. Eating two bananas a week reduced the risk by one-third.

Black sapote

Diospyros dignya

Also known as black persimmon, this small tree is a favourite in tropical and subtropical areas for its chocolate-like flavour; in fact, it is often known as 'chocolate pudding fruit', though some say the chocolate taste is imaginary and influenced by the sweetness and colour of the flesh. The fruit has green skin, even when ripe, and chocolate brown flesh. The most suitable cultivar for small spaces is 'Cocktail', which grows from three to four metres high and produces small oval-shaped fruit.

Plant your black sapote in a sunny spot protected from strong winds into well-prepared soil. Add dolomite or lime if your soil is acidic. Keep the plant mulched to conserve soil moisture. Fertilise after harvest each year by spreading decomposed manure under the mulch.

Black sapotes do not tolerate frost and young trees will die if exposed to temperatures below zero. Mature trees might survive a temperature as low as −2°C, but are likely to be badly damaged. This is not a plant for temperate zones or any areas subject to frost.

Fruit is usually ready to harvest from autumn to early spring. It remains firm on the tree. A guide as to when fruit is ready to pick is when the petals on top of the fruit begin to lift. Once harvested, fruit will ripen in a week or two at room temperature, often suddenly. It will store for several weeks in the refrigerator. Eat when flesh is soft. It can be enjoyed fresh, frozen for later use, or made into a milkshake. The fruit is high in vitamin C, containing perhaps four times as much as is found in oranges.

When the tree is two years old cut back the main stem (central leader) to encourage more fruiting lateral branches to form. This pruning also lets light into the centre of the tree and stops it from growing too tall.

Blueberry

Vaccinium spp.

There are blueberry cultivars suited to most areas of Australia. People in warmer zones need to look for low-chill cultivars such as 'Misty', 'Sharpblue' and 'Biloxi'. They are deciduous shrubs growing to only about two metres high and spreading to 1.5 metres, so make an ideal fruit for pots or small spots in the garden.

Blueberries are ideal for pots or small spots.

If your soil is acid, about pH 5.5, and not heavy clay, blueberries will probably thrive. Lower the pH, if necessary, by digging in acidic material such as peat, cocopeat, leaf mould, pine needles or any other organic matter that is low in pH. If unsure, test the pH with a kit from a nursery or department store.

Blueberries need loose friable soil and are unlikely to survive in heavy clay. If your garden soil is clay, it is preferable to grow blueberries in pots, enriching the potting mixture with acidic organic matter (see above).

If planting into the ground, prepare the planting hole as far in advance as you can with a combination of compost, decomposed manure and vermicompost. Do not add lime. Mulch with an acidic material. Fertilise twice a year, after the harvest and in spring before flower buds open, by spreading decomposed poultry manure under the mulch.

Blueberries begin to flower in early spring and fruit is usually ready to harvest from late spring to early summer, depending on where you live and the variety you have planted. The fruit forms in clusters. The largest and darkest in colour should be picked every couple of days. Protect the ripening berries from hungry birds by throwing a net over the bush when they are still green.

Fruit can be eaten raw when deep blue in colour. It can take a week or more for the flavour to fully develop once the fruit looks ripe, so experiment by picking a berry at a time until you know when they are ready. Berries will keep for a week or more in the fridge or freeze easily.

Keep the plant compact by pinching out the growing tips in summer, after the harvest. In winter remove any weak, damaged or cross-over branches and any growing into the centre of the bush. The bush grows naturally into somewhat of a 'V' shape, with suckers continually growing from the crown. Flowers are produced from near the tips of these suckers in the second year. Lower buds produce lateral branches that flower near the tips in the second year. After a few years each sucker becomes weaker and should be cut off at the base or to a strong side shoot.

Feijoa

Feijoa sellowiana

Often known as pineapple guava because of a perceived resemblance in the flavour, the feijoa has a reputation as being a very hardy fruiting plant. It is a shrub or small tree, growing to about four metres high. It is often regarded as a subtropical plant, yet will survive frosts as low as −10°C. It is drought-tolerant, but, of course, is more productive when irrigated. Feijoa is an attractive plant with beautiful flowers (the petals of which are fragrant and edible) and can be kept trimmed to make a good windbreak hedge.

Feijoas tolerate a wide range of soil types, but need good drainage. A slightly acid pH is preferred, so do not lime the soil unless it is very acidic. The plant needs to be well fertilised to fruit productively. Prepare the spot with compost and decomposed manure; poultry manure is preferred because of its higher nitrogen content. Keep well mulched so the soil remains damp and add rotted or pelletised poultry manure under the mulch in late winter and autumn. Keep the plant well watered until it is established and especially during flowering and fruiting.

Despite the advice in the preceding paragraph, I think feijoas must be one of the most forgiving fruit trees. I had one in a previous garden that produced quite prolifically, though fruits were on the small side. It was seldom irrigated or fertilised past the first summer, though it was always kept mulched and, no doubt, received nutrients from the decomposing material.

Fruit forms on new growth, so prune plants quite hard each year. If left unpruned, plants will only fruit at the tops of long woody stems. Train to any shape that suits you, but one main trunk with from four to six arms will give an open vase shape with good aeration and light penetration in the centre.

Flowers form in summer and the petals make an unusual sweet addition to salads. Fruit will mature throughout autumn and fall to the ground as it ripens. A sheet of shadecloth or similar around the tree at this time will make fruit collection easier. Fruit keeps well in the refrigerator for a month or more. Eat it by cutting it in half and scooping out the flesh with a spoon. It is a good component of fruit salad and can be blended into a drink of combined juices.

Strawberry or cherry guava (*Psidium littorale*) is a similar plant (in the same plant family as feijoa, but a different genus), but with smaller, sweeter fruits. It is recommended for subtropical areas, but will tolerate frosts as low as −5°C. There is a yellow-fruited cherry guava with even sweeter fruit, its leaves are a duller green colour and it is reputed to fruit even more prolifically.

Goji berry

Lycium barbarum

The goji berry is a relatively new introduction to Australia, but is rapidly becoming popular because of its reputed health benefits. The berry-like fruits are very high in antioxidants and vitamin C; growers claim 500 times more vitamin C than oranges. In addition, the fruits are a good source of vitamins A, B1, B2, B6 and E and are high in fibre.

Goji berry is a sprawling shrubby deciduous vine that likes to have a trellis or wall to climb up. To grow it in a pot and keep a bushy shape, pinch out the growing tips during summer and prune hard in winter when it is dormant. The plant is drought-tolerant once established and lives from five to eight years. Plants are said to survive temperatures from −27°C to +39°C. They prefer friable, well-drained soil, but have been known to grow in clay soil as long as it is well drained. They will not tolerate waterlogging.

Plant in a full sun position, protected from strong winds, but where there is afternoon shade in very hot weather. Keep well watered during the growing season, especially during hot weather. Mulch soil to keep in the moisture.

The small shiny red berries are oval-shaped and about a centimetre long with many small edible seeds in the centre. Eat them alone or in fruit salads.

Grape
Vitus vinifera

If you like grapes, or want to make your own wine, and have a sunny area and a strong supporting structure for the vine(s) to grow on, there is no reason grapes cannot be grown in a small to medium garden. You need to decide at the start whether the grapes will be for eating or for wine as there are distinct varieties. Wine grapes are generally too tart to eat and eating grapes are unsuitable for winemaking.

You need to choose the variety to suit your climate. Some can tolerate frosts to −10°C when they are dormant, while others have high mildew resistance and are suitable for subtropical humid regions. In general, winters need to be cool, springs wet and summers hot and dry. Some varieties for humid regions include: 'Pink Iona', 'Golden Muscat', 'Lady Patricia', 'Maroo Seedless', 'Chambourcin' (a wine variety), 'Flame Seedless' and 'Isabella Black'.

Gnarled old grapevines at a winery in north-east Victoria.

Vines are usually bought bare-rooted and planted in winter when they are dormant. They do grow easily from cuttings, so if you know someone in your area with a healthy vine this could be a source of cuttings and you would know what you were getting. Please observe restrictions on transport of vines as diseases can be spread and cause disaster for commercial growers.

Vines can be trained to grow over an arbour or pergola, they respond well to espaliering, or can be grown to camouflage a fence or shed. However you grow your vine, remember that they are long-lived and grow to be very heavy, so a strong supporting structure is needed. The trunks of the commercial wine vines in the photo show how thick the branches can become with age. Imagine the weight of vines like that creeping over an arbour!

There are many methods of pruning depending on how you want the vine to grow. For home use, train your vine to grow where and how you want it by cutting back to a bud pointing in the right direction. Grapevines are heavily pruned during winter, often leaving only a few canes or buds from which the next season's growth will develop. The photo shows a common method of pruning commercial vines.

These plants have very deep roots, which makes them good drought survivors; however, lack of water during flowering will dramatically reduce the yield. To prevent fungal diseases a dry climate is usually needed while the fruit is ripening, so water by drippers or other ground-level irrigation rather than by sprinklers. Unless the soil is very sandy and lacking in nutrients, grapevines need little or no fertiliser. If you do fertilise, choose a low-nitrogen product.

Cut the bunches of grapes when they are fully ripe as they do not become any sweeter once harvested. Birds love grapes and will get to them before you do unless you net the vines or cover the individual bunches. After harvesting they will keep for at least a couple of weeks in a cool spot. Try drying grapes to make your own sultanas.

Lemon
Citrus limon

Lemons are so useful in cooking, cleaning and first aid that every garden should have a tree. Now that they are available as dwarf trees and can be grown successfully in pots every garden has space for at least one lemon tree. Quite apart from their useful qualities, lemons, and other citrus trees, are very attractive plants with highly fragrant and edible flowers that are loved by bees and other pollinators.

Lemons have numerous uses in the kitchen and medicine chest.

Lemons can be grown in most areas of Australia, but they are frost-sensitive so choose a protected spot. If your lemon tree is in a pot, it can easily be moved to take advantage of the sun when needed or into shelter when frost is likely. Once established, frost hardiness is increased. Indeed, a straggly lemon tree can often be seen as the sole survivor in the backyard of long-abandoned farms, an indication of the plant's general toughness.

Plant your lemon tree into well-drained soil in a sunny position, but wind protection is appreciated, especially when the plant is young. Fertilise with decomposed poultry and other manures, compost and vermicompost under the mulch. Be sure to keep your tree well mulched as the shallow roots should not be allowed to dry out. Do not cultivate around the tree as damage to roots could occur.

Light pruning to remove straggly growth, cross-over branches and any dead or diseased areas will keep your tree in good health and growing as a dense bush instead of a straggly tree.

Some trees will produce fruit over an extended period, maybe even having more than one flush of fruit and flowers during the year, but the main crop will mature in late winter into spring. Ripe fruit will hang on the tree for some time and can be harvested when required. Pick fruits when still slightly green if you want to store them. Fruits will keep for weeks or months in a refrigerator. Alternatively, juice ripe fruits and store the juice in the freezer in ice cube trays for use in cooking or summer drinks.

There are several lemon varieties available: 'Eureka', 'Lisbon', 'Villa Franca', 'Verna' and

'Meyer'. The latter is a naturally occurring hybrid of a lemon and an orange. The tree is small and thornless, its fruit is sweeter than that of other varieties, it is more frost-resistant and copes well with humidity, making it a good choice for home use. However, if true lemon flavour is needed, in cooking for example, choose another variety.

Other citrus trees are available as dwarf plants. If your family enjoys citrus fruit, or you like to drink freshly squeezed juice, choose some of these: lime (*Citron aurantifolia*), orange (*Citrus sinensis*), pummelo (*Citrus maxima*), grapefruit (*Citrus paradisi*) or mandarin (*Citrus reticulata*).

Passionfruit

Passiflora edulis

It could be worth growing a passionfruit vine for the beauty of the flowers alone. The vine's fast growth and ability to screen a fence, shed or other eyesore, as well as the delicious fruit, make it well worth having. It takes up little vertical space and is easily trained to grow up a trellis or over a pergola or arbour. It is an evergreen plant, so will provide year-round screening, unlike a grapevine, which will only do this service for part of the year. Vines are renowned for being short-lived, so after about five or six years have another one waiting in the wings to replace the original.

Plant a young vine in spring into well-drained soil that has had organic material worked in. Fertilise regularly with a high-nitrogen product such as poultry manure to keep the vine growing vigorously and producing generously. This plant prefers slightly acid to slightly alkaline soil, so you might need to work lime into the prepared planting hole if your soil is very acidic. The roots are spreading, so keep the area under the vine weed free and well mulched. Passionfruit vines are only mildly frost-tolerant, down to about −2°C, and will appreciate some frost protection when young.

Train the vine to grow where and how you want it by tying it to the supporting structure and pinching out the growing tips when it reaches the stage where you want it to spread out along a wire or other support. Each winter cut the vine back very firmly to prevent straggly growth with a lot of dead wood.

In warmer areas the vine could crop nearly all year, with the majority of the fruit being ripe in summer and late winter. In cooler regions, expect to harvest a crop from late summer into autumn. Passionfruits have a hard skin that turns purple when the fruit is ripe. Fruit will fall from the vine and become wrinkled, but are still edible and can be stored for weeks at room temperature. The flesh will become dry if fruit is stored for too long.

Intriguing flowers and delicious fruit make passionfruit vines a popular garden choice.

When the crop is bountiful, the pulp can be scooped from the skin and frozen in ice cube trays for later use.

There is a yellow passionfruit (*Passiflora edulis* var. *flavicarpa*), which is reputed to be more disease-resistant than the common black passionfruit, but is more suited to the subtropics. This variety needs two plants to produce fruit.

The banana passionfruit (*Passiflora mollisima*) is an extremely vigorous, fast-growing vine producing generous crops of yellow, oval-shaped fruits. However, the flavour is quite bland compared to that of other passionfruits and it is so vigorous it will soon take over a small garden. If someone offers you one, refuse politely unless you have a farm-size garden.

Other passionfruits belong to different species and are frost tender, so are best suited to the tropics or subtropics. These include granadilla (*Passiflora quadrangularis*), sweet granadilla (*Passiflora ligularis*) and fragrant granadilla (*Passiflora alata*). Some of these vines produce very large fruits; that of granadilla, for example, can be as much as 30 cm in diameter, so a strong supporting structure is needed and perhaps a net to hold each fruit until it ripens.

Pawpaw

Carica papaya

This species is known as papaya elsewhere in the world and probably only in Australia is *Carica papaya* called pawpaw. It grows as a single-stemmed herbaceous tree, from three to 10 metres high, with a canopy of large,

Pawpaws take up little horizontal space in a small tropical or subtropical garden.

deeply lobed leaves clustered in a spiral at the top. Oval-shaped fruits, often quite large, form at the top of the stem below the leaf cluster.

Though the plant might grow in a protected microclimate in temperate regions, frosts and cold will damage or kill it and fruit quality is likely to be poor. Pawpaw is suited best to tropical and subtropical zones.

Pawpaws are easily grown from seed, but it is impossible to know for sure (though some ingenious theories have been propounded) whether seeds are male or female, so it is recommended to grow a cluster of several seedlings close together. One male plant will pollinate nine females. In female plants, large flowers form close to the trunk. Male flowers grow on stalks about 3 cm long. To complicate matters further, some plants produce both male and female flowers, and this might change on the same plant over time. No matter, just plant a few and see what happens. If you have too many male plants, remove them. Flowers can begin to form when the plant is less than a metre high. This is when you can tell whether they are male or female and discard any you don't want.

To be sure about the type of plant you obtain, you can purchase bisexual pawpaws, which will produce both male and female flowers on the one plant. Look for the cultivars 'Bisexual Yellow', 'Southern Red Bisexual' and 'Solo'.

Plant into well-drained soil prepared with organic matter. Add lime if your soil is acidic. A wind-protected spot is best because plants can be easily damaged when they are top-heavy with fruit. Keep well watered while fruit is forming and mulch around the base to conserve soil moisture. Spread decomposed animal manure under the mulch or use liquid fertiliser made from compost tea, worm juice or fish emulsion every few weeks.

Plants can begin fruiting from 12 to 18 months after planting. Harvest is usually from spring to early autumn. Fruit can be picked just before it is fully ripe and left to ripen at room temperature, but the best flavour is from fruit left on the plant to ripen fully. Ripe fruit is eaten raw or made into preserves; unripe fruit can be cooked and served as a vegetable. Both the flesh and the skin are good meat tenderisers.

It can be challenging to harvest fruit from a tall pawpaw. When the plant is about three years old you can cut it, in spring after the harvest, to a metre or two above the ground.

The white latex exuded by pawpaw plants is a skin irritant, so handle all parts with care.

Peach

Prunus persica

Peach trees can be very productive.

Peaches are one of the smallest of the fruit trees and, with dwarfing varieties now available, are a good choice for small gardens and pot growing. A sun-warmed peach fresh from the tree tastes like a different fruit entirely to most that are commercially available. Peach trees grow quickly and can be very productive.

Trees are planted in winter when they are dormant and should be in the ground as early in the season as possible to allow the roots to

Nectarines are smooth-skinned peaches.

become established before leaf buds open. Plant them in full sun with good air circulation into prepared soil.

Because of their high productivity, peaches need generous fertiliser applications and thrive on more nitrogen than most fruit trees. Spread decomposed poultry manure and/or blood and bone combined with compost or vermicompost under the mulch. Liquid fertiliser applications of compost tea, worm juice or fish emulsion every few weeks during flowering and fruiting will be beneficial.

The tree naturally grows into a vase shape, so prune to follow this, or train the tree(s) espalier style. Fruit is only formed on the last season's growth and the section of branch that fruited will never bear fruit again. This means that branches can be pruned hard each year to stimulate new fruiting growth. Remove each lateral shoot that has already fruited or cut it back to a new lateral shoot along its length. Cut back new growth in summer and do the main pruning when the plant is dormant. Thin out the fruit when it is about 2 cm in diameter, leaving fruits about 10 cm apart so they will grow to a good size.

Many peach varieties have a high chill requirement, with some needing over 700 hours of temperatures below 10°C. Gardeners in warmer locations will need to choose low-chill varieties such as 'Flordaprince', 'Tropic Beauty' and 'China Flat', all of which have a 150-hour chilling requirement.

Fruit tastes sensational when left to ripen on the tree, but the crop is usually so generous you will not be able to eat it all before it goes off. To enjoy the harvest over a longer period, pick the bulk of the fruit when most of it has turned cream or gold and there is a little 'give' to the touch. If the background colour is still mainly green, the peach will not ripen off the tree. Fruit can be left to ripen at room temperature or refrigerated and brought out to ripen a little at a time. You can still leave some on the tree to enjoy fully ripe.

Nectarines are smooth-skinned peaches (*Prunus persica* var. *nectarina*) and are grown in the same way as peaches.

Pineapple
Ananus comosus

Pineapples are fun to grow in any small space and look very decorative. There are rough- and smooth-skinned types and the leaves of the rough-skins are prickly, so avoid planting them near to where children play or too close to pathways. The rough-leaved type is said to produce sweeter fruit. They do need a tropical or subtropical climate, are frost-sensitive and need hot conditions to form flowers and fruit. They are very suitable to grow in pots or spare corners, or start them off in pots for

Pineapple plants are ideal for small spots in the tropics and subtropics.

decorative use and plant into the garden when they are well established. Plants can grow to a metre high, but are often shorter.

Well-drained acid soil is needed. Avoid planting pineapples in heavy clay soil because if the soil remains wet for long periods, plants are likely to die. Prepare soil before planting with decomposed manure or blood and bone. Frequent applications of a liquid fertiliser in the form of compost tea, worm juice, Bokashi liquid or fish emulsion will keep plants growing vigorously and producing tasty fruit.

Propagate from the tops or crowns of fruits you have eaten. Some people recommend leaving the pineapple top to dry out in a cool shady spot for two or three weeks before planting. Strip off a few of the lower leaves and plant pineapple tops about 5 cm deep. Mulch around the plants, but do not let the soil remain too damp or they will rot. Alternatively, pineapples can be propagated from slips or suckers of mature plants. Suckers form at the base of the plant and from the flowering stem, when they are known as slips or pups. If you know someone who grows pineapples, ask them to keep you some suckers for propagation. When growing your own plants, you can leave a sucker or two to develop the next crop, but remove all others. Only leave slips if you want them for propagation. When planting out slips or suckers, plant them about 8 cm deep. Tropical fruit nurseries, of course, are another source of plants.

It is a good idea to weed the area well beforehand and even use weed mat around plants because it can be a tricky job to weed around those prickly leaves.

Plants grown from crowns will take up to three years before fruit is ready to harvest; sucker-grown plants might be ready to eat in half that time. The fruit is ready to pick when it shows a tinge of yellow at the base and feels a little soft to the touch. The fruit will not become any sweeter once it is picked. Ripe fruits do not keep long, so enjoy them as soon as you can.

Plum

Prunus domestica and *Prunus salicina*

The two species of plums grown mainly in Australia are the European (*P. domestica*) and the Japanese (*P. salicina*). In recent years the Japanese species have become more popular and the Europeans, including gages and prune-types, are grown less often. However, many people like the sweeter flavour of such European cultivars as 'Green Gage' and 'Coles Golden Gage'.

In general, the European varieties fruit about a month later than the Japanese (which actually originated in China), are smaller

Luscious blood plums fresh from the tree.

trees with smoother bark, are slightly more frost-hardy, have a higher chilling requirement and tolerate heavier soil. Europeans all have yellow flesh; Japanese can have yellow or red flesh. The red-fleshed varieties are known as blood plums. Europeans should be picked when fully ripe; Japanese can be picked slightly green and will ripen off the tree at room temperature.

A couple of varieties with low-chill requirements that could suit people in warmer areas are 'Gulfruby' and 'Gulfgold'; both are Japanese types and will pollinate each other. Some blood plum varieties (also Japanese) for anyone who prefers red-fleshed plums are 'Elephant Heart', 'Frontier', 'Satsuma' and 'Mariposa'.

Plum trees grow to a maximum height of seven metres and are available on dwarfing rootstock, making them suitable for small gardens or pot growing. Except for cherry plums and the cultivar 'Santa Rosa', plums need a compatible cross-pollinator. Ask about this when you buy your tree. Fruit salad trees (multi-grafts) can have two (or more) compatible varieties grafted onto the one rootstock. Otherwise, in many areas there are enough plum trees around that you won't need to worry about buying two trees.

Plant trees during winter when they are dormant, in a sunny spot with good air circulation. Plum trees do not need heavy fertiliser applications, but prepare the planting hole with compost and well-rotted manure and scatter fertiliser under the tree once a year in spring.

The trees naturally grow into a vase shape. Prune after the harvest and again when the plant is dormant to encourage this shape and remove cross-over and damaged branches. Japanese plums fruit most on one-year-old growth, so prune them quite hard each year to encourage new growth. Europeans need less vigorous pruning.

Fruit flavour is best when plums are picked fully ripe; however, Japanese plums can be harvested slightly unripe and will keep for a few weeks in the refrigerator. They can be eaten fresh, cooked in a variety of ways, bottled or made into jam. Any excess can be cooked lightly and frozen in meal-sized portions.

Raspberry
Rubus idaeus

Raspberries and other similar berry canes are generically termed 'bramble' berries. They are good to grow on a trellis attached to a fence or shed wall. They take up little horizontal space, but can, after a few years, spread by suckers over more area than they originally did, so

Raspberries are delicious straight from the vine.

Bramble berry vines need a vertical supporting structure.

allow for this in your planning, or ruthlessly remove all suckers. They can be grown in a pot placed in a spot where the canes have vertical support as they grow.

Raspberries need as much as 1700 hours of chilling, so are best suited to cool and temperate regions. In warmer areas protection from later afternoon sun will be needed, perhaps from a large tree on the west side.

Raspberries need deep friable soil with plenty of organic matter. Start preparing the soil a month or two before planting if you can by digging in compost, blood and bone and decomposed poultry manure. When planting in a row along a fence or wall, dig a trench in the prepared soil about 15 cm deep and line the bottom with compost. Set the plants in the trench a metre or so apart and backfill around the roots. Spread more compost and decomposed manure over the top and mulch well.

If you are planning to grow raspberries, or any other bramble berries, along a dividing fence from a neighbour, it is a good idea to sink a length of iron about 40 cm deep along the fence line to prevent roots from growing into your neighbour's garden.

Plant canes in June or July and fertilise again in September. Keep plants well watered during dry weather. Tie canes to the wire support as they grow, either singly or in bunches. Once canes reach about two metres long, you can bend them in a semicircle and tie the end to the wire to keep a convenient picking height. The canes grow for the first season and fruit in the second. As soon as possible after the harvest, and certainly by June or July, cut off the old canes, those which have just fruited, close to the ground. There will be new canes growing from the roots, which will be the fruit-bearing canes for next season.

Fruit is usually ready to pick by early December and should be harvested every couple of days until about the end of January. It can be eaten raw or made into jam. To store some for later use, simply wash and dry it and freeze it in meal-sized portions.

There are autumn-bearing raspberries, generically known as everbearers. These produce fruit from first-year canes, so that a cane planted in winter will fruit in the following autumn. They might produce a light summer crop as well. The recommendation is to treat these as annuals, cutting all canes back to ground level in the winter, so new canes will be produced each year and crop from mid-February to April. If you really love raspberries, plant some of each so you are enjoying the berries from December to April. The varieties 'Everbearer' and 'Heritage' are the ones to look for. 'Heritage' has a low chill requirement, about 250 hours, so is a good one to try if you live in a warmer area and love raspberries.

Other bramble berries to try are blackberry (*Rubus* spp.), loganberry, youngberry, marionberry, boysenberry and silvanberry. The latter five are blackberry hybrids. All are treated in a similar manner to raspberries. Blackberries tolerate more heat than do raspberries.

Red Currant
Ribes rubrum

Red currant is a deciduous bush that is ideal to grow in pots or small shady or damp areas of the garden that might not be suited to other fruiting plants, though they will grow in full sun as long as there is afternoon shade. The bush looks very decorative when in fruit.

The red currant bush can grow from 1.5 to 2 metres high with a spread of up to a metre. Protect it from wind because the branches are brittle and easily broken.

The soil needs to be damp and well-drained with plenty of manure and organic matter incorporated at least a few weeks before planting. Keep plants mulched and spread fertiliser under the mulch in autumn and after the harvest.

This is an early ripening fruit and will probably be ready to harvest in mid to late spring. Harvest the whole cluster, not individual berries, by cutting it from the branch at the base when the berries are red and shiny. Birds like the berries, but it is easy to throw a net over the bush for the few weeks before harvest.

Keep the bush in a compact shape by pinching out the growing tips during summer. In winter when the bush is deciduous cut back any tangled or cross-over branches and open up the centre of the bush for good aeration and light penetration. Do not cut stems too far down because next season's fruit forms on the base of one-year-old stems and on spurs of older stems.

The fruit is eaten raw or made into jams, jellies and sauces.

White currants are very similar, the berries are just different in colour and sweeter in flavour.

Black currants (*Ribes nigrum*) have a stronger flavour and many people do not like them raw, but they are good in jams, jellies, sauces and drinks and are high in vitamin C. They can take a sunnier position than red currants, but still need plenty of soil moisture. They should be pruned heavily in winter, leaving shoots about 10 cm long for the next season's crop.

Strawberry
Fragaria × ananassa

Commercially, strawberries are grown on long hills with the soil covered in black plastic. This method warms the soil so fruit production begins earlier, prevents weeds and keeps the fruit clean. In the home garden, however, strawberries can be grown in a number of ways and are one of the most useful fruits for a small area. Grow them in the ground in a dedicated patch, as an edging for vegetable or flower beds, as a ground

An abundant crop of strawberries growing in an EarthBox®. (Photo courtesy EarthBox Australia)

cover under fruit trees or ornamental shrubs, in pots or hanging baskets.

Most people love strawberries, but so do many pests including slugs and snails, earwigs, birds and the family dog. The easiest way to ensure the crop is enjoyed by the human residents is to grow them in tall pots (out of canine reach) or hanging baskets. Use environmentally friendly snail baits or traps to reduce gastropod damage, and nets if birds are a problem. Strawberries are also prone to various fungal diseases. To minimise damage from these, keep good aeration around the plants, remove all diseased leaves as soon as they appear, apply seaweed emulsion regularly and use other organic fungicides as detailed in Chapter 7.

There are numerous varieties to suit all types of climates. Those available in your local nurseries should be ideal for your garden. If you plant two or three different varieties, you will have fruit over a longer time period during spring and summer.

Varieties for Queensland and warmer areas of New South Wales are 'Earlisweet', 'Redlands Crimson' and 'Maroochy Flame'. For New South Wales generally, try 'Naratoga', 'Narabelle' and 'Torrey'. Recommended varieties for Victoria and Tasmania are 'Red Gauntlet', 'Shasta' and 'Tioga'. 'Shasta', 'Torrey' and 'Tioga' yield well if they are planted in summer rather than the more usual time of autumn or early winter. There are new varieties available all the time, so if you love strawberries, experiment to find those that suit your particular situation and taste.

Choose a sunny spot, but afternoon dappled shade will be appreciated in areas where hot summer afternoons can be expected. Prepare the soil with decomposed animal manure and other organic fertilisers. Do not plant in an area where strawberries, raspberries or members of the solanum family (tomatoes, capsicums, potatoes) have been previously grown because of the risk of transmitting a viral disease.

Fertile, well-drained, slightly acid soil is needed. If your soil tends to waterlog in heavy rain, build up mounds or no-dig beds to plant your strawberries in, or put them in pots. Mulch will keep the berries clean and conserve water. Many people recommend using dry or semi-decomposed pine needles as a mulch. The acidity of the pine needles as they rot down and are incorporated in the soil benefits the plants and is said to improve flavour.

If you want to copy the commercial method, build up mounds or hills, prepare the soil and stretch heavy-duty black or clear plastic over the area. Drip irrigation or seeper hose can be laid under the plastic. Cut holes in the plastic to put the plants in. A third of the crown should be above the soil.

In hot climates, plant strawberries in March, warm climates from March to May and cool climates from May to July. Plants should flower from September and fruit will begin to mature in November. It takes from 20 to 35 days from flowering to fruiting, depending on the climate of your area and the particular seasonal conditions. Applications of seaweed liquid fertiliser every two or three weeks during flowering and fruiting are said to increase disease resistance and improve fruit flavour.

Most strawberry plants will produce runners. You want the plants' vigour to be going into fruit production rather than self-propagation during the spring and summer, so remove runners as soon as they form. If you want runners later in the season for propagation purposes, leave them to grow. Alternatively, you might have some plants dedicated to fruit production and some to production of runners for propagation. Do not let those for runners set flowers or fruit, nor those for fruiting form runners.

Most varieties will produce a second crop, the flowers of which begin forming further from the crown as the first crop of fruit is ripening. It is possible to obtain a third crop, depending on the soil and seasonal conditions, by cutting back all leaf growth above the crown in about January, after fruit production tapers off, and fertilising with seaweed emulsion and/or other organic fertilisers. In winter, cut off all leaves again and the plant will regrow from the crown for the next season.

Strawberries are prone to a viral disease called verticillium wilt, so are best removed after the third season and a new lot of plants started in a different area. You can remove first-year suckers and plant them elsewhere. If this is done each year, you are assured of a continuous supply of new plants and should not have to regularly buy them. I keep my own plants going indefinitely this way. However, if your plants lack vigour and show signs of disease, such as malformed fruit, remove them and start again.

Not only do strawberries taste great, they are very good for you, unless you happen to be allergic, as some people are. They are very high in vitamin C and also contain B vitamins, vitamin K, manganese, iodine, potassium, folate, omega 3 fatty acids, magnesium and copper. Eat them raw straight from the plant or store them in the refrigerator for a few days. If you have too many to eat at once, wash, dry and freeze them to make into jam in the winter when the weather is cooler. Frozen strawberries are a refreshing addition to summer champagne drinks or non-alcoholic punch.

Alpine strawberries produce very tiny intensely flavoured fruit over a long period and do not form runners. Mine seem to be hardier all round than the more common large-fruited varieties and are quite drought-tolerant. They are grown from seed and will often self-propagate, but mature plants are easily divided to obtain new ones. I have not found them to be as virus-prone as other strawberries, but this could vary depending on location and growing conditions.

BUSH FOODS

Try to find out the bush foods that grew naturally in your area; these will be the ones to plant in your garden, though many of these plants are quite adaptable. To obtain productive crops, feed, water and mulch bush foods as you would any other food crops, but do not overfertilise, especially with manures. Compost, Bokashi and vermicompost are suitable fertilisers. If you are happy to have a plant that survives tough conditions and might provide you with an occasional nibble, many bush food plants will fit the bill and cope with little watering or other care once established.

There are a number of fruiting small shrubs or ground cover plants that are very suitable for small gardens as well as some that have edible leaves, many more than I have described here. Find a bush food or native plant nursery in your area to ask about plants that might thrive in your garden.

Australian finger lime
Microcitrus australasica

The finger lime, or native lime, is a thorny shrub or small tree originating in the rainforests of subtropical eastern Australia. It grows from three to six metres tall and spreads from one to three metres. In frost-free areas it will grow as far south as Sydney. This plant likes fertile soil with plenty of compost and water and prefers to grow in light shade. The bush is slow growing and will probably not produce fruit until the fourth year. The finger-like fruits are 5 or 6 cm long and can be used as conventional limes. They can be used to make a distinctive-tasting marmalade.

Apple dumpling/common apple berry
Billardiera scandens

This twining plant can be used as a ground cover or trained to grow on an obelisk or

Sweet apple berry twining around an obelisk.

fence. It is found in eastern Australia from Queensland to Tasmania. It grows 0.9 to two metres tall and spreads from 0.6 metres to 1.5 metres.

This hardy plant grows in full sun or light shade. Think of its natural habitat twining along the ground or in the lower branches of eucalypt forests. The tiny berries should be left to ripen fully before being eaten. If birds steal your crop, pick the berries when green and ripen in a paper bag with a banana. The taste has been likened to either stewed 'Granny Smith' apples or kiwi fruit and aniseed.

Two related plants are sweet apple berry (*Billardiera cymosa*) and purple apple berry (*Billardiera longiflora*). Sweet apple berry will survive drier conditions than common apple berry, whereas purple apple berry needs cooler, moister conditions.

Broad-leaf palm lily
Cordyline petiolaris

This is a small strappy plant with glossy green leaves from coastal Queensland rainforests. It grows 40 cm to 80 cm tall with a similar spread. Use the leaves to wrap food parcels in a similar way to vine leaves.

Davidson plum
Davidsonia pruriens

This small to medium tree from the rainforests of northern New South Wales and Queensland grows to about six metres high, but can be taller, and spreads from two to four metres. Its preferred habitat is in a wind-protected warm area under the shade of taller trees, as it grows naturally in the warm temperate to subtropical rainforests. If your location has only occasional light frosts, it might be worth trying, especially when protected from frosts in the early years. It needs fertile soil with plenty of compost. Young trees can be grown in pots in a courtyard to keep them sheltered from strong winds, frosts and harsh afternoon sun.

The purple, plum-sized fruit has an intense sourish flavour and is used sparingly to flavour desserts. The fruits are covered in fine hairs, which must be scrubbed off before the fruit is eaten. Some people are allergic to the hairs, so wear gloves when handling them. When ripe enough to eat, the fruit begins to fall from the tree. Serve it stewed with your chosen sweetener or make it into jam or jelly.

Large kangaroo apple
Solanum laciniatum

This evergreen shrub is native to south-eastern Australia and New Zealand and is usually found in moist, cool areas. It grows from 1.5 to three metres tall and spreads from two to three metres. The fruit, which is really more of a vegetable in taste, must be very ripe and a deep orange-red colour before being eaten. It can be used in a similar way to tomato or eggplant, made into chutneys and sauces, or stewed as a dessert.

Bush tomato (*Solanum centrale*) and green bush tomato (*Solanum chipendalei*) are similar in appearance and use, but occur naturally in more arid conditions. They are smaller, more straggly shrubs and the fruits are smaller as

Fruit of the kangaroo apple must be very ripe before being eaten.

well. The fruits can be left to dry on the shrub, when they look like sultanas or raisins. Bush tomato fruits can be eaten with the seeds, but the seeds of green bush tomato are bitter and poisonous and must be removed.

Lemon myrtle

Backhousia citriodora

This small tree is native to coastal temperate to subtropical rainforests from southern New South Wales to Queensland. It grows from three to eight metres tall and spreads from two to five metres. It needs fertile well-drained soil in a warm sheltered spot and grows well in the shade of taller trees. It is frost-sensitive.

The aromatic leaves are used as flavouring for Asian dishes, fish or desserts and are steeped to make herbal tea. The leaves can be used fresh, dried or crushed to a powder. The seeds and flowers are used to make tea as well, usually mixed in with a few leaves.

Lemon-scented tea-tree

Leptospermum petersonii

This shrub or small tree is found on the east coast of Australia in the wet temperate to subtropical rainforests. It grows three to eight metres tall and spreads three or more metres. The leaves are steeped, either mixed with other teas or by themselves, to make a lemon-flavoured tea.

Lilly pilly

Acmena and *Syzigium* spp.

There are dozens of species of lilly pillies and all have edible fruit, though many grow into trees that are too large for a small garden. However, there are some attractive small trees that only grow two to three metres tall. I have a few *Syzigium australe*, 'Orange Twist', trees along one side of the driveway. They have glossy green leaves with orange new growth and produce pretty bunches of purple berries.

Lilly pillies often grow naturally near water courses, so they might not be suitable for the driest part of the garden, but with fertile, well-mulched soil, they should thrive in most gardens.

The berries can be eaten raw, but are very acidic and are best cooked with some sweetener, as in jams, jellies or sauces. There were some large trees growing in a supermarket carpark in my area. Each year I would see a couple out with their buckets harvesting the crop. I did wonder about lead and other possible contaminants in the berries, but now the trees have been removed.

Use midgenberry as a ground cover.

I suppose the fallen berries made too much mess.

Midgenberry/midjin/midyimberry

Austromyrtus dulcis

An attractive spreading shrub or ground cover, this plant is found in a limited coastal area of southern Queensland and northern New South Wales. It grows from 0.3 to 1.2 metres tall and spreads from one to three metres. It is very adaptable, but prefers to grow in compost-enriched soil in a shady spot sheltered from winds. It needs to be kept well-watered and mulched when young, is slow growing and will probably not produce much fruit until the third year, after which crops can be prolific. The plant is frost-resistant.

The grey/mauve fruit is delicious, but soft and easily bruised when ripe, so must be handled carefully. Eat it fresh, make jam or bake it into pies with other fruit such as apples.

Muntries/muntari

Kunzea pomifera

A very low-growing shrub suitable as a ground cover, muntries is found in limited coastal areas of southern Australia from Yorke Peninsula to the Glenelg River in South Australia and in the Victorian Mallee. It grows to only about 10 cm high and spreads from 0.9 to two metres. This hardy plant is frost-resistant and will tolerate salinity, strong winds and alkaline soil. Grow it in full sun. Fertilise plants with compost, vermicompost or a sprinkle of blood and bone.

The purple-red ripe berries are said to have the taste and texture of dried apples. Eat the

New leaves are a bronzy pink colour.

Another useful ground cover with edible berries.

Attractive leaf pattern of muntries.

Native raspberry is related to the familiar cultivated variety. (Photo courtesy Happy Earth)

berries fresh, or they can be dried, frozen, stewed or made into jam or chutney. Mix them with other fruits to incorporate into pies.

Native ginger

Alpinia coerulea

This clumping plant has soft, thick lance-shaped leaves growing from an underground rhizome. Native ginger is found growing as an understorey plant on the east coast from the tropics to almost Sydney. It grows 1.2 to two metres tall and spreads over two metres. It prefers a moist shady location under larger plants. White flowers are formed on spikes and followed by blue berry-like fruits.

Many parts of the plant are edible. The pith inside the fruit has a lemony taste. The young root tips can be used as a ginger substitute. Aboriginals wrapped meat in the leaves before cooking it in an earth oven. The gingery tasting seed pods are used as a spice or breath freshener.

Native raspberry

Rubus parvifolius

There are several species of native raspberries, which are closely related to the cultivated raspberry. This shrub is sometimes prostrate and found in both eastern Australia from Queensland to Victoria and in south-east Asia. It grows from 0.3 to 0.9 metres tall and spreads from 0.9 to three metres. It is best tied to a trellis, or otherwise trained to grow vertically.

Berries are similar to but usually smaller than those of cultivated raspberries and can be eaten fresh, frozen, or made into sauces and jams.

Prickly currant bush

Coprosma quadrifolia

This shrub is found in moist forests and near streams in south-eastern Australia. It can grow to about four metres tall with a spread of 1.5 metres. It is very hardy, either in shade or a

Prickly currant bush is a hardy attractive shrub.

sunny location. The small greenish flowers produced in spring become small, bright red berries in summer, but you need both male and female plants for fruit production.

Warrigal greens
Tetragonia tetragoniodes

Also known as New Zealand spinach, this prostrate spreading perennial is widespread in Australia and New Zealand, thriving in climates from temperate to tropical, and is one of the better known and more widely used bush foods. It is said to be the first native food plant from Australia to be introduced into Europe. The plant grows from 15 cm to 30 cm tall and spreads from 60 cm to 100 cm, though under favourable conditions it just wants to keep on spreading.

The dark green, arrowhead-shaped leaves are used as a spinach-like vegetable. It is best to lightly boil the leaves before eating them to remove the oxalate content, which is mildly toxic.

Warrigal greens are easy to grow from seed, are one of the most drought-tolerant vegetables, are ready to start picking in eight to 10 weeks, and keep continuously producing for months. My plants in a previous garden died back in winter, but always regrew in spring, whether from roots in the soil or from self-propagated seeds I am unsure; perhaps it was both.

This young plant will spread and spread.

Yam daisy/murnong
Microseris scapigera

The yam daisy is a small plant, similar to the dandelion in shape and flower. It was once widespread in temperate regions of south-eastern Australia where it grew in grassland and open forest. It will grow in any well-drained soil, but bigger tubers, the part eaten, will be produced in soil that has been enriched with compost or decomposed manure.

The tuberous roots are bitter when raw, somewhat like a radish in taste, but become sweet when slow-roasted or boiled and eaten as a vegetable similar to spicy sweet potato. Tubers can be dug up after the flowers die off, until the plant begins to resprout in autumn.

HERBS AND FLOWERS

Herbs and flowers are used to add flavour to foods and garnish them to make a meal more visually attractive. They can transform a meal from tasty and nourishing to superb. Most gardens will probably already have some of these useful plants. They are so easy to grow; if you think you don't have time or space for a food garden, try some herbs in pots to get you started. Most of the herbs have medicinal properties that they have long been valued for. If you become interested in this aspect, it will bring a new dimension to your food garden.

Let your preferred food style be your guide to choosing which herbs and flowers to grow. For Mediterranean food grow parsley, oregano, thyme, basil and garlic. For Asian food grow coriander, dill and lemon verbena. Grow rosemary and mint to flavour roast meats, and bay and sage for stews.

You probably already have some edible flowers in the garden, which can be used to garnish and add interest and flavour to your cooking. Roses, nasturtiums, fuchsias, pinks, lavender and violets are some of the commonly planted flowers that can be eaten. In addition, the flowers of many herbs and vegetables are edible, adding to their usefulness; these include zucchinis, chives, rocket, rosemary, basil, elder, fennel and lemon verbena. Even the flowers of some weeds such as dandelion, chicory and red clover can be eaten. Be aware that not all flowers are edible and some are quite poisonous, so be certain to identify plants correctly before eating their flowers, or any other part.

Basil, sweet

Ocimum basilicum

Sweet basil is a very fragrant annual plant growing to about 60 cm tall. It is easily grown from seeds or widely available at seedling stage from nurseries. In hot climates it might grow throughout the year, but for most areas it is a spring–summer crop. Grow it in pots or

Nothing enhances the flavour of tomato dishes like basil.

garden beds. Use it to flavour salads, vegetables, pasta or fish dishes. It is especially complementary to any dish containing tomatoes and is the essential ingredient in basil pesto.

This herb needs light well-drained soil and is frost tender, so do not plant it out in the garden until frosts are finished in your location. You can start some plants in pots in a protected spot and plant them in the ground later if required. When the plant begins to flower, pinch off the flower heads to keep good leaf growth for a longer period.

Leafy stalks can be cut and dried on wire mesh. I often drape stems over a clothes horse in an airy spot out of direct sunlight to dry them. Crumble dried leaves into an airtight jar to have a supply of this fragrant herb over winter.

In addition to its culinary uses, basil is valued as an insect repellent. Plant it among vegies to repel pests or in a pot near doorways to keep flies away.

There are several different basil varieties to choose from. Bush basil (*Ocimum minimum*) is a smaller plant than sweet basil. Purple basil (*Ocimum basilicum purpureum*) has purple or pinkish leaves and is an attractive fragrant plant, but the flavour is not very pleasant. There is a plant sold as perennial basil, but I did not find it to be so; maybe in frost-free climates it would last longer than a season. Cinnamon, lime and aniseed flavoured basils can be grown from seed, but are not often found in nurseries as seedlings. There is also a variety called 'Thai', which is a very ornamental plant said to have a sweet anise-clove fragrance and a slight taste of mint and citrus.

Bay tree
Laurus nobilis

The bay tree is a slow grower, but it does eventually grow to be quite tall, about 12 metres. However, it adapts well to pot growing and can be pruned to a round shape or grown as a standard (round head of foliage on top of single stem). The thick, glossy leaves are used to flavour a variety of foods, particularly casseroles, soups and stews. They are good to flavour fish, meat or poultry, or even milk puddings.

Bay trees are not fussy about soil type, as long as it is well drained. They originated in the Mediterranean region, so are best suited to sunny locations with mild winters. If summers are very hot, dappled shade in the afternoon will be appreciated, especially when the tree

Grow a bay tree in the garden or a pot.

is young. Once established, your bay tree will be quite drought-hardy, needing watering only in the hottest time of year.

The profuse creamy coloured flowers in spring attract bees and other pollinators.

Leaves can be dried on a wire rack or by hanging stalks from a ceiling beam or clothes line; however, as the tree is a long-lived perennial, once you have one established fresh leaves are always available.

Bergamot
Monarda didyma

Bergamot is one of the most attractive of the herb plants, having spectacular pink, mauve or red flowers in spring–summer, which are attractive to bees and other pollinators, including honeyeaters. It is a perennial that dies back in winter and reshoots from the roots again in spring. Both leaves and flowers are edible.

The plant prefers a shady position where the roots are kept cool, but is quite adaptable to a filtered sunlight location as long as there is afternoon shade in hot weather. Spread compost or vermicompost over the root zone when the plant begins to reshoot and mulch well during summer.

The flower stalks can grow to a metre or more in height, making bergamot a suitable background plant to grow behind lower growing herbs or flowers. When flowering has finished, cut the stalks back to ground level.

Use the leaves in salads, vegetable dishes, or with pork or veal. They can also be used to flavour sweet dishes or made into a refreshing tea. The flowers can be torn apart and used in salads. Both leaves and flowers can be dried on a wire rack and stored in airtight containers.

Calendula/pot marigold
Calendula officinalis

Often commonly referred to as marigold, this plant is valued for its sunny orange or yellow flowers that attract beneficial parasitic wasps. Both leaves and flower petals are edible (the centre of the flower tastes bitter, so pull the petals off) and can be used in salads or cooked dishes, though it is more commonly the flowers that are eaten today. It was traditionally used in stews as a substitute for the more expensive saffron to impart a golden colour. Flowers and leaves can be dried and stored for later use.

Calendula is a hardy plant that is easily grown from seeds and readily self-propagates. It does not seem to be fussy about soil type or position, but does seem to prefer sunshine to shade. Grow it as a border or scattered

Calendulas and nasturtiums beneath young fruit trees.

throughout the garden. Pull out plants when they begin to look straggly and use them as mulch to have a constant supply of new seedlings germinating. It is frost tender and will die back in winter but will come up again in spring if seeds are left around the garden. Grown in pots in a sunny courtyard, calendulas will provide a welcome splash of colour as well as a salad ingredient.

The flower petals are mildly antiseptic and contain vitamins A and E. They are often made into a cream that is one of the better known natural remedies for cuts, sores, nappy rash and burns. You can easily make your own skin remedy by putting fresh petals into a blender with enough apricot or almond oil to cover and processing until smooth. Store in a jar in the fridge. As a quick first aid for minor burns or stings, rub fresh calendula petals onto the affected area. This useful, cheerful little plant has other medicinal uses for anyone interested in this aspect of herbal lore.

Chives
Allium schoenoprasum

A clump or two of chives takes up little space in the garden and provides a reliable source of a mild onion flavour for cooking and salads. This handy perennial herb is hardy and will happily grow into a clump that can be separated to give you new plants to spread around. The common chives have attractive pink-purple pompom flower heads, which are also edible, having a very similar, though milder, oniony flavour to that of the strappy hollow leaves.

Chives can grow from 20 cm to 50 cm high, making them ideal as a border to garden beds where they will also perform the task of repelling insect pests. They prefer a light well-drained soil and a sunny position, but are very adaptable. Grow them in a pot close to the door so they can be snipped regularly for use in the kitchen. As well as their common use in salads, they are good in omelettes, stir-fries, soups, stews, rissoles, vegie burgers and other cooked dishes.

Garlic chives (*Allium tuberosum*) can grow taller than common chives and have a mild garlic flavour to the leaves and flowers. However, the flowers are white and not as attractive as those of the common chives.

Coriander
Coriandrum sativum

This frost-tender hardy annual is easily grown from seeds. It looks similar to parsley, to which it is related. Coriander grows from 40 cm to 60 cm tall with pale mauve to white umbrella-like flower clusters. Leaves, seeds and flowers can all be eaten. The leaves are often referred to as Chinese parsley or cilantro. There are two broad types: flat leaf and cut leaf. The flat-leaf type has a tendency to bolt quickly to seed, unless leaves are frequently cut to stimulate bushier growth over a longer time. The cut-leaf type (*Coriandrum sativum* 'Delfino') yields more leaves and is slower to bolt.

Coriander likes a sunny spot with moderately rich well-drained soil. Afternoon shade will be appreciated. It can be grown in a small spot or in a pot. The flowers attract beneficial predatory insects, so if you like to use coriander in cooking, grow several plants scattered throughout the garden. Begin to harvest the leaves when the plant reaches about 15 cm tall and snip them frequently to keep the plant going for a few months.

Let plants go to seed (they will of their own accord anyway) and collect seeds to flavour bean dishes, stir-fries and stews. The leaves are often used in Asian, Mediterranean and Latin American cooking and complement chicken, red meat and spicy dishes. The flowers are said to be slightly sweeter in flavour than the leaves and can be eaten raw or very lightly cooked.

A plant with a similar flavour, though belonging to a totally different genus, is Mexican coriander (*Eryngium foetidum*). This grows better in hot, humid climates than coriander and thus might suit many regions in Queensland.

Daylily

Hemerocallis spp.

Daylilies have strappy, iris-type leaves, can grow from 30 cm to over a metre tall for some species and have very showy flowers in a range of pinks, mauves, yellows and oranges. They are reasonably hardy once established and will spread to form quite large clumps, which can be separated to spread around the garden.

If you are looking for a very decorative flower that is also edible, look no further. Flower petals and buds can be eaten, as can the leaves and stalks and even the tuberous roots, not that many people want to dig up their

Versatile daylilies come in a range of colours.

lovely flowers for this purpose. The stamens can be used as a saffron substitute.

Grow daylilies as a border where they will flower for months every year during spring and summer, or to brighten up a dull corner of the garden. As a feature plant in a pot it will look stunning. As the name suggests, flowers only last a day, but each plant produces clusters of buds and throughout spring and summer there will be a constant supply of new flowers. It is quite a hardy plant, but will

Petals, flower buds, leaves and roots are all edible.

perform better if planted into moderately rich soil and watered every few days over summer. In a previous garden I had a plant that was given to me; I didn't realise its potential at the time, so put it into a corner where it was neglected. It still grew and spread into a large clump and flowered, albeit with small flowers. Now I have a cheerful border of these stunning flowers that repay my modicum of attention with plentiful large blooms.

The flowers are said to have a high mineral content and contain protein and vitamins A and C. Use flowers and buds raw in salads, or lightly cooked in stews, soups and meat dishes. Cut flowers in the morning when they are at their best; by the end of the day they will be wilting. Young white tubers (if you can bear to dig them up) can be eaten raw, after being well scrubbed. Older brown tubers can be roasted like potatoes.

Dill

Anethum graveolens

This straggly, ferny-leafed annual grows to over a metre tall. The leaves, seeds and flowers are all edible. The flower head consists of many tiny yellowish flowers in an umbrella shape. The flowers attract a range of beneficial insects. The plant is easily blown over by wind so plant it in a sheltered spot or stake it.

Grow dill in a sunny spot in well-drained soil that is not too acidic. Lime acid soil before planting. It is a hardy plant that will thrive just about anywhere and in poor soil, but the harsher the conditions the less leaf growth there will be and the sooner the plant will bolt to seed. Seeds that fall from the plant will readily self-propagate. To save the seeds for use in cooking, gently cut the heads off after the first few have fallen and dry them on a tray. Alternatively, if the seed heads are very dry, hold a container under the plant, bend the seed head over and shake it so the seeds fall into the container.

The leaves can be cut at any stage to accompany fish, lamb, chicken, egg dishes and cooked vegetables or to snip over a spicy salad, but the best flavour is when the flowers are just opening. Whole tiny flowers can be added to salads or the complete flower head included in pickled preserves. The seeds are often used in pickling, but are also a spicy accompaniment to cabbage, cauliflower, cucumber, bread and root vegetables. The flowers have a stronger flavour than the leaves and the seeds are stronger still.

The seeds have traditionally been used medicinally as an aid to digestion and a treatment for flatulence.

Garlic

Allium sativum

Garlic is probably the most frequently used culinary herb, being an ingredient in many styles of cuisine. As well, garlic has long been valued for its many health benefits, including being a natural antibiotic, reducing blood pressure and treating sinus conditions. The bulb is the only part usually eaten, though the leaves can be snipped and used in a similar way to chives or spring onions.

You can grow it from a bulb purchased from a nursery or supermarket, though the latter could have been treated with a growth inhibitor, so it is best to buy bulbs specially for propagation. If you know someone with organically grown garlic, that is a good source. Separate the individual cloves and plant them, root end downwards, about 5 cm deep and 15 cm apart into rich well-drained soil. Decomposed manure dug into the bed before planting will be beneficial. Plant in spring to harvest about six months later in summer.

Each clove will multiply into a cluster, making up a bulb. Harvest when the flowers begin to fade and the strappy leaves start to wither and droop. Pull or dig up the bulbs, shake off the excess dirt, leave them to dry in an airy spot, remove the leaves and roots and store in a cool dark place. Alternatively, plait the leaves together in bunches and hang in a cool airy spot. Either cut the leaves off and store the bulbs when they have hardened, or leave the plaits hanging for decorative as well as utilitarian effect. The bulbs will not keep as long if left hanging in a humid kitchen atmosphere.

Lavender

Lavandula spp.

Though widely known for their fragrant uses, lavender flowers are also edible. The flowers are loved by bees and other beneficial insects, though the perfume of the plant is said to repel pest insects. Lavenders are available in many varieties with different sizes, colours and perfume intensity. There is space in every small garden for a lavender or two.

There are three main groups of lavenders: the Spica Group, known as English lavenders;

Fragrant, pretty, insect attracting and edible lavender.

the Stoechas Group, variously known as French, Italian or Spanish lavenders; and the Pterostoechas Group, which are less hardy than the other two. The species most frequently recommended for culinary use is *Lavandula angustifolia*, commonly known as English lavender and belonging to the Spica Group.

Lavender's natural habitat, generally speaking, is a dry climate with poor rocky soil. So grow them in an open sunny position, preferably in sandy or gravelly, slightly alkaline soil. The soil must be well-drained. Overfertilisation and watering will result in a less intense perfume. Cut off any unused flower spikes in autumn and give the bush a light haircut in spring to keep it in good shape.

For use in cooking, cut the flowers when they first open and strip the tiny blooms from the stem. The flavour complements chicken, duck, desserts, biscuits and cakes. Lavender sugar to be used in meringues or biscuits can be made by blending flowers and sugar in a food processor. Seal in a jar for a week or two, then sieve the mixture and store in an airtight container.

Lavender oil can be used to baste poultry or as a relaxing massage oil for aching legs and backs. Fill a jar with clean flowers. Pour olive oil over until all flowers are covered. Leave in a sunny spot for four to six weeks, shaking every few days. Strain through muslin fabric or a coffee filter to remove the flowers and store the oil in an airtight container in the pantry.

Dry the flowers by hanging bunches of flower spikes in an airy place for a week or two. When dry, strip flowers from spikes and make into lavender bags to perfume clothing drawers and deter moths and silverfish. The easy way to make a lavender bag is to put a tablespoon of dried flowers in the centre of a pretty handkerchief and tie it up with a ribbon.

Lemon balm
Melissa officinalis

Sometimes called simply balm or sweet balm, lemon balm is a fragrant bush that grows to about 60 cm tall. The insignificant white flowers attract bees. It is a hardy perennial if grown in moderately well-fertilised, moist but well-drained soil. The plant might die if roots become waterlogged over winter. Grow lemon balm in a sunny or partially shady spot. Leaves will develop more fragrance in the sun. It is very suited to growing in a pot in a sunny courtyard where its citrus fragrance will be released as it is brushed against.

Young leaves are frost-tender, so plant lemon balm in a spot where it will not be exposed to frost, or protect it for at least the first winter. If grown in a pot, it can easily be moved as needed. After flowering, usually in late summer, cut branches back by about a third to keep a bushy compact shape, otherwise the plant can become straggly. In some areas the plant might die back to bare stems over winter. They can be cut to ground level and will reshoot in spring.

The leaves can be used fresh or dried to make a refreshing tea, or floated in fruit drinks. Lemon balm tea has traditionally been used to relieve symptoms of fever, colds and flu. Snip leaves finely into a fruit salad or vegetable dishes where a hint of lemon is called for to add a mild citrus flavour. Lemon balm leaves can also be used to flavour milk puddings.

Marjoram
Origanum majorana

This hardy aromatic herb can grow to 45 cm when in flower, but without the flower spikes it is much lower. Grow it in full sun in the front of a bed of herbs or flowers, in a small vacant spot or in a pot. It prefers moist, well-drained, slightly alkaline soil, but is very adaptable. Both flowers and leaves are edible and in addition to marjoram's culinary uses,

Marjoram flowers are edible and attract beneficial insects.

Marjoram stems cut for use.

the mauve flowers attract bees and other insects.

The leaves are used either fresh or dried to flavour a variety of foods, including poultry, fish, eggs, vegetables, soups, stews, scones, salads and dumplings. A tea made from the dried leaves is a traditional relief for colds and congestion. The flowers complement chicken, fish and vegetable dishes.

Leaves are best harvested before the flowers form. To keep a compact shape and prevent marjoram from becoming woody and straggly, trim it regularly. For maximum leaf harvest, cut off flower buds as they begin to form.

Oregano (*Origanum vulgare*) is similar to marjoram, but can grow taller and has a more intense flavour and aroma. Use it to enhance meat dishes, pasta, pizza, tomato dishes, zucchini, capsicum and eggplant. Golden marjoram (*Origanum vulgare* 'Aureum') has a slightly milder flavour, but its cheerful golden colour makes it a very pretty ground cover or edging plant. The pinkish-mauve flowers contrast beautifully with the golden foliage and have a spicy flavour.

Mint

Mentha spp.

There are numerous types of mints, though they all look similar. The leaves are varying shades of green, or variegated, and the flavours differ markedly. Depending on the species, mints can grow from several centimetres to over a metre in height. They have a variety of culinary and medicinal uses and the flowers attract beneficial insects. The leaves are the part most commonly used in cooking, but the flowers also are edible and can be incorporated into salads, savoury dishes or puddings.

If grown in the ground, mints can often spread and take over an area, so for a small garden they are best grown in pots. They prefer damp, well-drained, fertile soil in a sunny or dappled shade location. They will not thrive if exposed to full afternoon sun in hot weather, so make sure they are in shade at this time of day. They are shallow-rooted plants so need to be planted into soil containing organic matter, be well mulched and kept watered during hot weather. This is easily accomplished when they are planted into Waterwell-type pots or pots with large saucers.

Peppermint leaves make a refreshing tea.

The most widely grown mint species is probably spearmint (*Mentha spicata*), the one that is commonly used to flavour roast lamb, peas and potatoes or made into mint sauce.

Peppermint (*Mentha piperita*) is most frequently used to make a refreshing tea from either fresh or dried leaves. Drunk hot or cold, peppermint tea is said to be relaxing and to soothe indigestion and cold symptoms. This is the one grown commercially to produce peppermint oil.

Eau-de-cologne mint (*Mentha piperita citrata*), also known as bergamot mint or orange mint, has a very pungent perfume and a strong flavour. Use just a little in food, especially Mediterranean cuisine, or add a leaf or two to cold fruit drinks. The dried leaves can be made into scented sachets for wardrobes and drawers and are a good addition to potpourri.

The mints are reputed to repel pest insects, including cabbage moths, but if you try this, keep them in pots among the brassicas or you will soon have a bed of mint. Pennyroyal (*Mentha pulegium*), though being too pungent for most tastes, makes a good herb lawn and repels ants and fleas.

Nasturtium

Tropaeolum majus

This cheerful spreading annual will grow as a ground cover, or, if a supporting structure is provided, will clamber up it. As a ground cover, expect it to grow no more than 20 cm high, but it can spread several metres in a favourable spot. Flowers, leaves and seeds are edible. The flowers are usually shades of

Nasturtium flowers, leaves and seeds are all edible.

bright orange and yellow. Some varieties have variegated flowers or leaves. Cultivars with more subtle flower colours are available, but I have not found them to be reliable. The blooms are loved by bees, so take care when picking and eating them.

Used as a companion plant in the orchard or vegie garden, nasturtiums are said to repel borers, white flies and aphids. Allow them to twine up apple trees to repel borers. Grow them among brassicas to decoy cabbage moths, which seem to prefer nasturtiums to your broccoli and cauliflowers. If you are short of space, try growing some nasturtiums in a hanging pot to cascade downwards.

Nasturtiums are easily grown from seed, but can sometimes be bought as seedlings. Plant them in a sunny or dappled shade spot where afternoon shade is available in summer. Moist, well-drained soil is preferred, but do not use too much fertiliser. Nasturtiums are very frost-tender and generally regarded as annuals. Plant them when the danger of frosts is past. They are likely to self-propagate the following spring from seeds in the ground. I currently have a pot of nasturtiums in a sheltered position under fruit trees, which are in their second year and still thriving.

Both flowers and leaves have a peppery flavour which will enhance salads, dips, cheese dishes and vegetables, especially potatoes. The seeds can be pickled as a substitute for capers.

Parsley, curled

Petroselinum crispum

Parsley must be the most useful and well-known herb. Its fresh flavour complements a wide range of foods, it grows almost anywhere and self-seeds readily, and all parts are edible, though it is the leaves that most people are familiar with. In addition, parsley has a high nutrient value, being rich in iron and antioxidants and a good source of vitamins A, C and E and folate.

This biennial plant can be grown from nursery-bought seedlings or propagated from seed. If growing from seed, never let the soil

In flower, parsley attracts beneficial insects.

A lush bed of self-sown parsley.

dry out; cover the bed with shadecloth or similar to keep it moist between waterings. Seed can take two or three weeks to germinate. To speed up the process, soak it in water for 24 hours before sowing or, after sowing, water the bed with hot water from a watering can. I let plants go to seed and cut the seed heads to mulch other areas of the vegie patch. When the seedlings come up, I either leave them in place or transplant them to where I want them. Often, the seeds germinate so abundantly that I use most of the young plants as a green manure, only leaving a few to mature.

Parsley prefers a spot with morning sun and afternoon shade and thrives in moderately rich soil. However, I have found it to be very adaptable and even seen it growing in cracks in concrete. To extend the harvest and keep the plant compact and producing new leaves, cut the flower heads off as soon as they begin to form. Once the plant has flowered, the leaves develop a stronger, slightly bitter taste, but I still find them useful at this stage.

Use the leaves to complement egg dishes, pasta, soups, stews, cooked vegetables, salads, poultry, fish and red meat. Many health benefits are claimed for parsley including maintaining a healthy cardiovascular system and helping relieve arthritis. A tea made from the fresh or dried leaves might assist digestion and benefit kidney stones, though people with kidney disease should avoid consuming large quantities of parsley because it contains oxalates. Both the boiled roots and the blanched stalks can be eaten as a vegetable. Chew a sprig of parsley after eating garlic to sweeten the breath.

Italian parsley (*Petroselinum crispum neoplitanum*) has flat leaves, similar to celery leaves, a stronger flavour than curled parsley, and grows taller and germinates more quickly.

Rosemary
Rosmarinus officinalis

If you are looking for an attractive perennial plant that will survive tough conditions and

The plant is hardy enough to use as a hedge. This one is beside a concrete path and backed by a brick wall.

be useful in the kitchen as well, rosemary is the one. It will thrive and be even more aromatic in poor soil and hot sun and needs little watering once established. Often used as a hedging plant, rosemary can grow as tall as two metres, but is easily kept trimmed to be a more compact shrub and grows well in pots. In fact, it is an ideal pot plant for a sunny courtyard or rooftop where its beautiful spicy aroma will permeate when the plant is brushed against. There are several cultivars with varying intensities of blue flowers. Both flowers and leaves are edible.

The one 'must' for successful rosemary cultivation is well-drained soil. Plants are very likely to die if the roots become waterlogged.

Use the leaves and/or flowers fresh or dried to flavour roasts, any meat dishes, pasta sauces, eggplant, zucchini, potato, tomato, Brussels sprouts and cabbage. Snip leaves into bread, scones or pizza dough. Rosemary helps with the digestion of rich or starchy food and can be made into a tea to relieve headaches.

A young rosemary plant in the vegie garden.

An old belief was that rosemary twigs twined in the hair stimulated the memory.

There is a prostrate form of rosemary (*Rosmarinus prostratus*), which is a hardy ground cover or rockery plant and is edible, but the flavour is not as intense as that of the upright plant.

Sage, common
Salvia officinalis

There are numerous species and varieties of sage, many of them having culinary and medicinal uses, but common or garden sage is the one most often grown and used in cooking. Both leaves and purple flowers are edible and the flowers are loved by bees.

Sage grows 60 cm to 90 cm tall and its silvery leaves are an indication of its drought tolerance once established. Light, well-drained soil is recommended; do not over-fertilise or overwater. Sage does not like wet feet and excessive overhead watering can cause the leaves to mildew.

It is an attractive plant, especially when in flower, and will thrive in a pot in a sunny courtyard. Cut back the plant after flowering to keep a compact shape and prevent it from becoming woody and straggly.

Sage leaves, fresh or dry, are used to flavour pork, veal, duck, oily fish, soups, stews, onion, tomato, eggplant, cheese dishes and egg dishes. Snip leaves or flowers into bread, scones or pizza dough. Sage tea is recommended as calming and beneficial for the liver. Used as a gargle, it will soothe a sore throat. Sage is also said to be a memory enhancer.

Clary sage (*Salvia sclarea*) leaves were once thought to cure eye infections. Try them fried in batter to accompany lamb or as an appetiser. Flowers of common sage, clary sage and pineapple sage (*Salvia elegans*) make an attractive addition to salads.

Thyme
Thymus vulgaris

A sage plant close to the house is handy for plucking.

Thyme makes a hardy aromatic ground cover.

There are hundreds of species and cultivars of thyme, the most frequently used for culinary purposes being common thyme (*Thymus vulgaris*). The thymes are low-growing, hardy perennial plants, seldom reaching more than 20 cm in height. They have wiry stems from which develop tiny leaves and flowers. The blooms, usually purple, pink or white, are attractive to bees. Plant thyme as a border or edging species along a path, as a ground cover, to fill a small vacant spot, or in a pot. Combine it with rosemary and sage for an aromatic and hardy potted herb garden suited to a sunny courtyard or rooftop.

Thyme prefers sandy, well-drained soil in a sunny location. Do cut it back after flowering each year to keep it compact and bushy.

Flavour and aroma will be reduced if thyme is overwatered or overfertilised.

The flowers taste similar to the leaves, but are sweeter. Use both leaves and flowers, stripped from the stems, to flavour stuffing, meat, fish, vegetables, bread, scones, pizza dough, pasta sauces and any dish containing tomato. The flavour can be intense, so a little goes a long way. Thyme tea might help relieve symptoms of colds, sinus conditions, cramps and colic and aid digestion. Thyme is a natural antiseptic.

Some other thymes often used for culinary purposes are lemon thyme (*Thymus × citriodorus*), which has a pleasant lemony flavour and aroma, and the variety known as orange-scented thyme (*Thymus × citriodorus* 'Fragrantissimus').

A TASTE FOR ALL SEASONS

I belong to the KISS school of cooking: Keep It Simple, Sweetheart. I don't have time to prepare elaborate meals and you won't often find me spending precious gardening or writing time concocting complicated cuisine. Most of our meals are based around what is seasonally available from the garden.

Summer lunches are likely to consist of a salad sandwich or a platter of garden goodies, accompanied by cold meat and some delicatessen treats, served with crackers. Evening meals will usually be based around a fresh salad.

Cold weather favourites consist of a variety of soups for lunch and slow-cooked meals of meat and vegies in the evening. I love anything I can throw in the crockpot in the morning and leave simmering all day.

When you lead a busy life, as most of us do, it is very easy to resort to takeaway meals. That's OK, occasionally, but once you have fresh food available in the garden, healthy meals need not involve too much work. The secret is to be imaginative with what you have. Collect a variety of simple ways of preparing tomatoes, pumpkins, beans, potatoes, zucchinis and any other crops you have in seasonal abundance. Add flavour with your own herbs and variety and decorative appeal with judicious use of flowers.

The following recipes and suggestions might help. They are all gluten-free, and most are low in salt, sugar and cholesterol. I hope you enjoy them, but most of all I hope you enjoy devising your own favourites.

Adjust all quantities to suit your own needs and tastes and substitute ingredients according to what you have available.

Tomato paste

The summer months see our kitchen abundant with tomatoes. There are bowls of them everywhere. My favourite way of preserving those we do not immediately eat or give away is to make a paste that can be frozen to use later in the year for soups, casseroles, risotto and pasta sauces.

Process any quantity of fully ripe tomatoes in a blender. Pour into a saucepan. Bring to the boil and keep boiling briskly, stirring frequently, until the quantity is reduced by about half and the paste is as thick as you want it to be. Allow to cool. Pour into freezer containers. I use a variety of sizes, from ice cube trays for times when just a hint of tomato flavour is wanted, to about 500 mL for soup. Put in the freezer when cool. If you need to reuse the containers, transfer the frozen contents to plastic bags.

Totally herbaceous tomato chicken

This meal developed on a day in summer when I had planned to have roast chicken for dinner. The day started off cool, but was hot by afternoon and I was reluctant to have the oven on to cook the chicken. I decided to cook it on the gas hotplate. It could just as easily have been done in a crockpot and left to simmer all day. Note that zucchini will fall apart if cooked for too long.

Ingredients
1 roasting chicken, about size 17 (1.7 kg)
6 small onions, peeled
2 large carrots, peeled and cut into chunks
1 medium red capsicum, cut into chunks
2 cloves garlic, finely diced
1 generous handful chopped herbs: parsley, basil, marjoram
Generous slurp of tamari
150 mL red wine
500 mL tomato paste, as above
1 medium zucchini, cut into chunks
1 tbsp cornflour, approx.

Method
Lightly grease a heavy-based saucepan with olive oil. Put chicken in. Tuck onions, carrots and capsicum around the sides. Mix garlic, herbs, tamari and wine into tomato paste and pour over chicken and vegetables. Bring to boil over medium heat. Turn heat to as low as it will go and simmer, covered, for about 1¼ hours, turning chicken once during that time. Add zucchini chunks, stirring them into sauce. Simmer a further 15 to 30 minutes. Test chicken to see if it is cooked right through; if not, simmer a further 15 minutes. Taste sauce and adjust flavouring to suit. Thicken if necessary with the cornflour mixed to a smooth paste in a little water.

Let chicken rest for 15 minutes before carving. Serve chicken and sauce with vegies over basmati rice.

Zigzag tomatoes

This way of serving tomatoes is much easier than it looks and never fails to impress.

Ingredients
Allow 1 or 2 tomato halves per person, depending on the meal
Lettuce or rocket, shredded
Basil or mint, chopped
Chives, chopped
Vinaigrette dressing
Yellow nasturtium flowers or calendula petals

Method
Cut tomatoes in half by using this method: Hold tomato in your left hand (if you are right-handed) with the top facing up. At the halfway point insert the point of a small serrated knife at an angle of 45° and push it halfway through the tomato. Withdraw knife and make the next cut so it forms a 'V' with the first. Continue all the way around the tomato until you have two halves cut in a zigzag shape.

Serve tomatoes on a bed of shredded greens. Sprinkle them with the chopped herbs and dressing. Decorate with yellow nasturtium flowers or calendula petals.

Taste of summer basil pesto

When basil is plentiful, make it into pesto, which can be used as a dip, a salad dressing or flavouring for other dishes. If you have rocket in abundance, use it instead of basil.

Ingredients
2 cloves garlic
1 packed cup fresh washed basil leaves, roughly chopped
50 g pine nuts
100 g Parmesan cheese, grated
2 anchovy fillets, optional
Olive oil, as needed

Method
Place all ingredients in a blender, using just enough olive oil to make a paste. Process until it reaches the desired smoothness.

Fresh pesto, bean and carrot salad

For this recipe, use any quantities to suit yourself. You could just as easily serve it hot in the winter, perhaps substituting broccoli florets for the green beans.

Ingredients
Carrots, diced
Green beans, sliced into 2 cm lengths
Basil pesto, as above, without the anchovies if preferred
No-fat yoghurt
Basil, finely chopped
Spring onions, finely chopped

Method
Cook carrots and beans together in boiling water until just tender. Drain. Make a dressing from pesto and yoghurt with twice the amount of yoghurt as pesto. For example, 2 tablespoons of pesto to 4 tablespoons of yoghurt. Combine herbs and dressing. Stir through vegetables, cool and refrigerate.

Sensational summer salsa

In late summer I often have a plentiful supply of fresh tomatoes, cucumbers and capsicums. This simple dish is easy and very refreshing. Use quantities to suit yourself, but you need roughly 1 part cucumber and 1 part capsicum to two parts tomatoes.

Ingredients
½ cup capsicum, diced
½ cup cucumber, diced
1 cup tomatoes, diced
A few basil or mint leaves, finely chopped
A few nasturtium leaves, finely chopped
Balsamic dressing, enough to moisten

Method
Combine all ingredients about half an hour before serving for flavours to mingle. Serve spooned over cold meat or as a side salad.

Very vegie hotpot

Use whatever vegies you have available.

Ingredients
2 cups tomato paste, as above
2 cloves garlic, finely chopped
1 small hot chilli, finely chopped
2 tbsp parsley, finely chopped
2 tbsp spring onion, finely chopped
1 tbsp basil, finely chopped
1 cup green beans, sliced
1 cup carrot, diced
2 cups corn kernels
1 red capsicum, diced

Method
Preheat oven to 180°C. Gently heat tomato paste with garlic, hot chilli, parsley, spring onion and basil. Simmer 2 minutes. Put chopped vegies in a casserole dish and pour hot sauce over. Cook 1 to 1½ hours, stirring occasionally. Serve with boiled new potatoes, mashed potato or rice.

So sweet pumpkin soup
This is a favourite winter lunch. This quantity makes enough to last two people for several meals.

Ingredients
1.5 kg pumpkin, after peeling
750 g yellow sweet potato, after peeling
1–2 large onions
3 sticks celery
3 cloves garlic, more if you love garlic
1 tsp mustard powder
1 tsp sea salt
1–2 cups coconut milk, optional

Method
Cut pumpkin, sweet potato, onions and celery into chunks. Roughly dice garlic. Put vegies into a large saucepan and just cover with water. Bring to the boil and cook until tender. Strain liquid from vegies, keeping it in a separate container. Process vegies in batches, with each batch just covered in enough of the cooking liquid to bring it to the consistency you prefer. Return to the heat, add mustard and salt and adjust seasoning to taste. If you want to add coconut milk, replace some of the cooking liquid with it during the blending process. If you prefer a spicier taste, add a hot chilli to the vegies or some sweet chilli sauce to the blended soup.

Creamy easy potato salad
The fresh herbs give this salad a flavour boost; if you have your own potatoes available, it is even better, and you can be sure it contains no gluten if that is an issue. If you use commercial mayonnaise, which I do, read the label to ensure there are no wheat products used. For variety, add walnut and/or finely diced celery or apple, substitute finely chopped dill leaves for the herbs in the recipe, or use an olive oil and vinegar dressing to replace the creamy one given below. If you have plenty of eggs, gently stir quartered hard-boiled eggs through the finished salad.

Ingredients
20 whole small new potatoes (chats) or small 'Kipflers', or 5 halved medium-sized red-skinned potatoes such as 'Desiree'
½ cup low-fat mayonnaise
½ cup no-fat plain yoghurt
2 tbsp finely diced herbs: basil, mint, parsley, spring onions
1 tbsp pine nuts

Method
Scrub potatoes and put them in a large saucepan, cover with water, bring to the boil and simmer until just tender. Meanwhile, make the dressing: mix remaining ingredients in a small bowl or jug. Drain cooked potatoes, tip them into a bowl. If you have used halved 'Desirees,' dice them to the required size, leaving skin on. Stir through the dressing so potatoes are generously covered. Cool and refrigerate.

Aromatic rosemary potatoes
The smell that wafts through the kitchen when this is cooking is sensational. Use more

rosemary if you love it, but it can be overpowering.

Ingredients
4–6 small new potatoes or 'Kipflers' per person, scrubbed
2 cloves garlic, finely diced
2 sprigs rosemary, about 5 cm long, leaves stripped from twigs and roughly diced
2 tbsp olive oil, approx.

Method
Preheat oven to 200°C. Lightly oil a medium-sized casserole dish or baking tray. Place potatoes in dish. Combine garlic, rosemary and oil and pour over potatoes. Stir through so potatoes are well coated with oil. Cover and cook until tender, stirring once during the cooking time. This will take 45 to 60 minutes. If you prefer potatoes to be browned and slightly crisp-skinned, leave the lid off the casserole dish and turn the oven to a higher setting for the last 10 to 15 minutes of cooking time.

Broadly beany
This easy and tasty way of cooking broad beans works just as well with zucchini when it is in abundance. For variety, add tomato paste and/or basil pesto to taste.

Ingredients
1 large onion, diced
2 cloves garlic, finely diced
2 cups broad beans, shelled
2 tbsp parsley, finely chopped
1 tbsp olive oil, approx.

Method
Preheat oven to 180°C. Stir-fry onion and garlic in a small amount of olive oil until onion just changes colour. Put all ingredients into a medium-sized casserole dish and mix well. Cook about 30 minutes or until beans are tender.

Chock-full-of-goodness frittata
Use any vegetables you have available, allowing about a cup per person. This will serve four and you probably won't need much else. Include the cheese if you aren't concerned about cholesterol.

Ingredients
1 large onion, diced
2–3 cloves garlic, finely diced
1 cup corn kernels
1 cup peas
1 packed cup chopped Asian greens or silverbeet
3–4 sticks celery, diced
6 large eggs
600 mL milk, or combination milk and no-fat yoghurt
Generous slurp of tamari
2 tbsp parsley, finely diced
200 g grated tasty or low-fat cheese, optional
olive oil

Method
Preheat oven to 180°C. Stir-fry the onion and garlic in a small amount of olive oil until the onion just changes colour. Lightly oil a large casserole dish and layer the vegies in it, pressing them down, but not too firmly. Beat eggs and milk/yoghurt together with tamari. Stir in parsley and cheese. Pour milk and egg mixture over vegies. Cover and cook until frittata is firm in the middle, about 1½ hours, uncovering for the last 15 minutes to brown the top. You can sprinkle the top with extra

cheese and let it melt and brown over the top if cholesterol is not a concern.

Brassy brassica pasta

This makes a filling meal for four and is especially delicious when you have your own broccoli and cauliflower. For a variation, add chopped cooked chicken or bacon to the vegie mixture and heat through. Of course, use ordinary pasta if you are not gluten intolerant. To flavour the vegies use any of the suggestions below. The incorporation of broccoli cooking liquid depends on how moist you like your pasta.

Ingredients
1 pkt gluten-free pasta
1 cup broccoli florets, lightly cooked
1 cup cauliflower florets, lightly cooked
1 medium onion, diced
2 cloves garlic, diced
2 tbsp parsley, finely chopped
Olive oil
100 mL broccoli cooking liquid, optional
Generous slurp of tamari, or 2 tbsp basil pesto, or ½ cup tomato paste
½ cup low-fat fetta cheese, diced into 2 cm cubes

Method
Cook pasta as per directions. Cook broccoli and cauliflower. Stir-fry onion, garlic and parsley in a little olive oil. Tip cooked vegies into pan with onion and garlic. Add enough cooking liquid to moisten. Slosh in tamari (or desired flavouring) to taste. Stir this mixture through cooked, drained pasta. Add fetta just before serving and stir through.

FINAL WORDS

I am not a pessimist, but neither am I blinded by unrealistic optimism. Financial crises come and go, and so will this latest one, perhaps having taught us all some lessons about living within our means. I do not think oil is going to 'run out' any time soon. However, despite the drop in price at time of writing, caused by a world financial slow-down, it will inevitably become more difficult and expensive to access. My son Bradley says, 'the Stone Age didn't end because the world ran out of stones'. It ended because people discovered new ways of doing things, new technologies. Perhaps the Oil Age will not end because the world runs out of oil, but because of new and better technologies.

I believe there will be new technologies, but there is also bound to be a transition period of adjustment and social inequalities along the way. Inevitably, this will have flow-on effects on food production, as will the ongoing effects of our changing climate.

My message is: take back the power, grow as much of your own food as you can, and you and your family will be in a better position to adapt to changes, whatever they might be.

APPENDIX 1
Suppliers and information

Aquaponics
www.backyardaquaponics.com.au

Bokashi Bucket
Tel: (02) 9591-1699
www.bokashi.com.au

Dwarfing Rootstock Fruit Trees
Kendall Farms
Tel: (07) 4779-1189
www.kendallfarms.com.au

Daley's Fruit Tree Nursery
Numerous food plants suitable for tropical and subtropical areas.
PO Box 154 via Kyogle 2474
Tel: (02) 6632-1441
www.daleysfruit.com.au

EarthBox Australia
Tel: (03) 9378-4700
Email: cd@earthboxaustralia.com
www.earthboxaustralia.com

Eco Bag Industries
PO Box 3100
Victoria Point West, Qld 4165
Tel: 1800-638-628
www.ecobagindustries.com.au

Fruit salad trees

Fruit Salad Tree Co
'Willow Creek'
Gulf Rd
Emmaville, NSW 2371
Tel: (02) 6734-7204
www.fruitsaladtrees.com

Hydroponics information

Australian Hydroponic and Greenhouse Association
www.ahga.org.au

Western Australia
www.hydroponicsolutions.com.au

Hydro Masta, a Sydney-based company
www.hydromasta.com.au

Open-pollinated seeds

Bay Seed Garden
PO Box 1164
Busselton, WA 6280
Tel: (08) 9752-2513

Digger's Club
Heronswood
105 Latrobe Pde
Dromana, Vic 3936
Tel: (03) 5987-1877
www.diggers.com.au
Email: orders@diggers.com.au

Eden Seeds
MS 905
Lower Beechmont, Qld 4211
Tel: (07) 5533-1107
www.edenseeds.com.au

Gourmet Gardens
PO Box 1892
Esperance, WA 6450
Tel: (08) 9071-6512

Greenpatch Organic Seeds
PO Box 1285
Taree, NSW 2430
Tel: (02) 6551-4240
www.greenpatchseeds.com.au
Email: enquiries@greenpatchseeds.com.au

Kings Seeds
PO Box 975
Penrith, NSW 2751
Tel: (02) 4776-1493

New Gippsland Seeds and Bulbs
PO Box 1
Silvan, Vic 3795
Tel: (03) 9737-9560
www.newgipps.com.au
Email: newgipps@bigpond.com

Phoenix Seeds
PO Box 207
Snug, Tas 7054
Tel: (03) 6267-9562
Email: phnxseed@ozemail.com.au

Yilgarn Traders
333 David Rd
Waggrakine, WA 6530
Tel: (08) 9938-1628
Email: yilgarn@midwest.com.au

Seeds and organic gardening supplies (including Chinese water chestnuts)

Green Harvest
PO Box 92
Maleny, Qld 4552
Tel: (07) 5435-2699
www.greenharvest.com.au
Email: inquiries@greenharvest.com.au

Seed Savers' Network

For information about seed saving and to see if there is a group in your area, the first port of call is the Seed Savers' Network.

PO Box 975
Byron Bay, NSW 2481
Tel: (02) 6685-6624
www.seedsavers.net
Email: info@seedsavers.net

Soil analysis

SWEP Analytical Laboratories
Specialising in soil analysis for organic systems.
PO Box 583
Noble Park, Vic 3174
Tel: (03) 9701-6007
www.swep.com.au
Email: services@swep.com.au

Wet Pot
61 Charteris St
Paddington, Qld 4064
Tel: (07) 3217-5383
http://wateringsystems.net/
Email: wakelingmark@yahoo.com.au

APPENDIX 2
Bibliography

Bartholemew M (2005) *Square Foot Gardening*. Rodale, United States.

Blazey C (1999) *The Australian Vegetable Garden*. New Holland, Sydney.

Fanton M and Fanton J (1993) *The Seed Savers' Handbook*. The Seed Savers' Network, Byron Bay, NSW.

Glowiski L (1991) *The Complete Book of Fruit Growing in Australia*. Lothian Books, Melbourne.

Grass Roots magazines, numerous issues, but particularly issues 178 and 182 for the wicking bed information. Grass Roots Publishing, Seymour, Victoria.

Handreck K (1993) *Gardening Down-Under*. CSIRO Publishing, Melbourne.

Hemphill J and Hemphill R (1978) *Herbs and Spices*. Paul Hamlyn, Dee Why West, NSW.

Horsfall M (2008) *Creating Your Eco-Friendly Garden*. CSIRO Publishing, Melbourne.

Horsfall M (2003) *The Miracle of Mulch*. New Holland, Sydney.

Kapitani A & Schultz R (2006) *Succulents for the Garden*. Schultz Publishing, Victoria.

Kapitani A and Schultz R (2007) *More Succulents for the Garden*. Schultz Publishing, Victoria.

McVicar J (1997) *Good Enough to Eat*. Kyle Cathie Limited, London.

Mollison B (1979) *Permaculture Two*. Tagari Books, Stanley, Tasmania.

Mollison B and Holmgren D (1978) *Permaculture One*. Corgi Books, Transworld Publishers, Melbourne.

Romanowski N (2007) *Edible Water Gardens: Growing Water-Plants for Food and Profit*. Hyland House, Flemington, Victoria.

Smith K and Smith I (1999) *Grow Your Own Bushfoods*. New Holland, Sydney.

Tankard G (1987) *Tropical Fruit: An Australian Guide to Growing and Using Exotic Fruits*. Viking O'Neil, Ringwood, Victoria.

Woodrow L (1996) *The Permaculture Home Garden*. Penguin, Ringwood, Victoria.

(2003) *Flora*. ABC Books, Ultimo, NSW.

(1974) *How to Grow Herbs*. Lane Books, California.

(1991) *The Home Vegetable Garden*. 8th edn. NSW Agriculture & Fisheries, NSW.

INDEX

animals 36–8
   fish 39, 41
   goats 38
   guinea pigs 37
   poultry 36–7, 38
   rabbits 37
   sheep 38
aquaponics 39–41, 89, 97, 116, 125
   indoors 53

balcony, courtyard, rooftop 20, 22–3, 42, 72, 165
   body corporate approval 23
   council approval 23
   food crops for 94–5
   hydroponics/aquaponics for 97
beneficial insects 29, 35, 88, 121, 122, 126, 128, 129, 143, 198, 199, 201
blossom end rot 163
Bokashi 65, 72–3, 154, 180, 187
   uses for 73
borage 35
bush food, growing & using 187–92, see also bush tucker
   apple dumpling 187
   Australian finger lime 84, 187
   broad leaf palm lily 88, 188
   Davidson plum 27, 188
   large kangaroo apple 84, 188
   lemon myrtle 28, 84, 189
   lemon-scented tea-tree 28, 189
   lilly pilly 120, 189
   midgenberry 27, 88, 190
   mountain pepper 28, 84
   muntries 27, 28, 87, 88, 120, 190–1
   native ginger 84, 87, 191
   native raspberry 191
   prickly currant bush 27, 84, 191
   sweet apple berry 87, 90, 97, 188
   warrigal greens 26, 27, 33, 87, 88, 97, 120, 192
   yam daisy 87, 192
bush tucker 12, 16, 23, 26–8, 84, 87, 88, 89, 90, 91, see also bush food, growing & using
   antioxidants in 28
   drought tolerance 28, 120
   edible leaves 27–8
   fruit producing 27

carbon/nitrogen ratio 59–60
   nitrogen drawdown 60–1
clumping bamboo 35

compost 35, 65–70
   cool 67
   easy 67
   hot 67
   less work 68
   lime, dolomite, wood ash 68
   micro-organisms in 68–9
   mini heaps/bins 69–70
   nutrients in 66
   rotating bins 68
   speeding up 70
   tea 73–4
   what can go in 69
crop rotation 93–3, 95
   hints & options 95
   how to 94
   plant families 93–4

deciding what to grow 24–31
   be realistic 24
   crop selection 24
   food preferences 24
diversity 29
dwarfing fruit trees 34, see also fruit, dwarfing rootstock

Earthbox® 21, 42–3
earthworms 34, 35, 41, 47, 48, 49, 58, 59, 70, 73, 75, 109, 128
   castings 72
   vermicompost 70–72

fertiliser
   Bokashi 72–3
   compost 65–70
   compost tea 73–4
   fish emulsion 63–4
   for fruit trees 83, 84–5
   for pots 77–9
   from fish 39, 40, 41
   from poultry 86
   green manures 75–6
   green weed tea 74–5
   homemade 5, 65–76
   humus 79–80
   in planting hole 85
   manures 37, 38, 64–5
   manure tea 74
   mulch 79
   mycorrhizal fungi 60

nitrogen   7, 9, 39, 58, 59, 60, 61, 63, 64–5, 67, 68, 75, 76, 80, 84–5, 86, 131, 146, 150, 151, 168, 172, 176, 179
   organic   65
   overuse   65
   phosphorus   61, 63, 66, 72, 64–5, 66, 72, 84–5, 128
   potassium   61, 64–5, 85–5
   seaweed emulsion   39, 62, 63–4, 65, 67, 70, 77, 85, 96, 106, 129, 146, 154, 184, 185
   vermicompost   62, 65, 70–72, 76, 77, 78, 106, 153, 154, 172, 179, 187, 190, 195
flowers as food   16–18, 19, 193
flowers, growing & using   193–206, *see also* flowers as food
   calendula   195–6
   daylily   197–8
   lavender   199–200
   nasturtium   202
food among the flowers   16
frogs   29, 123
frost protection   84
fruit   24–7, 35
   berries   26
   cacti & succulents   26
   compact cultivars   26
   dwarfing rootstock   25–6
   for pots   96
   tropical   27
   vines   26
fruit, growing & using   165–85
   acerola   165–6
   alpine strawberry   185
   apple   166–7
   apricot   167–8
   babaco   168–9
   banana   169–70
   blackberry   183
   blackberry hybrids   183
   black currant   183
   black sapote   171
   blueberry   171–2
   feijoa   172–3
   goji berry   173
   grape   174–5
   lemon   175–6
   passionfruit   176–7
   pawpaw   177–8
   peach   178–9
   pineapple   179–80
   plum   180–1
   raspberry   181–2
   red currant   183
   strawberry   183–5
   white currant   183
fungal diseases   127–8
   fruit trees   127
   sprays against   127–8
   vegetables   127

garden ponds   29
green manure   35
grey water   112–5
   cautions   114–5
   from bathroom   114
   from kitchen   114
   from laundry   113–4

hardy food plants   119–20
   bush tucker   120
   fruits   120
   vegies   120
herbs & bush tucker among the shrubs   23
herbs, growing & using   193–206
   basil   193–4
   bay tree   194–5
   bergamot   195
   calendula   195–6
   chives   196
   coriander   196–7
   dill   198
   garlic   198–9
   lemon balm   200
   marjoram   200–1
   Mexican coriander   197
   mint   201–2
   parsley   203–4
   rosemary   204–5
   sage   205
   thyme   205–6
homemade fungicide sprays   129–30
   bicarbonate of soda   129
   compost   129
   milk   129
   seaweed   129
   vegetable oil   130
homemade insect control sprays   128–9
   chilli   129
   eucalyptus   128
   garlic   128
   molasses   128
   oil   128
   pyrethrum   129
hydroponics   41–2, 43
   indoors   53
   nutrient strengths   42
   plant combining
   Verti-gro® system   42

indoor productivity   51–53
   aquaponics/hydroponics   53

mushrooms   52
sprouting   51–2
wheatgrass   52

lateral branches/growth/shoots   163, 167, 168, 171, 172, 179
lawn   23–4
   design ideas   90–91
   herbs   88
   productive possibilities   89–90
   replacing   88–91
   vegie patch over   91–4
lizards   29, 123
location   15–16
   fruiting plants   15
   overhanging trees   15
   vegies   15

marigolds   35, 86, 124, 195, *see also* flowers, growing & using
mulch   10, 16, 23, 31, 34–5, 38, 42, 43, 44, 59, 60, 61, 62, 67, 70, 71, 72, 75, 76, 77, 79, 80, 84, 85, 86, 94, 96, 103, 104, 109, 120, 127
   and pH   58
   lucerne   127
   mound, moat &   84
   sheet   88, 109, 110–11
   water under   116
multiple uses   34–6
   borage   35
   clumping bamboo   35
   dwarf fruit trees   34
   fruit trees   35
   marigolds   35
   native shrubbery   35–6
   peas & beans   35
   pumpkin vines   34–5
   vegetable crops   35
Mycobacterium vaccae   11
mycorrhizal fungi   60, 80

narrow strips   87–8
nasturtium   86, 87, 202
nitrogen drawdown   60–1
nitrogen fixation   75
no-dig beds   45–9
   best yet   48
   how to make   46–8
   planting out   48
   tank bed   49
   what to use   46
nutrient deficiencies   63

part of the picture   29–31
peas & beans   35

permaculture   33–9
   animals   36–7
   multiple uses   34–6
   perennial species   33
   poultry & vegetable dome   38
   swales   38–9
   zones   33, 36
pest control   120–9
   birds & beneficial insects   121–3
   codling moth   125–6
   coloured sticky traps   126
   companion planting   124
   crop rotation   121
   earwigs   125
   frogs, lizards, spiders   123–4
   fruit flies   125, 126
   fungal diseases   127–8
   healthy soil   120
   helpful insects   121
   homemade sprays   128–9
   organically acceptable commercial   126–7
   physical barriers   124
   pluck & squirt   121
   poultry   123
   slugs & snails   125
   timing   120–1
   traps   125–6
pH   47, 57–8, 61–2, 68
   and mulch   58
   in pots   77
   managing   57–9
   vegetable tolerance to   93
plants for birds & insects   29–31
pollination   5
pots   20–1
   care   95–6
   climbers in   97
   concrete   20–1
   Earthbox®   21
   fertilising   77
   fibreglass & clay   21
   food crops in   94–5
   fruit trees for   96
   glazed clay   20–1
   hanging   21
   pH in   77
   plastic   20
   practicalities of   78–9
   reusing   20
   stackable plastic   21
   tall plants in   97
   terracotta   20–1
   vegetables for   97
   watering   119
poultry   35, 36–7

for pest control　86, 123, 165
　　　manure　64, 85, 86
propagating mix　104, 105
　　　homemade　105
propagator　105–6
pumpkin　34–5, 155–7

rare & unusual foods　28
reasons to grow　3–13
　　　blandness & obesity　4
　　　carbon sink　8
　　　chemical content　7–8
　　　children　12–13
　　　ecological footprint　9–10
　　　economy　4
　　　environmental health　8
　　　exercise　11
　　　feel-good factor　11
　　　food miles　10–11
　　　freshness　5
　　　greenhouse gas emissions　9
　　　heirloom varieties　4
　　　human health　8
　　　increasing food prices　5
　　　nutrition　5–7
　　　organic　4
　　　salicylates　3
　　　stress & health　12
　　　taste　3
　　　time lapse　3
　　　toughness　3
　　　unripe harvesting　3
　　　variety　12
recipes　207–12
　　　aromatic rosemary potatoes　210–11
　　　brassy brassica pasta　212
　　　broadly beany　211
　　　chock full of goodness frittata　211–12
　　　creamy easy potato salad　210
　　　sensational summer salsa　209
　　　so sweet pumpkin soup　210
　　　taste of summer basil pesto　209
　　　tomato paste　207–8
　　　totally herbaceous tomato chicken　208
　　　very vegie hotpot　209–10
　　　zigzag tomatoes　208
replacing a tree or shrub　83–4
replacing flowering annuals　86–7
rocks & logs　29, 123

seedlings
　　　growing your own　104
　　　in propagator　106
　　　propagating mix for　104, 105

　　　transplanting　106–7
seeds　99–104
　　　care of seedbed　103–4
　　　direct sowing　102
　　　F1 hybrid　101
　　　in dug beds　102–3
　　　in egg cartons or newspaper　107
　　　in Jiffy Pots　108
　　　in no-dig beds　103
　　　lifespan　101
　　　open-pollinated　4, 99–101, 163
　　　outdoor or indoor sowing　101–2
　　　planting　104–5
　　　selecting to save　100
　　　soil temperature for germination　102
soil improvement　55–81
　　　acid or alkaline　57
　　　biota　58
　　　Bokashi bucket　72–3
　　　bury waste　70
　　　carbon/nitrogen ratio　59–60
　　　compaction　80
　　　compost　65–70
　　　compost tea　73–4
　　　drainage　80
　　　fish emulsion　63, 64
　　　green manures　75–6
　　　green weed tea　74–5
　　　homemade fertilisers　65–76
　　　humus　79–80
　　　managing pH　57–8
　　　manures　64–5
　　　manure tea　74
　　　mulch　79
　　　mulch & pH　58
　　　mycorrhizal fungi　60
　　　nutrient deficiencies　63
　　　nutrients　61
　　　organic fertilisers　65
　　　seaweed emulsion　63–4
　　　vermicompost　70–72
soil structure　56–7
　　　gypsum　57
　　　improving　56–7
soil texture　55–6
　　　clay　55
　　　loam　55
　　　sandy　55
　　　silt　55
square foot gardening　50–1
　　　plant spacing for　51
superfoods　6

tiny spots　87

uses for plants   31

vegetables   99–107
  for pots   97
  hybrid   99
  open-pollinated   99–101
  planting   92–4
  preserving the past   99
  replacing a lawn   91–4
  rotation   93–4, 95
  selecting seed to save   100
  shade strategies   98
  tolerance to acidity   93
  top 10 for nutrients   133
vegetables, growing & using   133–64
  Asian greens   133–5
  beans   135–6
  beetroot   138
  broad beans   137
  broccoli   139–40
  buk choy   133, 134
  capsicum   140–5
  carrot   141–2
  Ceylon spinach   161
  Chinese mustard   135
  Chinese water chestnut   143
  choy sum   135
  cucumber   144–5
  lettuce   145–7
  mizuna greens   135
  onions   148–9
  pak choy   133, 134
  peas   150–2
  potato   152–5
  pumpkin   155–7
  radicchio   147–8
  radish   158–9
  rocket   147
  silverbeet   159–61
  spinach   161
  spring onions   150
  tomato   161–4
  tree onions   150
  watercress   147
  Welsh onions   150
vertical growing   18, 20
  green walls   20
  lattice   18, 20
  metal fences   18
  peas & beans   35
  reinforcing mesh   18
  rotary clothesline   18
  verandah posts   20

warrigal greens   27, 192
water   112–20
  bales   117
  choose hardy plants   119–20
  collection   113–14
  dripper irrigation   119
  dripper & seeper hoses   118
  Eco bags   117–18
  grey   112–15
  innovative watering   116–19
  juice bottles   117
  leaky buckets   117
  pipe method   116–17
  self-watering plant guards   117
  Smart WaterMark   118
  sun & wind protection   115–16
  tanks   112
  watering pot plants   119
  Wetpots®   117
  wetting agents   118
weeds 109–11
  control   109–11
  edible   109
  in no-dig beds   110
  in pot plants   110
  sheet mulch   110–11
  solarising   110
wicking beds   43–5
worm farms   70–72

zoning   33, 36

Other titles available from
CSIRO PUBLISHING GARDENING GUIDES:

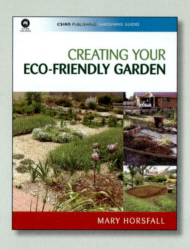

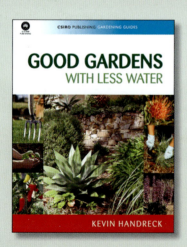

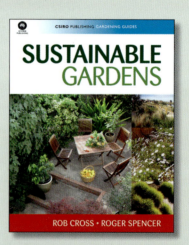

www.publish.csiro.au